What Business Ow
About *Grow Your I*

This book clearly explains time-tested marketing concepts and relates them strategically to small business. What I love is how Jon is so clear that marketing is a series of ongoing events (rather than a one-time or occasional action) to create and nurture relationships with your current and future customers.

Jon McCulloch is indeed the Evil Bald Genius — follow his advice, learn his strategies, embrace his philosophy on positioning and personality. Then take action on what he shares with you in this book and your business will succeed. I can say this because I've done it, and it works!

Angie Mattson, Your Organized Guide, Inc.
www.YourOrganizedGuide.com

Jon McCulloch has provided a complete marketing blueprint for small businesses in one book. It's all there.

Not only does he tell you what you need to do, why you need to do it and how, he also gives you the tools to manage time in your business to get all of this done and provides oodles of detail on the really practical stuff you need to get around to as part of it all.

For anyone willing to absorb and apply what is shared in this book, it really is a complete recipe for growing your business.

Flor McCarthy, McCarthy & Co. Solicitors
www.mccarthy.ie

There isn't a single sentence in this book that wouldn't be incredibly useful to any business owner. Jon McCulloch has crammed a fantastic amount of information into this guide, all backed by hard data and evidence, and refreshingly free of bullshit.

Jon McCulloch's talent lies in being able to explain the logic behind each element so you really understand why you need to master it, and can easily see how to apply it within your own business and industry.

For a start-up company, following this step-by-step blueprint will enable you to properly structure your business and marketing strategies from the outset, avoiding the usual mistakes that most new business owners make, and for an established business looking to grow, *Grow Your Business FAST* provides a powerful checklist of what still needs to be done and what can be achieved.

This isn't a get-rich-quick guide, but a study in how hard graft can be most efficiently directed for the quickest results. *Grow Your Business FAST* should sit on every business owner's desk and be referred to often. Even the Contents Page is a joy to read and a useful business tool in itself.

It's not often you can describe a business book as riveting but Jon's writing style meant I read the book from cover to cover over one weekend.

A fantastic, *enjoyable* read. The mind boggles as to what else Jon McCulloch has up his sleeves.

Michelle Knight
www.talladiumuk.co.uk

This book is jam packed with useful stuff so much so you start to feel that time to do this will be an issue, then he even gives you tips on how to fit it into your day or sometimes night.

Kevin Hever
www.cornerstonefinancial.co.uk

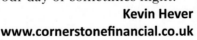

Jon McCulloch is not your typical entrepreneur. He understands — really understands — how to create practical business success applicable to any and all businesses. And all of the strategies he teaches he has used himself to create his own highly successful business.

In *Grow Your Business FAST* Jon goes through all the things you really need to know to create a successful business. For me one of the most important chapters was 'getting it all done' and his 'daily strategy for success'. Implementing the advice in this chapter alone will make your business ten if not a hundred times more likely to succeed. I read a *lot* of books - yet I have learnt more about creating a highly successful business from Jon McCulloch than from anyone else. Buy this book and so will you.

Dev Lall FRCS
www.privatepracticeexpert.co.uk

This is the first book I have ever read that grabs you by the throat and makes you understand how, without vigorous, intelligent marketing, anyone running a micro or SME business is wasting his or her time. The Evil Bald Genius does not do pussyfooting: be warned.

Unlike the thousands of mealy-mouthed marketing authors in the past who try to sell you half-assed marketing "solutions", the EBG shoves his methods right in your face and makes you see how they'll work for you.

And he has hundreds of stonking success stories to prove that they work. *Grow Your Business FAST* is not for the faint-hearted, but if you're faint-hearted, you won't go far in business anyway. This book is a brilliant piece of prose that will turn you into an evil genius of a marketer, too.

Suzan St Maur, Online business writer and best-selling author
www.HowToWriteBetter.net

This book comes with a big promise — and it's a promise fulfilled. Packed with tested strategies, Grow Your Business Fast tells you in plain language how to get more leads, produce more sales and make more money. And in business, that's really all that matters.

Its easy-to-read style means you can whip through the whole book in a day or two, though putting just 20% of the strategies to work is probably enough to revolutionise any small business — and very quickly at that.

Steve Prescott
www.steveprescottmarketing.co.uk

This book is one of the best I have read in a long time. Written with expert knowledge on a subject that many business people think they know but nearly always get it wrong.

The character of the writer flows off the pages. It is written with honesty, integrity, wit and a down to earth, no bull attitude, putting the real facts of business life on the table for all to see.

I would recommend this book to anyone who needs to get a better understanding of the whole concept of marketing and its key function in business. It is a must to any small business looking for a key insight into the world of marketing. I will be recommending it to all my clients and may even use this as a free book to every new client.

I could mention 5 or 6 elements from my first read of this book, but I have to start with ROI (return on investment), this alone is the key to me building my business. I know how long we retain our clients and that could be worth over £50,000. Its time for me to find some an impressive "attention grabbers".

David Taylor, Sheridan Accounting Solutions Limited
www.sheridanaccounting.co.uk

In an era of clueless Social Media experts spouting endless nonsense like "brand awareness" and "engagement", Jon's *Grow Your Business FAST* lifts the lid on what really works and gives specific advice as to how any small business can ramp up their profits within a short period of time.

It's an unfortunate fact that most businesses have been lied to by everyone from newspapers trying to flog them advertising space to these aforementioned 'Social Media' experts. For most SME owners this has led to almost a morbid fear of marketing, coming to think of it as something of a black art, something that they just aren't supposed to figure out.

I should know, I used to be one of these people.

But it doesn't have to be that way. Instead, by learning how to concentrate your efforts on the fundamentals of marketing and developing strategies like Premium Pricing that attract a better class of higher paying customer, your business can begin to turn itself around and grow like you've never imagined.

One word of warning though, Jon's advice is often quite brutal and unforgiving, but rest assured you're always getting the gods honest truth. When there's money on the line, that's the way it should be.

Keith Commins,
www.pearldesign.ie

Finally a book that is easy to understand, cuts through the BS and gives practical advice.

With *Grow Your Business FAST* Jon has hit the 'how to' marketing sweet spot.

I am undertaking the actions in this book on a daily basis.

It's like a boot being applied to my, sadly no-longer-pert, derriere.

Kat Smith, Hair Organics
www.hairorganics.co.uk

A feast of direct response marketing tips, skills and strategies you can actually use, *Grow Your Business FAST* is *essential* reading for any business owner. Jon's been battling it out in the front lines, discovering what really works, so you don't have to. Everything is presented in a clear and conversational fashion.

There's no fluff, no filler and no need for quantum leaps in your knowledge to use what Jon shares to your advantage. If you actually apply what you read to your business, your competitors won't know what hit them.

Marcus Santer, founder and chief instructor at Qigong15.com, the home of Qigong goodness

G *row Your Business FAST* is by far the most powerful Business Book that I have had the good fortune of reading (and I have read quite a few).

This book is a must for every business owner, who is serious about surviving during the economic downturn, whilst growing their business and increasing profit.

Grow Your Business FAST not only asks the question of Why we need to grow our businesses? but also delivers the step by step methods of HOW to grow your business.

Reading and learning is simply not enough. You MUST take action and implement.

I have read, learnt and implemented the techniques and strategies, and within 3 months, my New Business pipeline is healthier than ever, my customer list has increased by over 60%, my online communication click through rates have increased x 6, my turnover has doubled and my customers are spending more than previously.

Damien Mooney, Full Potential Marketing Ltd www.fullpotentialmarketing.co.uk

G YBF is the essential guide to small busir marketing. Jon takes you through a' vital steps you must know as a small b owner to be able to do effective marketin. works — and which your competitors neve. understand.

One particular section of the book which simply is excellent, and will shake the world for me owners, is the part about the deadliness of low prices. Jon b. explains why competing on price will lead to a slow, painful c for your business — and gives you the strategies and step-by-ste. guides you need to build a solid business where you no longer have to struggle with competing on low price and getting tiny profits.

I wholeheartedly recommend you read this book today, as every day going by without you taking action is a day you'll lose money.

Vegard Svanberg, Monsternett AS (in Halden, Norway)
www.monsternett.no

I hadn't expected to read a marketing book based on 'stool samples' but, turns out it's good shit.

Grow Your Business FAST goes beyond the usual 'what to do' and delves into the 'how to do it', which I think I why too many people including myself normally never get round to action after reading other books. I feel like I've had a slap around the face to get on and do stuff, just so long as I measure the results. I can't help but think this book will do anything else but bring in more sales.

Dave Carr, Quantum Digital
www.quantummobilewebsites.co.uk

Good: it reads easy and flows well

The bad: it kicks you in the nuts [immed]iately by giving you some straight to the [poin]t facts, take it or leave it. (I hope anyone [that]'s my competition would leave it!)

The ugly: you realise if you want to get ahead, [y]ou simply got to get off your arse and start doing some of this stuff.

I have to say *Grow Your Business FAST* is a brilliant book and I'll be using it as a business reminder manual as well as a blueprint to remind me of the stuff that I'm sure I'll miss trying to setup or grow my business.

I genuinely hope my competition do not get hold of a copy of this book.

Ed Farshi
www.piccolo.uk.com

Grow Your Business FAST, covers absolutely everything you need to know about moving up to the next level of growing your business.

There are lots of tips and advice that can be implemented straight away without having to spend fortunes and the information about driving highly qualified internet traffic to your website is bang up to date. The knowledge Jon McCulloch shares, I'm sure comes from years of hard work, trial and error and constant testing which means it's a "done for you" invaluable resource you can refer to again and again.

Jon's style of writing is unique and very easy to read, the only hard thing I found was putting the book down.

A brilliant marketing and copywriting master class for anyone who's serious about growing their business.

Mo Yusuff, Club Row Creations
www.clubrowcreations.co.uk

My head is spinning... I cannot believe how much wealth building material Jon has managed to cram into this compact volume!

The style is reminiscent of Dan Kennedy's books: upfront, non-apologetic, and telling the reader how things are - only with much more oomph...

You will find zero filler here... just pages and pages stuffed with proven business building strategies. I have a private collection of at least 150 books in the marketing genre, and I'm telling you; this book ranks in the top five when it comes to the foundations of growing a successful business in minimal time.

Kirk Bardsley, direct-response marketer/copywriter
www.KirkBardsley.com

If you've previously trusted graphic designers, web designers, or the art department of newspapers and magazines to produce your advertising, and you're frequently disappointed with the results, this book will blow your mind!

Jon McCulloch gives you a complete overview of the kind of people you need (not want) to be selling to, how to craft a marketing message that appeals directly to those people, and how to choose the most effective media to deliver your message.

Jon's strategy for using email is probably the quickest, easiest, and most profitable thing you could ever do for your business, and I would happily bet none of your competitors are using this method.

Entering into the world of direct-response marketing is like going on a journey. And if you follow the steps laid out in *Grow Your Business FAST*, you'll probably look back on this day in the future and think to yourself "That was the day everything changed...".

Andrew Gardner
www.boutiquephotography.com

Timing is everything, last night I was away from home on business, sat in a hotel not much to do, so I started to read, and read, and read. I think I started about 9.00pm and fell asleep still reading about 2.30am.

What a read!

I'm sure this was his intention but reading *Grow Your Business FAST* is just like sitting talking to Jon over a pint. It flows, the arguments make sense, and even when your mind questions things Jon seems to answer these as well. There are so many nuggets in there that need to be referred to over and over again.

One thing I am going to do, (tonight probably) is go through it all again and write down bullet points from it, reminders if you like, which I know will keep me going.

What I found most helpful was although a lot of the subject matter was known to me, I found when I was honest with myself, that I was only going part of the way — 60, 70% is not good enough, and already I have identified ways I can make my business better. After all I am not in the Licensing Business, I am in the business of marketing my Licensing Services.

Now the hard work begins. I am going to take 5 ideas at a time, perfect them, then move on to the next 5 and so on. Number 1 is undoubtedly to create a set of rules for myself. Easy to ignore when you work for yourself on your own.

Stewart Gibson
www.gpretail.co.uk/licence-applications

Grow Your Business *FAST* is a very entertaining read — not like the normal stuffy books on this subject.

I've read many before and attended a lot of seminars but this is the first one I've come across that covers it all — and by covering it all it puts everything into perspective and in its place.

Steve Barnett, Hexagon IT
www.hexagon-it.co.uk

Fucking brilliant! *Grow Your Business <u>FAST</u>* will definitely help SME business owners if they apply it! It's chock full with real-world advice which is immediately actionable! I think it's superb.

Two Gems worth noting upfront which get me salivating each time I think back to them are Pareto's 80/20 rule which in a sense really could be the magic bullet used to transform a business; and the second is Premier Positioning. In a nutshell this book has helped me quickly and easily identify the most important parts of my business (80/20 Rule). Spending time on these areas will get me exponentially better results and by choosing to position myself and business at the premium end of my market I am getting the best possible return on that activity. Genius!

The more business owners that this book gets in front of the better!

Brett Smart
www.findatenantonline.com

GYBF is a great piece. GYBF reads like a conversation with Jon. GYBF is clear, concise, and the condensation of so much business wisdom that GYBF must be leapt over like a tiger, and then methodically gone through like a tortoise...

The one thing that particularly jumped out at me was King of the Hill. It has shown me what I must do and will establish me as *the* expert in adult orthodontics!!!! Thanks, Jon.

Christopher West, Lotus Othodontics
www.lotusorthodontics.com

A WESOME - I tell you *Grow Your Business <u>FAST</u>* has fired me up all over again about the truth of the matters of business, clients and life

There is so much in there — in addition to the amazing business wisdom, fabulous and devastatingly simple copywriting tips, it's got so much life assistance and mindset improving information I reckon it should be called *Grow Your Business (and Sort your life out!) <u>FAST</u>*.

Already an addict of the EBG style, I love the fact that it doesn't sugar coat a single thing - and that it speaks to the reader as an adult. I also love the fact that this is NOT a "done for you" solution builder but a "do it yourself - and here's how" solution builder. That said, you were a lot tamer than usual!

The one thing that jumps out at me is how simple you have made growing a business — this allows the reader to really focus their efforts on implementation - as what you have written is so easily understood.

I think it's a great place to start for a new business owner — as it's all in there and (not that I'm accusing you of plagiarism) it lends from and simplifies enduring principles from some of the greats, which will make it a must have guide for Business Owners who refuse mediocre.

It's structured in a logical way which really helps a business owner to build on the principles step by step.

Olayinka Ewuola
www.eaglessl.co.uk

J on McCulloch's *Grow Your Business <u>FAST</u>* is a Must Have for anyone starting up or running a small business! Definitely not a book for a 'wish list' — you need it and you need it NOW! Einstein said, "If you can't explain it simply, you don't understand it well enough."

The EBG ably demonstrates his understanding of the topics and ideas in this book, which are all grounded on well-established business and marketing theories. Using examples from his own and others experiences Jon has created a fantastic blueprint for you the small business owner, to adapt and implement immediately.

The hardest thing to do is translate theory into practice, I know this from my own experience - moving from 'teaching' to 'doing'. If this book had been available about 3 years ago it would definitely have saved me making lots of costly mistakes.

Lesley White, NK9D Ltd
www.nk9d.co.uk

C alling Jon McCulloch's new book a blueprint is spot on because all the necessary info is right there in a neat and potent package.

It was a fun and easy read too - I (unintentionally) knocked it out cover to cover in one evening.

No bullshit either. Just EBG telling you what you need to do to grow your business fast. (Honesty and integrity are beautiful things aren't they?)

My favourite sections were "Email Marketing" — one tip there helped me bring in an extra $1,150 for a client last week — and the "Premiere Positioning" and "Premium Pricing" sections... worth their weight in gold. What I learned there will be a major force behind the changes and new business I'm starting this summer.

Andy Moose, 'cigar smoking email writer'
andymoose.com

For the small business owner *Grow Your Business FAST* is a must have "how to run a business" manual. People get manuals for car repair (Haynes) and for DIY(Readers Digest) generally giving them tips on how to save money.

GYBF helps them make money but just as important how not to waste money on pointless advertising and marketing (by giving them examples). Most business books are based on theory but this is a hands on in the trenches book. And it is not a book for dummies but a serious attempt to show people how to run their business.

It is for start ups and more established businesses who may be struggling. Also great tips on how a business owner can grow and develop as a person (so not just about growing the business).

Key points for me were:

- Easy to read and to follow the flow of the book.
- Balanced opinion throughout the book. Jon tells you about the importance of testing and not just taking his word as gospel.
- Explains the myths and misconceptions out there which are probably in the mind of the business owner.
- Pointing out the pitfalls and how to overcome them (with examples).
- Focusing on the important numbers... ROI and lifetime value of a client.
- Dangers of Social Media.... not to disregard it but to be aware it will not solve all their problems (balanced opinion).
- Minute details... even down to the font type and the line length of adverts and sales letters making them easier to read for the end user.

I have been a following Jon's work for years so much of what he says I am familiar with. However the book highlighted a lot of stuff I know but am not implementing... a kick in the backside for me!!

Will be my go to book in growing my and my clients' businesses.
Robert Cartoon, Cartoon Coaching and Consultancy
www.wildwoodrooms.co.uk

I'm a newbie to marketing and loved *Grow Your Business FAST*.

Jon's intelligent, practical and honest approach sets out a common sense reason for marketing your business and how to go about it. Law school doesn't teach you how to run a business let alone how to deal with marketing it!

A Key point for me was positioning and pricing and how to go about it. Seeing in print the actual effect of a 10% increase AND decrease in pricing was a reality check and really made me stand back and look at my business afresh. The real scary bit was that it's so easy to get caught up in the fear of losing a client because of pricing but, as you rightly point out, there are clients that need to be lost and every business has them!

I think the book is a must for any business owner who wants to get the edge over the competition. Whether you intend to implement ideas and strategies yourself or intend to bring in marketing experts you need to have an understanding of the fundamentals and what you should be doing.

Teresa Payne, Parfitt Cresswell Solicitors
www.parfittcresswell.com

I just hope my competition don't get hold of this powerful book! I've read hundreds of business building books over the years. Most are boring and rarely get finished, but Jon, your book is like a breath of fresh air, and written in a way that kept me wanting more, full of practical information that works.

For me being reminded of the importance of focusing your marketing message directly to your chosen and highly targeted market was invaluable.

Thanks a million Jon.

Paull Newsome, County Flat Roofing,
www.countyflatroofing.co.uk

Buying business books is often like a "Schrödinger' Cat" experiment. Before you open it it's potentially the best business book you've ever, ever read, or, more likely, yet another trite rehash of some college professor's tired anecdotes about how a successful company that bears no relation to yours did 'it'.

Jon McCulloch's GYBF is not Schrödinger's cat.

What you get in this book is an extraordinary blueprint of how you can make your business soar. Make no mistake however, Jon does not offer a 'magic bullet', he offers a tough and intensive programme that is tried and tested. The difference between his ideas and almost every business book out there is that his ideas and this plan work, for everyone. You just have to put in the work. There is no other way.

Paul Bond,
www.brixworkwear.com

The good news is that almost any business that gives people what they want can still make a profit. The bad news, as Jon McCulloch points out, is there will be hard work involved and there are no magic bullets.

But if work doesn't scare you and you just want to know how to grow any business, then it all comes down to marketing and knowing the numbers. And that's great news because it means Jon's blunt, no-nonsense, no-fluff blueprint is all you need to turn your business into the profit-making machine it should be.

Roy Everitt, Cinnamon Edge
www.cinnamonedge.co.uk

What a great read. *Grow Your Business* *FAST* drove home a simple but very crucial message for our vintage bike business: all customers are not equal. We absolutely must stop trying to be all things to all customers and concentrate our efforts on the 20 % of clients who account for 80 % of the sales.

Of course I knew this already, intellectually, and had started to do something about it by compiling a Best Customers list made up of the 20% of top spenders each month. But I haven't targeted the list in any way and consequently haven't yet reaped the rewards.

A quick check of figures proves Jon's point: we have over 5,000 clients on our database yet the combined annual spend of the 250 clients on the Best Customer List represents 70 % of our total annual turnover.

I'm flabbergasted. And very determined to find ways to a) deter small spenders and time-wasters and b) improve rapport and services with our best customers initially via a new monthly printed newsletter. This must be the key to success.

Thank you indeed, Jon, for such valuable insights.

Lorraine Harris, Classic Motos France
www.classicmotos.fr

Jon strips away any false notions you may have had over what the universe owes you (and your business). His advice is accessible, pragmatic, hard-hitting, and grounded in an ultra-realistic picture of how things actually work — not how you might think they work or want them to work. If you read this book and then ignore its ideas, prepare for stagnation or worse. If however you implement its ideas, prepare for success!

Bren Cullen, SurveyGuru
www.surveyguru.com

Jon has captured what every business person needs to understand and know about growing a business and how marketing is fundamental to business success.

Grow Your Business FAST is straight talking and easy to understand, if not a bit uncomfortable at first. I wish I had this book when I was at college and starting my career — I would have saved so much time and effort.

Jason Hier
www.roelto.com

You can spend your whole life reading business books and never getting things done. Or you can sidestep all the endless guff and just get the practical, transformational stuff from Jon McCulloch. 'Grow Your Business Fast' touches on so many aspects of running a successful business.

There's a whole bag of quick wins, business changing principles and foundations in deeper topics like copywriting and web traffic generation. Frankly, I've never seen a book that gives so much value across so many fields... but as a member of Jon's inner circle, it's what I've come to expect!"

James Daniel — Copywriter
www.earthmonkey.co.uk

I have read any number of books on marketing, but this book by Jon McCulloch is nothing short of a Masterclass in how to grow your business. Moreover it is so well written, it reads like a novel. Jon is one of those people who says it as it is, not for any other reason than he has found out what works by doing it himself.

By implementing just a couple of the ideas you will see a significant improvement in your business. I know that we have! We are going to recommend the book to all our clients.

Peter Robson, Your Niche Business
www.yournichebusiness.co.uk

I am a very keen and capable golfer but I didn't get to that standard without some very good coaching from the pro at my club. If you are looking to start out in business, or grow your business, then doing so without the help of this book would be just like turning up at the first tee with all your new golf gear, having never had a lesson in your life, and expecting to shoot below par (in golf below par actually means you are very good).

Get this book if you want to get good at running your own business as Jon is a complete pro and will show you exactly how to avoid the hazards and keep the ball bang in the middle of the fairway.

Aarif Merali, d2rCrossmedia,
www.d2rCrossMedia.com

R ight from the get go there's no time wasted on warming you up and it jumps right into the action steps (a style I personally enjoy). I hate chit-chat. I wish someone had written something like this a few years ago. There is no hype and it's a complete no-nonsense approach with a step-by-step guide — like a paint by numbers blueprint, albeit with very straightforward advice which is typical of Jon's style:

- Several things guaranteed to not make you any money.
- The hardest, most time-consuming and expensive (and least profitable) thing all businesses tend to do in their marketing first and how to avoid it and increase your ROI dramatically.
- The 4 Simple Keys that make *any* marketing message extremely effective (and even irresistible).

And a lot more before you even touch page 40. The section of polarizing your audience is best explained by Jon who does it quite a bit himself. Then you move on to other topics like Premier Positioning including

- What is so attractive about a "Rolls Royce"?
- How you can increase your profits by 39% or more by making this simple tweak to your prices.
- The MOST effective marketing vehicle with perhaps the best ROI and why your competition isn't using it.

And there's a lot more such as how to get your ad prices as cheap as you possible, how to get it all done — even if you take baby steps, and there's an appendix which could have been the topic for another book — How to write a profitable ad or sales letter. This belongs on the desk of every business owner (and more important, in their heads after they've read it).

Sanjay Pande
DirectMarketingBlueprints.com

Grow Your
Business
FAST

The Quick, Dirty, and <u>Uncensored</u> Secrets to
Extraordinary Small Business Success
Despite Recession, Crap Governments
and Tight-Arsed Banks

Jon McCulloch
The Evil Bald Genius

Published by
Impression Publishing
www.ImpressionPublishing.net

First Edition published 2013

Printed and bound in Great Britain by
www.printandpublish.co.uk

A catalogue record for this book
is available from The British Library
ISBN 978-1-908374-96-7

Contents

Contents

Contents

Preface

Congratulations... And welcome to my world. By making the effort to get this book in your hands, you just made a huge leap forward in your business life. It might not feel like that right now, but by the time you've finished reading it and started putting the strategies to work in your business, you're going to be so far ahead of your competitors they really won't know what's happening.

I'm Jon McCulloch, a.k.a. *The Evil Bald Genius*, and in joining me for the next 300 or so pages you've just let yourself in for an unimaginable and life-changing experience (and one not for the faint-hearted). More about why they call me the *Evil Bald Genius*, or *The EBG* for short, in a moment.

Because before we get into that, I have a lot of ideas and concepts to share with you during our time together, and your understanding all of them is vital to your business success. I promise to share *everything* with you: the good, the bad, *and* the ugly.

And you'll learn something from all three.

Even more important than that... if you *do* put them to work for you, you're very quickly going to be making more money with less work, less hassle, and fewer headaches.

Assuming that's what you actually *want* of course. Because, presumably you've invested in this book because you want to grow your business and you know you're not quite hitting the mark yet. You know there's a lot more opportunity out there for making money, ethically, legally, and morally, but the precise details of the "how to" is somehow eluding you, tantalisingly just out of reach. You can see it... hell, you can taste and smell the money... but you can't quite touch it yet.

If that's so, then you're in exactly the right place.

Because the secrets I've uncovered after many years in the trenches, helping business owners just like you grow their businesses and dramatically increase their profits, are waiting here for you to plug straight into your own business... *starting right now*. It's no exaggeration to say some of the profit-boosting strategies you'll find within these pages could be making you more money within five minutes of you reading them.

Everything I've included in this book has been tested and proven by me and my clients over the years, in both boom- and bust-economies. That's a story in itself, and one to keep you right on the edge of your seat as it unfolds. It's been a wild time, but a fun one, as you're going to see for yourself as we get to know each other. In the meantime, buckle up, let go of the sides, and enjoy the ride.

Yadda, Yadda, Yadda

Yet, I do know you've likely heard all this before, people swearing to share with you the secrets to Life, the Universe and Everything, only to find they promise much and deliver nothing.

And maybe *Grow Your Business FAST* is more of the

same-old, same-old? Just the same trite yadda, yadda, yadda you hear every day?

Look, I know it's easy for me to say this... but you've probably never come across anyone quite like me at all before.

Yes, I also promise much.

But then I deliver even more than I promise.

Yet I don't expect you to take my word for this. Anyone can make any claim they like, especially now we have the Internet where having a slick and professional website means nothing, since even a half-witted teenager can throw one up overnight and have it looking most convincing.

Truth is, I have a group of more than 135 Entrepreneurs I coach and mentor and the comments I get about the quality and power of what I share with them is humbling, even for an Evil Bald Genius. More than 85% of the people I allow in to my Inner Circle stay for at least a year in an industry where the average for this kind of group is 50% over just two months. My results are off the scale. And, no, I'm not trying to get you to join, so I'm not even going to share the URL with you right now. It's invitation-only and we don't even know each other yet. Perhaps some time in the future *if* you qualify and you want to apply for a place, then maybe you can. Moreover, I've worked with many multi-millionaire Entrepreneurs on both sides of the Pond over the years, men and women who understand business themselves and yet are willing to pay a short, irascible bald guy 4,000 miles and a half-dozen timezones away a small fortune (at a truly *ruinous* exchange rate) to help them grow their businesses rather than rely on home-grown talent.

There has to be a *reason* for that, and it's not my height, good looks, or natural charm.

Those reasons will become apparent as you read this book.

But in the meantime, I ask you *not* to believe me blindly

about anything you read here. I *want* you to be sceptical, questioning and even cynical. I don't expect you to take anything I say at face value, so please, examine everything with all the critical thinking skills you can muster, and then *test it for yourself* in your own business in the harsh and unforgiving reality of the marketplace and see if I'm right or not.

Why do I say this?

Two reasons.

First, I prefer to be correct than "right". I have a perfectly healthy ego, but I'm more interested in the *truth* than anything else. So if I'm wrong about something, I want someone to tell me.

And secondly, you're going to find what I have to share with you makes a substantial and dramatic difference to your business, your profits, and your life.

But *only* if you *take action*!

If you think I or anyone else can somehow teach you a magic spell that'll make you rich overnight and with no work... then you're reading the wrong book and learning from the wrong guy, and the best thing you can do is send this book back to me for a refund.

Finally... before we begin...

Why Do They Call Me the Evil Bald Genius?

Well... first let me just say all three are true to some extent, depending on your perspective.

They call me a Genius because I'm pretty smart when it comes down to it. Not to brag or anything, but it's a fact, as you'll come to discover for yourself as you get to know me better.

Why Bald?

Obvious, really. Although it's strictly untrue because I actually shave my noggin. If I left it to sprout for long enough, I'd have hair just like normal people do.

And Evil?

It's really just a bit of fun, and it refers to some of the fiendishly clever but simple strategies I use in my own business and share with others to help them grow theirs. Many of them are here in this book.

But I've also had the epithet levelled at me because I'm an atheist libertarian. It seems some people can't get their heads around the idea I don't go around killing little old ladies and kicking puppies because I'm not afraid of an afterlife filled with imaginative and inventive devils and demons wielding red-hot pitchforks and pokers[1]. And there are yet others who find my principles of self-reliance and a refusal to be responsible for others' problems to be personally offensive. Why this is I can but imagine, but I suspect it's because they can't intimidate me with their guilt-trips and so seek to insult me instead.

Whatever. It's all water off a duck's back to me, and I find it all rather amusing. So, I positively embrace the "Evil" moniker as my own.

But, *really* Evil?

Well, just read the rest of the book, put the strategies to work for you, and *then* make your mind up.

A Few Notes Before You Get Started

1. English is a funny language in that there are no gender-neutral third-person singular pronouns. So

---

1. And if the only reason you don't do evil things is a 2,000 year old book written by bronze-age goat herders says it's naughty, then you really do need help.

instead of writing barbaric and ugly phrases like "he or she", "his or hers", or, vilest of all, "s/he", I've taken the traditional route, old fart that I am, and used the masculine throughout. If this offends you, then you're going to hate the rest of the book, of that I'm certain.

2. I swear a lot... and many of the words I drop into conversation have found their way into this book. Please don't read this book and then write to me and complain about my bad language. Not only do I not care, but you'll just invite mockery and make yourself look stupid.

3. I'm not interested in your "feedback". If I get something objectively wrong, by all means correct me. But if you're just giving me your unsolicited opinions on how I ought to run my business or communicate with my audience, please don't bother. Your opinions are irrelevant. There's an excellent clip here from Howard Stern that sums up my feelings perfectly: www.jonmcculloch.com/gybf/howard-stern

4. Any mistakes you find are entirely mine and mine alone. You are free to send comments and corrections to me here: gybf@jonmcculloch.com. Don't hold your breath waiting for a reply, though. Consider this as a "thank you" in advance.

Chapter 1

Grow Your Business *FAST*

This book has one purpose: to *Grow Your Business FAST*. That's it. That's why I've written it, and that's what it's intended to do for you. It's not for entertainment or intended for anyone with merely passing and idle curiosity about what's required to take pretty much any small business and dramatically improve its fortunes, and vastly increase its profits — all ethically, morally, legally, and entirely above board.

But you need to understand much of what you'll discover here in our time together is going to be very uncomfortable for you; some of it may even be offensive, and you might be tempted to ignore the message because you don't like the me, the messenger, or the way I present myself.

That'd be a shame, but if you do have that reaction you'll not be the first, nor will you be the last.

And I really don't much care if I offend you or not: the truth is here, and it's up to you to heed it and succeed, or ignore it and perhaps allow your business to become one of the 80% going bust in the first five years of trading because you insist on seeing the business world as you *think* it is rather than how it *actually* is.

Nor is this a book stuffed with woolly theories, vague hypotheses, and half-baked ideas about what works or doesn't work in the unforgiving reality of the marketplace. Nor is it written by some pompous old egghead, snug and warm in his tenured University professorship, who's never actually run a business of his own out here in the real world.

Because everything I share with you in *Grow Your Business FAST* has been "battle-tested" and proven to work by me, personally, as well as thousands and perhaps even *millions* of business owners just like you from all over the world — of every race, in every culture, and of every religious persuasion (including those of *none*, like me).

And it works.

In short, what you have in your hands is a complete Blueprint for all serious and determined business owners who are sick and tired of working ever longer hours for less and less reward, running faster and faster just to stand still, who want to make more money with less work, less hassle, and fewer headaches selling their products and services at higher prices than their competitors to premium-quality customers and clients not only glad but actually *eager* to pay whatever price asked of them.

Best of all… the strategies, tools, tips and techniques I share with you in these pages are so simple and easy, you can start putting them to work in your business *today* and see increased profits *tomorrow*, or even sooner. Most of what you do to grow a business takes time, but some of the simplest strategies I share with you take effect literally[2] instantly.

---

2.   And I use the word in its correct sense.

The Prize: Sovereignty

Ultimately, the intended end result is to deliver into your hands a business where you have what I call *Sovereignty* — doing *what* you want, *when* you want, with *whom* you want, at the *price* you want... and only *if* you want to do it at all.

In business terms this means being able to pick and choose among the people who are queuing up to buy from you, and realising at a deep and visceral level you are not dependent upon or beholden to any one customer or client. Yes, you do need customers and clients, but no *one* individual or company should have the power to hold you to ransom with the promise of fees, contracts and purchases, or future orders. If you find yourself in that position, then you don't actually have a business at all — you have what we can describe as being a terrible *job* at the very best; what we can call it at worst is unprintable.

But, here's my promise to you: if you follow the steps I lay out in *Grow Your Business FAST*, then Sovereignty is well within your grasp. And by the time you've got to the end of it and got to grips with the sometimes uncomfortable and counterintuitive truths I share with you, you're going to have all the strategies, tools, tips, and techniques at your fingertips to put to work and make it happen for you.

Because the truth is, the secret to business success in any economy, regardless of recession, crap governments and tight-arsed banks, is actually no secret at all.

The Dirty 'M' Word No One Likes to Say

The difference between successful businesses and unsuccessful ones is effective[3] marketing — and what works

---

3.   And in this case "effective" means "profitable"

and doesn't work in marketing has been known for a long time. And it all boils down to a surprisingly small number of equally surprisingly powerful *fundamentals*.

What's more, these fundamentals never change, and there are never any new ones. That's why they're *called* fundamentals. So next time you see someone promising a "brand new way of marketing", and you've got to buy this funky new widget because all the old ways of marketing no longer work, just take pause for a moment and think about what they're really saying[4].

Truth is, most of the time they're just repackaging something old in a new way. We see this all the time with the Internet — every time a new technology becomes available, or cheap or simple enough for the business owner in the street to use, some slimeball stands up and claims he has discovered the brand new, never-seen-before *One True Way of Marketing*.

And it's all bullshit.

Marketing is Marketing is Marketing

As long as you're selling to human beings the fundamentals will always, I repeat, *always* be the same. You'll discover why this is as we go through *Grow Your Business FAST*, and you'll soon be proving it for yourself, but just for now I simply ask you to take it on trust. Any differences you discover or perceive will be differences of style, not substance.

---

4. True story: one loathsome, lying sack-of-shit marketer sent out an email to his list saying "If you're not using Facebook you won't make any money online this year. Simple". Thing is, he was hawking an affiliate product, yet his *own* product was a Wordpress plugin to help with keyword research for Search Engine Optimisation. So, what's he saying? His own product isn't going to help you make any money... or he's lying about the Facebook thing? You couldn't make it up, could you?

In fact, some of the most powerful marketing strategies I know date back over 150 years and spank the pants off the more modern methods, most of which have gained traction among business owners because they're cheap and easy, and require very little thought or effort. But more on that later.

Now, I know the very word "marketing" conjures up some very negative images in most people's minds. Most people when they think of marketing imagine fast-talking BMW-driving yuppies with big mouths and even bigger expense accounts swaggering from wine-bar to sushi restaurant pontificating on "brand-identity", "brand awareness", "getting out there", and other meaningless crap.

Fortunately, while these lamentable creatures do exist, they have very little to do with the kind of marketing I'm talking about in *Grow Your Business FAST*, which is the kind of marketing driving the engine of small business, and which in turn keeps the economy trundling along, and to everyone's benefit. We call it *direct response marketing* because in every single thing we do we ask the prospect, customer, or client to take an immediate and direct action we can measure. We are not interested in pouring good money after bad into marketing we cannot tell is working for us.

But that's not all.

Because on top of the common misconceptions held by business owners of what marketing is, I often hear people on the other side of the counter say marketing doesn't work on them.

Well, perhaps; perhaps not.

But I think it's much more likely they don't understand what marketing *is*. Because when I dig a little deeper and try and find out what they actually mean, it turns out they are invariably talking about the hard-sell tactics you sometimes come across, or the cheesy kind of marketing built on tricks and gimmicks, dripping with false sincerity.

In other words, they're saying the kind of marketing they don't like and doesn't work on them... they don't like it and it doesn't work on them. This kind of statement is hardly pushing back the frontiers of human knowledge.

We, all of us, have marketing strategies we detest and that leave us cold. Take me, for example. I can't stand telemarketing calls, cold or otherwise. The way I run my business means no-one calls me without an appointment. Not even my solicitor, my bank manager, or my accountant do that. So when the phone does ring and it's a marketing call, even if it's from a firm I do business with, they get short shrift.

In other words, telemarketing doesn't *ever* work on *me*.

But this doesn't mean telemarketing doesn't work anywhere at all, because it obviously does. I personally know people who have kicked off their own businesses by making literally thousands of cold-calls. It's not something I'd want to do, and it's not something I'd respond to favourably, but that's not the point.

It *works*.

It just doesn't work on everyone who receives a call, and for many reasons, it might not work for every business (and the only way to know if it's going to work in *your* business or not is to test it and see what happens. That's an important observation we'll see cropping up all over the place as we get into the detail of how to market your business effectively).

These people who claim marketing doesn't work on them are probably sincere in their beliefs and in what they say, yet they're not only misinformed or uninformed about what marketing actually *is*, but they're also wrong about it not working on them.

They just don't realise what's working on them because

they have no reason to notice or object to it. When things go smoothly and we're having a good time, we scarcely notice it other than to feel good.

Understanding this is crucial for your success as a marketer, because then you'll understand what anyone but your target market thinks or feels about your marketing strategy, tactics, and implementation is irrelevant — and the only vote worth counting is a vote your customers and clients make with their wallets. I say this because you are inevitably going to get a lot of pissers and moaners, even in your target market, and you'll be tempted to believe their negative reactions are representative of the whole. They are not. Focus on your sales, and to hell with the rest.

More on this later, but for now, just embrace the fact marketing as a strategy for selling more products and services works on *everyone*, because it's really about helping people solve their problems. And we all like to have our problems solved, don't we?

Alas, this isn't the worst of our problems, because we have to contend with…

The Myth of the Better Mousetrap

There's a small but sizeable minority of business owners who, for reasons I have never quite been able to fathom, seem to believe their products and services ought to "sell themselves", like a better mousetrap is supposed to.

Authors, painters, chefs, and other arty people are particularly prone to this, and they frequently wax lyrical justifying the reasons they have for not marketing their work effectively, while at the same time complaining to anyone who'll listen about how little money they're making.

These two things are not coincidental.

I suppose in an ideal world the sheer power of Art would magically reach out and draw the Enlightened in; but the world isn't like that.

As I hinted a few pages back, at the root of many a business owner's problems is a refusal to see the world accurately. They insist instead on trying to shoehorn their own subjective experience of and beliefs about reality into some warped idea of how they think things *should* or *ought* to be, hoping reality will comply.

Sadly, this refusal to deal with the world as it *actually is* rather than how they *think* it is, *should* be, or *ought* to be, is a guaranteed path to ruin, and is, in my opinion, one of the chief reasons 80% of businesses go out of business within the first five years of trading.

And like it or not, if people aren't buying form you, it's your own fault (and even of it wasn't you're still the one responsible for fixing things).

FACT: Your Business Lives or Dies on the Strength of Its Marketing

Because, marketing is the *one* and *only* thing bringing people through your door.

And… marketing, in effect, is *everything* and *anything* about you, your business, your products, and your services, your prospects, customers, and clients perceive about you.

You might want to think about that for a moment.

It does *not* mean you have to put up a façade and pretend to be something you're not. On the contrary, one of the most effective marketing strategies you'll ever put to work for you is to let your personality permeate everything you do. Most business owners won't have the spine to do this because they (correctly) think it'll drive some people away. While this might be a frightening prospect, it's actually A Good Thing, as I hope you'll come to understand, because it's far more important to think about the people it'll actually *draw* to you. I cover this in a lot more detail in a later chapter.

But what it *does* mean is if you want to succeed in business you have to consider the people who are paying your wages: your customers and clients. After all, they are the *only* reason your business exists. What I'm talking about here is unparalleled and unmatched levels of service with your customers' and clients' needs ahead of everything else, *including* your own immediate profits.

I'll explain more about this later, but right now let me just put your mind at rest, because I am not talking about your becoming a doormat and buying into the soul- and business-destroying idea "the customer is always right". That way lies madness and poverty.

Rather, I'm talking about attracting customers and clients who see you in an entirely different way, as a trusted advisor to be respected and heeded rather than the hired help to be abused and discarded as soon as a cheaper option comes along.

I am reminded of a quote at this point, one I think you'd do well to print out and stick on your wall where you can see it as you go about your day's work:

> *There is hardly anything in this world which some man cannot make a little worse and sell a little cheaper and the people who consider price alone are this man's lawful prey, as it is unwise to pay too much as it is to pay too little.*
>
> *When you pay too much you lose a little money that is all.*
>
> *When you pay too little you sometimes lose everything,*

> *because the thing you bought was incapable of doing the job it was supposed to do.*
>
> *The common law of business balance prohibits paying too little and getting a lot, it cannot be done.*
>
> *If you deal with the lowest bidder it is as well to add something extra for the risk you run and if you do that then you will have enough to pay for something better ~ **John Ruskin 1819-1900***

Mr. Ruskin had this one dead right, and as you'll discover for yourself by the time you reach the end of this book, finding those men and women to whom price is not nearly so important as value is a lot easier than you might think.

In the meantime, just remember:

- **No marketing means no traffic.** No people coming into your store, no phone calls, no mail, and no visitors hitting your website.

- **No traffic means no sales.** You can't sell to people who aren't there talking to you on the phone or writing to you, or aren't face to face with you in the flesh, or virtually, online.

- **No sales means no profits.** I hope you can see this is self-evident.

- **And no profits very quickly means no business.** I hope this is self-evident, too. Even non-profits and charities need to keep the lights burning and their staff paid.

So, given you have to be marketing effectively if you want your business to thrive and prosper, rather than just grind itself (and you) into the ground before going bust... and given you're marketing anyway, by default, simply because you and your business exist, whether you like to think that or not... doesn't it make sense to ensure you've actually got a handle on it all and you're marketing deliberately with a proven strategy and to a definite plan, rather than letting it just "happen" by accident?

The only sane answer to that is, "Yes, EBG, it does".

What Kind of Business Do You Really Want?

Over the years I've worked with hundreds of business owners and helped *thousands* in one way or another. And while they've all had different aspirations and motivations, not a single one of them has ever said to me they wanted to work harder than they were doing, have more hassles and headaches, and endure it all for less reward.

Instead a common refrain was, in effect, they wanted to be making more money with less work, less hassle, and fewer headaches, *and* they wanted to enjoy doing it. Sure, the audience is somewhat self-selecting and biased towards business owners who want or need help, but within it there lurks an important point: we all want to be doing better in our businesses, even if we're going OK now. No one wants to take a pay cut, and we'd all like to be paid the same or more for doing even less work. Moreover, you can't stand still in business even if you want to: if you're not moving forwards with the world, you're effectively falling behind.

It might surprise you to discover I, myself, am not motivated just by money. Yes, I like making money and you won't see me selling myself cheap, because doing that heaps all manner of other problems upon us aside from the cut in income. I am unashamedly proud of being the highest priced copywriter and marketing consultant in Ireland and the UK, and quite possibly in the whole of Europe.

But it comes down to far more than just the Groats[5].

See, when you're a business owner the buck stops with you. If you don't make a profit, then you don't eat. Your employees share none of this risk and get paid regardless, of course[6]. The moment they don't get paid or things get too tough, they're off to another job.

And very quickly, unless you keep on top of things, your business starts to run you instead of you running it. And I know from personal experience how draining and demoralising this is. It begins to take over your entire life. It affects everything, from your health to your relationships with others.

Yet it almost always comes down to two things:

1. Bad customers or clients.

2. Not making enough money.

And each feeds into the other if we're not careful and suck us down into a spiral of misery and despair.

Fortunately there's a simple cure for both of them, and instead of having a business hanging like the proverbial millstone around your neck, it's surprisingly easy to have one giving you the personal Sovereignty you hoped for when you started your business in the first place.

Sounds like a tall order, perhaps, especially if you're struggling in your business and at rock bottom right now, but I promise you change can come remarkably fast once you

---

5. I use Groats here because this book is going out to an international audience and I am not going to sit here and type "dollars, euro, or pounds" over and over again. So mostly I'll use "Groats", OK?

6. And yet even though they *don't* share the risk many of them still clamour for "profit sharing" because that's, you know, "fair". It's only fair if they agree to take a pay *cut* when things aren't quite so rosy. Suggest that, though, and all you hear is crickets.

start taking action.

A Word of Warning

Several words, in fact.

Despite the promises I've made you, I also need to be clear about something: you're not going to turn your business around and make it a monumental success just by *reading* this book.

It's a very practical Blueprint to turn your business around and dramatically improve your profits and the quality of your life.

But you have to *take action...* and every action brings an equal and opposite reaction.

So my first warning is...

Fact of Uncaring Reality No.1: Nothing Comes Without a Price

And business success is no exception.

The price of a successful business is discipline, more than a little hard work, many late nights, and frequent setbacks and disappointments; but a struggling, so-so business has a price all of its own — and perhaps the unceasing pain of regret, the headaches, the frustration, and endless fruitless hours scratching around to make a profit is a price you've already keenly felt being extracted from you an inch at a time.

More than that, there's no guarantee you won't ruffle a few feathers and even make one or two enemies, particularly among your competitors. And you're *definitely* going to need a thick skin, because, as does anyone who becomes successful at anything, you're going to draw more than your fair share of criticism, sniping, and envious and back-biting comments.

There's also a good chance you're going to run into a lot of resistance from friends and family, maybe even your spouse. Chances are your employees aren't going to be too keen on some of it, either.

All of this is unavoidable.

A large part of the secret of business success is to stop trying to be everything to everyone. If you try to be all things to all men and women, you very quickly end up being nothing of consequence to anyone.

You can't please or even serve everyone, so it's just as important to say loudly and clearly to whom you *don't* want to sell your products and services, as it is to say to whom you *do* want to sell them. And that can be emotionally very difficult, especially in the beginning when you've been used to taking every customer or client who came along because you were afraid of losing their business. You also need to stop being nice just for the sake of being nice. Nothing wrong with good manners, but compromising your integrity for fear of offending someone (especially someone who isn't giving you money) is a waste of time and energy.

So before you *agree* to pay the price... are you *sure* you're *willing* to pay it?

Secondly...

Fact of Uncaring Reality No.2: You Are Not a Special Flower

As I mentioned above, everything I share with you in *Grow Your Business FAST* has been proven to work in the real world of small business in probably every single country in the world, and in hundreds, perhaps thousands, of industries and niches.

So while it's *possible* you have somehow contrived to be in a business and dealing with customers and clients in a way you can truthfully say "My Business Is Different", it is *highly unlikely* — to the point where it's vastly *more* likely you're just plain wrong and are merely feeling uncomfortable about what needs to be done and hiding behind a shield of irrationality.

Because you are not a Special Flower.

The reality of the market will be utterly heedless and uncaring of any sincerely held belief you have of deserving a break, or how people "ought" to buy from you just because you "need" the sales[7]. That's not how business works, and avoiding taking the marketing bull by the horns and wrestling it to the ground because you believe, for all sorts of manufactured reasons, marketing simply doesn't work or ought to be unnecessary in your industry or niche, is guaranteed to make your business crash and burn.

Human beings are wired up a certain way. It's how we've evolved[8]. And marketing systems and strategies have themselves evolved to influence people to react in certain ways, ways dictated to a large extent by the way we're wired up. In other words: if you're dealing with actual human beings and you've not discovered some strange race of aliens to sell to, then what I share with you here will work for you, of that I am certain.

Which leads me neatly to my third warning.

---

7.   Governments, unions, and other busybodies spend most of their time dreaming up all sorts of schemes to make marketplaces "fair". Some fool here in Ireland even proposed a legal "maximum wage" not so long ago. None of this meddling *ever* works and *never* can, for reasons we'll come to in another chapter.

8.   Unless you *really* believe the Earth was magicked into existence 6,000 years ago and all the evidence we have to the contrary is wrong, misinterpreted, or some kind of scientific conspiracy... in which case you have problems I really can't help you with.

Fact of Uncaring Reality No.3: Stuff Doesn't Do Itself

Nothing I share with you will work to any degree or in any respect whatsoever unless you actually put it to work in your business.

If you leave this book lying on your desk or stuck on your bookshelf, then, even if you agree with every word I say and see the value in it, nothing is going to change for you.

If you keep doing the same things you've been doing in your business up to this point, then you're going to keep getting the results you've been getting. Moreover, if you follow the herd and mimic, ape, and mirror your competitors, you're going to get pretty much the same results *they* get, too. As Einstein said, "Insanity is doing the same thing over and over again and expecting different results".

At this point you can probably see the truth in this and make a silent promise to yourself: "this time is going to be different". But the chances are it won't be, not unless you radically change your past behaviour. If you're anything like me you've bought "how to" books before, read them, seen the wisdom therein and... done absolutely nothing further with what you've discovered. I know a guy, already very successful and wealthy, who has a garage full of unopened courses and programmes, covering everything from copywriting to Internet marketing. He's spent more than $100,000 on it all, and by his own admission, it's money wasted.

It's an easy trap to fall into, though, because of the emotional comfort we get from the buying process. We tell ourselves, even if not in so many words, "if I just buy this product... it'll solve all my problems".

I can tell you from long and painful experience that doesn't work.

And... it's never going to work.

So, please, whatever you do… do *something*.

Anything.

Take just one thing I share with you in *Grow Your Business FAST* and give it a try.

And how do you choose what to do, and, more important, what to do first?

Well, my fourth warning is this…

Fact of Uncaring Reality No.4: Strategies and Principles Work; Tactics Sometimes Don't

What I mean by this is for every part of the *Grow Your Business FAST* Blueprint, there are a dozen different ways of putting it into action. And while they all work, not all of them are going to work the same way for everyone every time. You may even find some of them might not work at all in your particular case. This is no different from two people having the same bug but responding slightly differently to different treatment.

The cure is available, though — we just have to go about it slightly differently. But here's the thing: if you don't try for a cure, you won't get one. Few things in life are certain. Death and taxes are two of them; and there's a third: *uncertainty*. One thing you can be certain of is life and business are full of it.

There's one thing I've noticed about business owners all over the world: when it comes to this marketing lark they love to talk about it and get all moist about the possibilities, but no matter how much they love the concepts and ideas, and ostensibly agree with and embrace the need to test things, when it comes to the crunch they falter, beset by doubts and fear of failure.

Get used to failure, Bubba, because my fifth warning is…

Fact of Uncaring Reality No.5: Most of What You Do Is NOT Going to Work

It's true.

As a veteran marketer, I can tell you a sales letter sent out in the post is doing *very* well if it makes a sale to five people in a hundred. You can make a *lot* of money very quickly with a conversion rate of that size. But look at the other side of it: 95 out of 100 are still *not* buying from you. Whatever you're offering them has failed to tickle their fancy. It's even worse if you are selling face to face — just imagine how demoralising it can be, if you let these things get to you, to find 95 people out of 100 reject your sales pitch.

To look at it all in a wider context, what professional copywriters, who love to crow about their amazing successes, don't tell you is perhaps seven out of eight campaigns either flop or just about break even, and only one in eight hits that profitable sweet spot.

But that's when the magic happens... because when you *do* find those sweet spots, they'll pay you back for the failures many times over. You can make a fortune on that 87.5% failure rate.

The annoying thing is... it's impossible to tell ahead of time what's going to work and what's not. That's why we have to keep testing stuff until we find what works. Yes, I can look at your ad or sales letter or website, and tell you with great confidence whether it's a good one or a bad one. But — and here's the crucial point — even if it's a good one, *it can still bomb*. In other words, I can tell you if your ad is *good*; I cannot tell you if it's going to *work*.

In fact, there is only one certainty I can offer you.

And that is... you will fail to achieve every result you don't go for.

So, every direct mail letter or postcard you don't send, every email blast you never do, every book or "special report" you don't write, every video you never make, every irresistible offer you don't test… every single one of them will make you no money at all.

That I *can* guarantee.

Fact of Uncaring Reality No.6: There Are Two Big Mistakes You're Making In Your Business Right Now

Most business owners make one of these two very common mistakes with their marketing — and the real problem is many of them make both of them at the same time.

The first mistake they make is having unrealistic expectations. I know we're all impatient for success, but it takes time and it takes effort. It can be a lot easier than we think, and it can come a lot faster than we'd believe, too, but it comes neither effortlessly nor overnight.

Why anyone thinks it should is a mystery, but it's a situation not helped by the number of over-hyped sales letters out there on the Internet making all sorts of bizarre claims.

And the second mistake they make, which really follows on from the first, is they give up too quickly. They'll, say, pick a strategy like direct mail and send out one piece to a small list. And when they don't make the Big Bucks as promised by the sales letters and the "cookie cutter" systems they peddle, they simply give up and move onto the next Bright Shiny Object.

Unfortunately, outrageously profitable marketing systems are built piece by piece over a period of time. They do not spring into being overnight and almost never turn an enormous profit from the outset. Sometimes you don't even manage to break even. The marketing "gurus" who sell you the lie overnight success is likely, or even possible, hide from you the sweat they put into doing the groundwork to make their ridiculously profitable systems possible.

A good example is my wife's blog.

This is just Mrs. EBG's "hobby blog" yet it's enormously profitable for her, and she regularly releases $47 ebooks to her email list and makes a healthy $12,000 or so over a weekend.

And from the outside it looks so easy — easy enough anyone can do it. But what they don't see or think about is the 180 or so blog posts she wrote to get "authority" in her niche; they don't see the hundreds of forum posts she made for the same purpose; they don't see the *daily* emails she writes to her list to grow and nurture the relationship with her readers; they don't see the *research* we both put into it even before she bought the domain name.

All this takes time and effort, and you'll find it's what's behind every "effortless" and "overnight" success.

So man up[9].

Grow a pair[10].

And stop dithering and waiting for the certainty no one with integrity can offer you.

Fact of Uncaring Reality No.7: There Is No "Secret of Success"... Except This One

Virtually every business owner I talk to is searching for that one thing, the secret sauce, the silver bullet, the Holy Grail, or whatever metaphor you like to use, to fix their business and send their marketing off into the soft-focus sunset on My Little Pony where presumably everyone will live and profit happily ever after.

---

9.   Or woman up.

10.   Or the equivalent.

Well, we can dispense with that nonsense right now. As adults and business owners we don't need fairy tales.

Fact is... the secret of success is there is no secret, not in the sense of a magic spell or shortcut. Loads of people will offer you one and even take your money in return for some bulllshit mumbo-jumbo promise, but they're liars, every single one of them.

Everyone knows deep inside it really boils down to hard work and finding a few things that really work and repeating them over and over again until we master them.

It's really that simple.

The trouble is, this view is very unpopular. And it's unpopular to the point where some people get angry with me, personally, for pointing it out to them[11].

Imagine everyone who ever read this book somehow got together in a room[12]. If I was then to conduct a survey, a rough headcount, I can tell you right now what we'd get in the way of results.

Around 20% of the people there would hate the book and everything in it. Maybe 5% of them would hate me, personally, too, and disagree violently with everything I said. Then, maybe 60% would agree with me to a greater or lesser degree, but not feel strongly either way. And maybe the top 20% would love it and declare themselves my loyal fans, some of them to the point where they'd offer to bear my children.

Now imagine we fast-forward a year and we get only those loyal fans, the top 20% back into the room again and ask them what they've done over the past 12 months.

And this is where it gets depressing and frustrating.

---

11. Which makes about as much sense as blaming me for getting wet when I've pointed out it's raining.

12. Which could be a very small room, for all I know about the future.

Because once more I can tell you what the results would be.

Probably 20% of them would have gone to work and put the ideas I share with you here to work in their businesses, and a small percentage of them, maybe just 1%, would have done *everything* and a whole lot more besides. Then 60% of them would have done a bit here and a bit there, but never really knuckled down to it. And finally 20% of them would have done Jack shit.

Nothing.

Oh, they'd have a whole bunch of "reasons", but they'd really just be excuses; and as someone once said to me: "excuses are like assholes: everyone has one, and they all stink".

All these different people would nevertheless have one thing in common: they'll all get the results they deserve for their efforts over the long haul.

In a later chapter we look at this strange but predictable distribution of numbers in more detail but the important thing to realise for now is the only way to make all of this work is to apply the strategies and, in time, master them. Use makes master, after all.

At first it's going to be hard.

Very hard.

Everything is going to be new to you and much of it counterintuitive and very uncomfortable.

And what you'll do is concoct all sorts of reasons in your own head why these uncomfortable ideas and strategies won't work in your particular business, even without trying them. I mean, there's no *point* in trying them, because you somehow magically "know" they won't work, don't you?

But... no.

You don't. I don't know whether any given strategy will

work for you or not, no matter how well it's worked for me and others — but *you* don't know it, either.

You *can't* know it.

What you'll actually be doing at this point is avoiding doing something just because you find it uncomfortable but want to justify that irrational decision to yourself.

While this is understandable, and it's something we all do, I'm afraid it's not going to help you grow your business (or do anything else worthwhile, either).

As I've often said, marketing is actually pretty boring, because once you find what works, you just keep doing it. For me, the excitement comes from finding ways to make what's working already work even better.

But if you're looking for that one easy and effortless answer to your problems, you're going to be disappointed. And I strongly urge you to face that disappointment and get over it right now and then move on.

The only way to succeed in business is with dogged stubbornness and refusing to give up.

After all, you don't fail until you stop trying to succeed.

Summary of Chapter 1

1. **The ultimate prize in your business is Sovereignty.** That means doing *what* you want, *when* you want, with *whom* you want, at the *price* you want… and only *if* you want to do it at all.

2. **Marketing is the most important activity in your business, bar none.** If you're not marketing effectively, pretty soon you won't have a business at all.

3. **Marketing works on everyone.** We're all wired up more or less the same way and we all have the same emotional triggers. The differences are in how strongly we react to them and how we pull them.

4. **You are not a Special Flower.** The universe isn't harsh or inimical; rather it simply doesn't care about you. To succeed you need to see the world as it *is*, not how you *think* it is, *want* it to be or think it *ought* to be.

5. **Get used to failure.** Because you won't succeed at anything without it.

Chapter 2

How Business Really Works

The very first thing we need to do is give you a whistlestop edjumacation in marketing and how it relates to business success, because, to stress the point once more (I can never *over* stress it), marketing is what puts bread on your table and bacon in your belly.

But before we dig into marketing and the systems we can put together to make our businesses super-effective and profitable, there are some fundamentals of business success we need to look at first. After all, there's no point in soliciting loads of business if we can't service it, or if it isn't profitable, is there?

Because if marketing is the engine driving your sales and profits, then the fundamentals I share with you in this chapter are the fine-tuning and the super-charger designed to give you the maximum gyrations for your Groat.

And the first thing we need to understand is the *real* business you're in.

What Business Are You Really In?

It's likely I don't know you, but if I did and I knew

roughly what your business was, the odds are I could play the mind-reader and guess your answer to that question with near 100% certainty.

- **If you are a photographer...** you'd tell me you were in the photography business.
- **If you are a builder...** you'd tell me you were in the building business.
- **If you are a butcher, baker, or candlestick maker...** you'd tell me you were in the butchering, baking, or candlestick making business.

And you'd be completely wrong.

Because the real business you're in is the *marketing* business.

So a photographer is really in the business of *marketing photography*; a builder is really in the business of *marketing building services*; and you can, I hope, figure out for yourself what business butchers, bakers, and candlestick makers are in.

At this point there's a good chance you're disagreeing with me. No worries. You're allowed to make mistakes — and if you are disagreeing with me about this, you are making a *big* one. I'll explain why that is. But if after you've read the next few pages you still disagree with me, then the best advice I can give you is close your business and get a job.

Oh, and pass this book on to someone else.

Why Are You Selling Stuff?

The simple answer is to make a profit.

But while that's the truth, it's not the *whole* truth.

See, making a sale to someone once is actually pretty easy if that's all you want to do. If you're not too concerned about your reputation or your customers' and clients' satisfaction, you can simply promise one thing and deliver something far inferior, while running away quickly with their money.

We see this all the time, especially with the lowest of the low, the spammers selling knock-off drugs, fake designer watches, and other crap on the Internet. They send literally millions and millions of emails, and while their response rates are a fraction of a fraction of 1%, their marketing costs are so low — bulk email is dirt cheap, after all — they need make only one sale per million emails or so to make a profit.

While I'm by no means comparing your average business owner to a spammer, they do share one thing in common: they run their businesses with a view to making single sales to a steady progression of new customers.

Once you cut through all the complexity, there are just three fundamental ways to grow a business with your sales:

1. Sell to more customers and clients.

2. Sell more to the customers and clients you get.

3. Sell at a higher profit.

In my work as a marketing consultant and business mentor, probably the most common problem business owners come to me with is the one of how to get new customers and clients.

The trouble is, this is the hardest, most time-consuming and expensive, and *least* profitable one of the three, because selling to your existing customers and clients and increasing your prices are both easier than getting new business by an order of magnitude.

Existing customers and clients are around five times as easy to sell to as new ones, and spend on average twice as much; and increasing your prices by just 10% on a 35% margin increases your profits by a whopping 39% on the same volume of sales (we look at this in detail in the section on *Premium Pricing*).

Yet, business owners ignore and overlook these untapped profit-goldmines hidden in their customer and client lists and devote most of their energy into getting fresh people into the business.

Sure, this is necessary to some degree because of natural attrition, but for the most part, especially for a business seeking to grow quickly and easily, and at low cost and risk, the quick and easy profits are to be found in your existing customers and clients.

This, though is predicated on three things:

1. You have served them to a high enough standard they *want* to buy from you again.

2. You are growing, nurturing and maintaining an ongoing relationship with them (in other words, don't expect people to buy from you repeatedly if they hear from you only once a year when you want to sell them something).

3. You are making relevant offers to them (that is, you are asking them to buy from you and you're asking them to buy stuff they actually want).

The answer to all of this is *follow-up*, and we'll look at that in detail in a moment, but first I want to give you a different philosophical perspective of what happens when you sell something the first time.

Most business owners see marketing and sales as an *event* rather than a *process*. And this is a huge mistake, because it focuses our attention on the *sale* rather than the *relationship*.

So instead of that, I encourage you to see it as the *beginning* of a long-term relationship you're going to have with that customer or client over many years, because *the vastly greater part of your profits are in the long-tern relationship you have with customers and clients and not in the initial sale.*

Or, another way of looking at it is we're not pumping money into marketing to make sales; rather, we're doing it to *invest in relationships with customers and clients.*

Some marketers phrase it slightly differently and say we're "buying customers", but I think it's worth going a step further to say we're actually "investing in relationships with them".

Making a sale to someone is easy if you don't care about your profitability, because you can just drop your prices until you're the cheapest around and you'll find all the scummy price-buyers flocking your way[13].

But, to hammer home this point again, the long term profits are always in the long-term relationship you have with customers and clients and not just the first sale. Because over the long term they will:

1. Buy from you over and over again.

2. Spend more with you when they do.

3. Refer friends, family, and colleagues to you.

What's more, any marketing you do to them will cost you less and be more effective, to boot.

Very few business owners get this idea, and it's costing them a fortune because they are spending all their time and energy getting new business and letting their existing clients wander off to suppliers new.

---

13. Good luck with that.

How Business Really Works

Lifetime Customer and Client Value

So now we come to the idea of *lifetime customer or client value* — how much is an average customer or client worth to us over the time they have a relationship with our business? If you don't know this number then you need to get it, and quickly, because it's fundamental to everything we do in our marketing.

I'll give you an example from my own business as a copywriter. I very rarely take on new writing clients now, but if I wanted to, these are the numbers I'd use. And when you've inwardly digested them, I invite you to think about why I am so much more successful than the vast majority of my copywriting competitors even though any *objective* difference in our copywriting abilities might sometimes be small.

My ideal copywriting client is already running a successful business and has ample cash-flow. This is important because I am not in the game of accepting challenges — I have no desire to go into a foundering business and try to fix it while being hounded by someone who's just dropped his last £20,000 on a sales letter. He is ideally working in a market with an "easy sale", such as weight-loss, and have customers and clients with a high lifetime value. He must also be fully acquainted with marketing the EBG Way and have bought into the ideas I'm sharing with you here in *Grow Your Business FAST*.

For that reason my writing clients, historically, have been worth an average of something like £60,000 a year to me, and none has been worth less than £25,000 in recent times[14].

Question: if a client is worth *on average* £60,000 a year to

---

14. One exception is a client I "fired" because we simply didn't "gel". He was perfectly OK and would have been a great client for the right person, but I wasn't that person.

me, how much money would I be willing to invest to get one of them on my books?

Answer: a lot. If I arbitrarily set my preferred Return on Investment (ROI) to be 500%, then I'd be willing to invest £12,500 to get a new client.

And I can do a shitload of marketing for £12,500. For example, I could compile a short-list of a dozen potential clients I'd like to work with, and invest £1,000 each in trying to win them over.

Just imagine what I could put together for them for that kind of money. I could probably Fedex every single one of them a very impressive "attention grabber" for a fraction of that. Or how about sending them a full-sized dustbin with a Kindle Fire inside which has a pre-loaded sales video and loads of samples and things on? I mean there is *no way on Earth* they could ignore a full sized dustbin delivered to their office, is there? Where the hell would they put it? How would they get rid of it even if they wanted to ignore it? The point I'm making here is twofold: first, it's an example of utterly outrageous marketing; and secondly, very few of my competitors would have the balls to spend this kind of money on getting a new client because they don't understand the principle of *lifetime customer and client value*.

This is NOT Just for Evil Bald Geniuses

The example I've just given you above is extreme and you might be thinking you can't do the same because, you guessed it, "my business is different".

No it ain't. No matter what business you're in the concept of *lifetime value* applies.

And once you know the lifetime value, you can decide how much you're willing to invest to get a new client.

Working Out the Lifetime Value of Customers and Clients

To do this accurately you need historical data. And if you don't have any, you'll have to make some educated guesses. The point is, even if you can't get the number exactly right the first time around the loop, anything you have is going to help because anything measured improves.

A good example, from my own business once more, is my Business Supremacy Inner Circle. I know from the first couple of years' data my retention rate is 85% for a 12-month period. And with each month that passes my data gets more and more accurate. This means for every 100 people who become Members, 85 of them are still there a year later[15]. What this then allows me to do is set an amount I'm prepared to invest to get a new Member. I'm not going to share the numbers because they're commercially sensitive, but I'll give you the meat of it:

- **I've arbitrarily decided I want to be in profit on receipt of the second month's dues.** This tells me how much I'm prepared to pay to get a new Member of the Inner Circle.

- **I know people who join my email list join my Inner Circle at a rate of about 5%, and with some traffic sources this is more like 50%.** This, in combination with the figure above tells me how much I'm prepared to invest to get a subscriber to my email list.

---

15. This is outrageously far off the scale, by the way. In my industry the *typical* figures are 50% over just *two* months, meaning half of the people who join leave after just eight weeks. My retention rate is so high because of some very specific and deliberate things I put into the programme when I designed it.

How Business Really Works

Just note this is taking into account the Inner Circle monthly fees only — it doesn't take into account product sales I make to these same people.

We've taken this to the point where I know how much I am prepared to spend to get a new person to join my email list, because I know the law of averages means each subscriber is worth a certain amount of money, statistically speaking.

Can you see what we've now done and how important it is?

And can you see how you can do the same kind of thing in your own business?

All you need to do is figure out approximately how much a new customer or client spends with you over a set period and how profitable that is, decide how much you're willing to invest to get another one to do the same... and... that's it.

Changing your view to see it in this way is profound change in your thinking and it's going to have an enormous and positive effect on your profits.

First, it's also going to make your whole business and marketing machine far more robust and effective because it means you're necessarily going to be doing more marketing to existing customers and clients to make the most of your relationships with them rather than putting all your time and energy into getting new faces into your business.

And secondly, your competitors are not going to have a *clue* what you're doing. From the outside they'll see your business is far more successful and they'll notice you're doing a lot more marketing which they'll know must be costing you an arm and a leg. And they'll likely do one of two things: they'll either copy you as best they can... and get it completely wrong because they don't *understand* what you're doing; or they'll mock and criticise you for spending loads of money on marketing in a business they "know" can't sustain it[16].

I strongly urge you to re-read this section, and repeat it as many times as you need to until you truly grok[17] it. It's important.

The Two Most Important Numbers in the Universe

The last thing for us to look at before we move on to the specifics of effective, powerful, and profitable marketing is a quirky bit of mathematics cum almost-spooky universal-weirdness.

Bear with me, and keep hold of your hat.

Ever heard of Vilfredo Federico Damaso Pareto?

No disgrace if you haven't. Few people probably have, although you may be more familiar with the eponymous *Pareto Principle*, sometimes called the *Law of the Vital Few*, but most commonly known as *The 80/20 Principle*.

Way back in 1906, when he was a lecturer in economics at the University of Lausanne in Switzerland, he famously observed that in Italy just 20% of the population owned 80% of the wealth. That was a startling observation, but what's even more startling is the same observation holds true for every other country, too.

In fact, over 100 years on, we now know every system we

---

16. One fellow I know but won't name would deliberately run very expensive double-spread ads in magazines knowing they'd be completely ineffective. Why did he do this? Because he knew his competitors would copy him the next month and blow a vast amount of money they couldn't afford to lose on ads that could never work. This is just one way he dominated his market (and he could afford to invest this money in crippling his competitors because he understood marketing and was making money hand-over-fist in other areas).

17. From Wikipedia: "When you claim to 'grok' some knowledge or technique, you are asserting that you have not merely learned it in a detached instrumental way but that it has become part of you, part of your identity".

---

have data for is like this and it applies not just to economics but to every area we care to look at.

For example...

- Look at the population of any country you'll see 80% of the population live in just 20% of the major cities.

- 80% of crimes are committed by just 20% of criminals.

- 20% of your clothes you wear 80% of the time.

- 80% of the wear on your carpets happens to just 20% of the area.

- Dig into your website logs and you'll see 80% of your organic search traffic comes from just 20% of your keywords (and 80% of your visitors spend most of their time on 20% of your pages).

- On Facebook, you'll do 80% of your interaction with just 20% of your "friends".

- If you use Word or other word processing software, you'll find 20% of the functions get 80% of the use. I'm an ex-programmer, and back in 1997/98 I was working on a system in London, and it turned out everything in the system was ultimately routed down to a bottle-neck, all handled by one function. It necessarily had to be this way because of the way the system had to work (it was a trading engine and so trades had to be executed strictly sequentially in the order they were submitted by the traders). So, the speed and efficiency of the entire system (and the hardware that we had to buy, which was about a million pounds a time) was entirely determined by this one function. Much of the time we spent perfecting the system was spent making this one function as fast and efficient as possible.

- When I worked as a bouncer it was very quickly

obvious 99% of the trouble was always started by the same very small number of people (and 99% of the fights were always about just one thing: *women*).

- In your car, 80% of the wear and tear comes from just 20% of your driving (accelerating and decelerating for the most part).

- 80% of the pleasure you get out of life comes from just 20% of the things you do (and likewise the misery you experience).

So that all applies to life in general. But what about your business in particular? Well...

- You make 80% of your sales to just 20% of your customers and clients (and 80% of your profits come from just 20% of your products and services).

- 20% of your customers and clients take up 80% of your time. Unfortunately, this is often the worst 20% who are also responsible for 80% of your hassles and headaches.

- 80% of the work you do on any project gets done in just 20% of the time you allocate to it (usually the last 20% as the deadline approaches).

- 80% of new business comes in from just 20% of your marketing.

- 80% of your results in any areas of your work occur in just 20% of the time you spend working on them (which leads us to the horrible and inescapable conclusion that 80% of our time is wasted).

Now, a couple of things to note here before we go any further are the numbers aren't usually exactly 80/20, although they're often eerily close, and they don't have to add up to

100, either. They can be 60/40, 90/10, 99/1 or even 83/13.

The point is the *principle* — a small number of causes have a vastly disproportionate influence on the effects. And this is true for all systems, so far as we can tell.

An Inescapable Truth

The most effective things we do are actually *vastly* more worthwhile than the rest because we get most results from a very small amount of work. But, *how* much more worthwhile are they?

This is where is gets extremely difficult to accept. And, even when you see the maths, you can accept it intellectually and you can even do the numbers yourself, but emotionally it's a hard truth to swallow.

Let's imagine we're doing 100 hours of work and in that 100 hours of work we produce, say, 100 units of achievement (it doesn't matter what that is, we're just talking hypothetically here, abstract stuff).

So, 100 hours of work gives us 100 units of achievement. If 80% of our achievement comes from 20 hours of work that means we're getting 80 units of achievement out of just 20 hours of work. That means we're clocking up achievements at a rate of four per hour. Again, it doesn't matter what they are. It could be sales made, holes dug, trees chopped down, tonsils cut out, teeth pulled, scrotums lasered, or whatever: the point is we are realising four achievements per hour, in just 20 hours of work, to give us a total of 80 achievements.

This means the remaining 20 of our achievements come from the remaining 80 hours of work, which is just a quarter of an achievement per hour.

And, if we take the first number, which is four achievements per hour, and the second number, which is 0.25 achievements per hour, and compare them... we can see four is 16 times bigger than 0.25.

So, from our *most* effective hours we're getting 16 times the achievements we're making from our *least* effective hours.

You Can't Argue With This

These are the numbers, and the numbers cannot lie.

But most people have trouble accepting this emotionally because we assume and instinctively *feel* there must be a linear relationship between the work we do and the effects we get — and, as I've just shown you, there isn't.

So, if we earn £100 for five hours' work, say, we will tell people "I've been paid £20 an hour". And, that's true when we submit our bill to the client or whatever. But if we look at it a different way and look at what we've *earned* (rather than what we've been *paid*) we'll find we've maybe earned £80 for one hour's work and just £20 for the remaining four hours' work.

We are psychologically predisposed to assume the linear relationship between effort and results. We assume if we want to double our income we need to work twice as hard, twice as long, or maybe a combination of the two.

But we don't.

What we need to do is spend more time on the really high value stuff — the stuff earning us £80 an hour — and as little time as possible on the low value stuff — the stuff earning us just £20 an hour.

This is all very *logically* easy to accept but, in practice it's deeply uncomfortable for us to accept *emotionally*, and to carry out in practice, because it means that we have to do some fairly shocking things to really get the benefit of it all.

And just *how* shocking you'll see in a little while.

But let me demonstrate what I mean. And this is where you're probably going to start feeling quite uncomfortable — because what I'm going to go through now is not out of the question, and certainly not out of the bounds of possibility for you if you're following *Grow Your Business FAST* diligently. And I know from experience it's not something nice to contemplate even if logic is telling us it makes sense.

If we use the numbers above, and for the sake of argument we're going to say your numbers actually are 80 and 20, and they're not 70/30 or even better 90/10 etc., then you'd probably agree with me that if you had 20 clients or customers then it means just four of them are worth 80% of your income.

Now, imagine I said to you: "Well, in that case I want you to write a letter to the bottom sixteen telling them that you don't want to deal with them anymore".

If I told you to do that you'd probably feel quite ill.

But you can see from the numbers it makes sense.

How to Make 90% of Your Income in Just 10% of the Time

Some years ago I had a very high-end Mastermind group and one of the guys who was in it had a son whose business was selling expensive model cars and stuff. These were not cheap toys, either. We're talking hundreds of pounds for them (and some of them were over £1,000).

He also had a store, a shop, in one of the shopping arcades in his town. It cost him a certain amount each week in rent, and he was there from 9 till 5, six days a week, Monday to Saturday.

And he was struggling to increase his business.

On looking more closely at his numbers it turned out 90%

of his income and his business, came from online sources.

And that was from natural search and nothing to do with Adwords at the time — this was just from natural search, referrals from websites like bulletin boards, and forums. And of those online sales, most of them came from South East Asia.

The best thing of all was, because this particular hobby was really big out there, not only were the majority of his *sales* coming from there, but they tended to have a much bigger transaction size than people just dropping into his shop. In other words, casual "drop in" traffic seldom bought anything, and when they did, they tended not to spend much.

And, of course, with rare exception, these online sales were all taking place during the night when he was asleep, and he'd wake up in the morning to find he's sold another £1,000 model car, as opposed to standing at the counter while some customer comes in and just wants to talk all day, and perhaps leaves without buying anything.

I said to him, "Hypothetically, if you could stop working in your shop, and could close it down, so you didn't have to stand behind the counter from 9 to 5, every day from Monday to Saturday; and could instead box up all your stuff in a garage, or a lock-up, or premises elsewhere and simply package it up and send it out as you sold it...if you could do all those things, and your maximum monetary cost for doing that was 10% of your income... would you do it?"

And he said, "Yeah, of course I would".

So I said to him, "Well, that's easy, then. Just close your shop and focus on your online business".

And it was an incredibly emotional moment for him. He could see the sense in it, but it was an extremely emotionally difficult thing for him to contemplate, even though it made perfectly logical sense.

How Business Really Works

What the 80/20 Principle Means for You

Right now you can probably see the power of the 80/20 Principle but might be thinking it's just a curious oddity, something some people find occasionally useful. But understanding and embracing it is actually vital to your business success and you're going to see it cropping up over and over again as we go through the rest of this book. I cannot possibly over emphasise how important it is for you to grasp this fully. Understanding and putting the 80/20 Principle to work in my own business has been probably *the* most important factor in my success.

It's meant I don't waste my time and energy on low-value tasks, poor quality clients, or anything not aimed at taking my business forward towards the goals I've set for it.

For now, just understand the bottom line is this:

- Small chunks of your time and effort are incredibly valuable.

- Some tasks are incredibly valuable.

- Some of the things that you do, some of the little habits you get into (or can get into) are incredibly valuable.

- Most of what you do is pointless, and the time you spend doing it is wasted.

- A natural consequence of all this is it's always going to pay you to put your time, energy, effort, and budget into those activities giving you the most favourable results, and bugger the rest.

You'll come to a greater understanding as we move forward. For now, though, just take my word for it.

It's OK.

You can thank me later.

A Personal Note

The universe is fundamentally unfair. It would be nice, perhaps, to imagine we're all part of some plan or other but there's no evidence to suggest that's true.

Things just go on as they are, evolving and unfolding along fairly well understood and to some extent predictable lines, and we, for good or ill, sometimes just get in the way.

Is this fair?

Nope.

My son was born with cerebral palsy.

Why?

No one knows, despite all the tests and whatnot.

Is it fair?

Definitely not. How could it be?

But that's not the point.

It is what it is, and there's nothing we can do about it, save help him play the hand he was dealt to the best of his abilities.

And that, in microcosm, is how it is for all of us. Sure, we can nibble around the edges maybe and perhaps make some small general improvements in the world as a whole and society in particular, but in the grand scheme of things we're stuck with what the universe throws at us.

What this means in broad terms is good things happen to bad people, bad things happen to good people, and we all have shit come our way.

In business terms it means 80% of businesses fail in the first five years, and of those who remain, the top 20% enjoy 80% of the success.

This, too, is probably unfair.

And it all looks designed and it's tempting to imagine we can radically change things by imposing order from the top down if only we can find the right combination of rules, regulations, and laws.

Alas, all these attempts are doomed to failure because economies and societies are examples of what we call *complex adaptive systems*. Without getting into the maths of it all, what it means is these kinds of systems *look* designed and planned, but in reality they get their order from the actions of the large number of elements comprised in the whole all following a relatively small set of surprisingly simple rules.

This is how ant colonies, bee-hives, and termite hills all manage to look like they've got some guiding intelligence behind them. Human societies and economies are more complex, of course, but that's mere detail: the principles are the same. So to change the structure of how businesses perform on the whole, you'd have to change the behaviour of a large majority of the *individual* business owners. And that simply isn't going to happen, or a least, not any time soon. So once more, we're stuck with it.

In other words *we cannot change the numbers... but we can decide which group we want to belong to.*

Whether you make a conscious choice or not, you're still choosing. If you choose to ignore what I share with you in this book and squeamishly avoid marketing because you don't want to draw criticism, or you think selling is somehow tacky and wrong, or you think it's just "unfair" and wrong to make more money than your hard-working competitors who "deserve" the same success you might enjoy, you are choosing to remain among the 80% who won't get the results they want and need from their marketing. Your choosing not to become exceptionally good at marketing and growing an incredibly profitable business won't stop anyone else from making a different choice and enjoying the profits you could be enjoying. Nor will it help anyone else who chooses the easy and most commonly trodden path of mediocrity.

In short, your choices won't help or hinder anyone but you. Their effect on the market and society as a whole will be as close to zero as makes no difference.

And, while you are free to choose anything you like, you're not free of the consequences of the choices you make.

So choose wisely.

Summary of Chapter 2

1. **Your *real* business is a marketing business.** This is true no matter what niche, industry, or "thing" you do.

2. **The only reason you are in business is to sell things at a profit.** Even if you have high-ideals and want to change the world, you have to make a profit else you won't be helping anyone.

3. **The greater part of your profits is always to be found in your long-term relationship with your customers and clients.** Focusing on making the immediate sale "off the page" is almost always a mistake and drastically cuts your potential profits.

4. **The two most important numbers in the universe are 80 and 20.** Because 80% of your "effects" come from just 20% of your "causes".

5. **Most most of what you do and the time you spend doing it is wasted.** The speed and level of your success will increase dramatically if you take the time and make the effort to focus your time and energy on the small number of things that really matter.

Chapter 3

Effective Marketing
Made (Dead) Easy

Effective — and that means *profitable* — marketing is actually very simple. Lots of people go out of their way to complicate things, frequently because they want to sell you something to scratch the itch they've just given you, but we can really boil it down to just four things:

- The right message
- Presented in the right way
- To the right person
- At the right time

Once you truly understand and embrace this, you'll realise the rest is all rather boring and repetitive, and surprisingly formulaic. It's all just a matter of getting these four elements aligned as best you can. When you do that, the results are staggering; when you don't, then you're in for a lot of frustration and worry, and you'll eventually go broke.

Just to get you to see the truth of this quickly, imagine trying to sell pork sausages to vegetarians, Bibles to atheists, and cigarettes to a non-smoker.

But while those are obviously not going to work, it's what most business owners are doing to some degree or other, even if they're doing it accidentally and unknowingly — and it's why their marketing doesn't get them the results they want and need. Profitable marketing at its simplest is just avoiding getting those four things terribly wrong. Just managing to do that is going to make an enormous difference to your business.

And you might be tempted to doubt how simple it all is if you've read marketing books before, but just bear in mind the vast majority of them are written by academics in universities who haven't actually done any of this marketing stuff in anger[18].

But, while it's *simple*, it's not always *easy*.

Many things can come up to derail you, and none is so pernicious as your own preconceptions and reactions to other people's comments and opinions.

Because once you start putting what I'm sharing with you in this book to work in your business, I guarantee you're going to get resistance from your friends, family, colleagues and employees, and a whole heap of criticism, derision and withering comments from your competitors.

And given time, it can all become somewhat wearing. That's why you need the thick skin I mentioned before.

But stick with it. To paraphrase Dan Kennedy, a true marketing genius if ever there was one:

> *"If you've not pissed someone off by lunchtime every*

---

18. And if they have, you'll find it's been with the big companies with the multi-billion Groat brands, and for reasons I'll make apparent as we go through this book, that's an entirely different world which bears absolutely no relation to the real world of small business marketing at all.

Effective Marketing Made (Dead) Easy

day, you're not doing much of anything at all".

When I start getting angry and indignant emails from people on my list, telling me I've offended them in some way — usually by taking their favourite Sacred Cow and butchering it on the altar of reality — I know I've done something right.

And my sales reflect this.

So forget everything you think you know about marketing and pay attention.

The Three-Legged Stool of Marketing

I'm going to steal shamelessly from Dan Kennedy once more. He describes your marketing efforts as being like a three-legged stool, with the legs representing your *Message*, *Market*, and *Medium*.

- **Message...** what you say to your market to get them to buy from you.
- **Market...** the people you want to get your message to.
- **Medium...** how you get the message to the market.

And, just like the stool and its three legs, if any one of these elements is missing, broken, or defective, then the whole thing comes crashing down. Just as with a stool, no one leg is any more important than another, and they all play their part in supporting both the other two and your marketing as a whole.

However, you do have to approach them in the right order, even though getting it right is always going to be an iterative process where you start with your best-guess and improve things: your message is what you say to your market to get the people in it to buy from you; and the more exactly you

can define your target market, the more accurately you can
target your message; and the more accurately you can target
your message, the better choices of media you can make to
reach them.

The mistake most business owners make is to start with
the medium. In other words, they'll pick a marketing channel
(or more likely be sold one by a fast-talking advertising rep
from the local newspaper) and then try to figure out how to
shoehorn the message into it and hope it gets in front of the
right market.

So the medium is really the last thing to look at, because
you can't know how to reach the people you want to reach
until you know who and where they are.

Other than that, there are arguments for starting with
either the message or the market. I, personally, prefer to start
with the message, because for me running my business is
about running the business *my* way. But I obviously can't do
this in isolation from my target market because the message
is *also* targeted at them. It's kind of a "chicken and egg"
thing, but they really go hand in hand.

If you're in an established business you should have plenty
of experience, personal knowledge, and data you can mine to
tell you who your best kinds of customers or clients are. Once
you know that, it's easy to figure out what you said to them
to get them to do business with you, and so what you need to
say to people just like them to get them to do the same.

But at the same time, part of your message is about what
you personally want from your business and that's often
independent of the kind of people you want to be doing
business with.

The long and the short of it is figuring out your message
and market is an iterative process, and a job in constant
progress.

Effective Marketing Made (Dead) Easy

One Simple Change to Utterly Transform Your Marketing

So, we've just seen how marketing works, the three component parts and elements you have to put together in the right order before you can start making money.

But they're really just the *structure* of marketing, and not the strategy. The next question, then, is how do we make all these elements work for us?

The traditional method of marketing works like this:

1. You get a prospect into your business. It might be a visitor to your store or website, someone calling in by phone, or perhaps even someone you're visiting on a sales call.

2. You try and sell them something right away.

3. You make the sale and bank the money, or you don't. Either way, they go off somewhere else, and you bank the money and then move on to getting the next customer or client.

And there's no doubt this approach works to some extent, both online and offline. After all, this is how most businesses do it, including the ones managing to last longer than those first five years[19] But the problem with it is in the numbers, particularly if you're selling online where shopping around with your competitors is quick and easy.

We've also seen how the greater part of your profits is always to be found in your list of existing customers and

---

19. There's a thought... maybe the fact most of these businesses all do things the same way has some bearing on the fact they all get more or less the same results and why 80% of them share just 20% of the success. Maybe the successful 20% are, you know, doing a few things, like, *differently*?

clients and getting new ones is hard work and comparatively expensive.

So what I'm going to share with you now is a very simple but fundamental and profound change you can make to the way you do business that's going to give you a dramatic increase in sales and profits. What's more, if you do it the right way it'll also have a knock-on effect on those ongoing sales to your existing customers and clients.

I can sum it up in one line: *instead of trying to sell to prospects immediately, begin your relationship with them by giving.*

Lead Generation Marketing

This is nothing new and although I wish I could, I cannot take the credit for it. In fact, when I say it's "nothing new" I really mean it's been around for *decades*, possibly *centuries*, even if some people have in recent years given it a new, funky name and claimed it for their own.

We tend to call it *Lead Generation Marketing*, and here's how it works in very broad outline:

- You put an ad in people's way with an offer of information on a topic. This can be online or offline.

- They have the option to respond in some way (email, web-form, by post, telephone, or whatever) and request this information in return for their contact details. They are, in effect, raising their hands and saying, "Yes, I'm interested".

- When they respond you give them the information, and that begins the relationship you have with them.

- You then grow and nurture that relationship and market and sell to them *over time*.

Like I said: all very simple. And it works exceptionally well. If you're selling stuff off a website, say, it's not unusual to see your sales conversions leap from around 1% to 10% or even more. I am involved with one business, Mrs. EBG's blog, where she gets sales conversions of up to 47% when she offers a new product to the list she's grown in just this fashion. This simply would not happen if she was offering these same products to "cold" traffic just happening by her website.

There's a second reason for collecting details, aside from the fact it increases your conversion rates, and that is it vastly increases your marketing ROI.

Here's why: everyone who comes to your business costs you something to get them there. If you're running an ad in the newspaper and it costs you 1,000 Groats, and on average it means you get 10 people through your door and one of them buys something, your cost of acquisition for a new customer is 1,000 Groats. Depending on what you're selling and what your margin is, that might be perfectly acceptable.

But it also means nine people are coming into your store and walking out without buying anything. If your ad was 1,000 Groats then each of the 10 people it's driven has effectively cost you 100 Groats to get to your business.

In other words, you've just thrown 900 Groats away.

But consider now if you're making an effort to collect names and contact details in return for something of value. You might still make only that one sale on the day, but of the other nine at least half of them might give you their contact details, giving you another bite of the cherry. If you can go on to convert just one of them to a sale you've just halved your cost of customer acquisition, and doubled your conversion rate.

That's it, in a nutshell. And we can apply it in principle

Effective Marketing Made (Dead) Easy

to any business, even though you mostly see it online with the ubiquitous "optin pages" or "squeeze pages". These are simply web pages where you're invited to enter your name and email address in return for some information such as a free report, or a series of informational emails[20]. It's all very simple and straightforward, and you can use these kinds of pages even if you're using offline marketing methods by sending people online from postcards, letters, and ads.

So, if it's all that simple and effective, why don't more business owners do it? I can't answer that. My guess is it comes down to one of these three things:

1.   They don't know about it.

2.   They know about it but don't *understand* it and think it's too expensive, too complex, or flat out doesn't work.

3.   They know about it but for some arbitrary reason assume they can't do it themselves[21].

Whatever the reason, the fact is very few businesses put any effort whatsoever into generating leads of any kind. I've been living in Ireland now for six years and *not once* has any shop, store, restaurant or other establishment asked me for my contact details; and of the hundreds I've bought stuff from, both online and offline, I can think of only *one* which has ever bothered to grow and nurture any kind of relationship (and they sell batteries and obscure electrical equipment, not the kind of thing anyone would imagine marketing in that

---

20.   In fact, the chances are excellent you're reading this because you went through this same lead-generation process with me after seeing an ad of mine online or receiving direct mail. Lead generation marketing is the *only* kind of marketing I do. That alone should tell you something.

21.   Remember: "my business is different"

---

way, eh?).

What Can You Give Away?

Pretty much anything you like. There are no hard and fast rules about this, but for best results you want it to be something that doesn't cost you the Earth and yet has a high perceived-value to your prospects.

For more years than I care to remember now, in the online world it's been the ubiquitous "free report". Some people claim these are becoming less effective now because people are more wary and they're no longer such a new idea. I suppose this might be possible in a few isolated cases, but it's by no means a universal truth, and I know loads of businesses in all kinds of different niches and industries where the "free report" is doing just fine.

But even if the "free report" is less effective than it was, we don't have to stop there and the only limit on what you can offer to begin a valuable relationship with a new prospect is limited only by your imagination.

For example you can offer:

- Free report
- A free email series
- A book (that might ring a bell, depending on how you got this one)
- CD or DVD (or offer them free access to an online video or audio)
- Free sample of whatever you're selling
- Free trial (of a service or software)
- Free consultation
- Some other free information resource (for example a butcher can give away simple recipe books, a baker

can give away free baking guides, and a candlestick maker can give away free guides to all the different kinds of wax in your candles).

Fact is, any business can do this and most probably should. There are perhaps exceptions, to be sure, most notably with ecommerce websites where visitors are often ready to buy right away, but even if you're in that kind of business it's still going to do you well to see your making a sale as you actually being paid to generate a lead, because, to repeat the mantra, the greater part of your profits is always in the long term relationship you have with customers and clients.

I recently spoke to a fellow who runs a very successful laptop repair business, a business where if asked about lead-generation I'd have said it would probably be difficult because if you have a broken laptop, you want it fixed yesterday. But then I'd have been wrong, because he's doing very well with it.

This is a perfect example of why everyone needs to *test* these things no matter what business you're in, how convinced you are it's not going to work, or, indeed, what anyone[22] tells you about your likely chances of success or failure.

The general principle here is of *educating our prospects instead of trying to sell to them right away*. Trying for an immediate sale with no thought to the future relationship is tactical thinking, not strategic thinking. What's more, while you might make sales to the people ready to buy right now, you'll miss out on all those sales to the people who are not *quite* in the right place yet.

You can never over-educate or over-inform your target market, but many business owners are reluctant to engage

---

22. Including me.

---

in this at all this because they're afraid once they've done that their prospects will just vanish off the radar looking for someone to sell them the stuff cheaper.

This can happen, of course, but when it does it's generally because you've given them too much of the wrong thing, or you've been *telling without selling*. I'm not suggesting for a second you should treat them to everything for free and hope some of them are decent enough to buy from you.

What you need to be doing is giving them enough to be useful but without giving away the farm. Getting it right is a matter of experience, but a very powerful rule of thumb which is going to be dead right in almost every case is *give them the Why and the What, and charge them for the How.*

So, their car is misfiring with a certain sound, you tell them *why* it's doing it and *what* they've got to do to fix it... and here's a manual you can buy showing you exactly *how* to do it.

Or maybe they want to write a bullet-proof Will to protect their children's interests even if one of them dies and remarries, so you tell them *what* they need to do and *why* they need to do it, but if they want the specific *how* to do it, then they have to pay you.

You get the idea, yes?

It's very simple and very effective, and I guarantee virtually none of your competitors will be doing it.

This is, however, just the first part of the process. Getting people's details in exchange for something of value is one thing... but what do you do with 'em, when you've got 'em? After all, unless you're utterly new in business or you've not yet started, you undoubtedly have existing customers and clients.

Question is...

Why Are They Not Buying More from You?

When I ask business owners this question, the most common answers I get are:

1. "They can't afford to — we're in a Recession you know."

2. "They don't want to. Because if they did, they would."

3. "I don't know."

The first of these is just incorrect; and the last... well, it's just pathetic. But in a sense it's good, too, because it means for the business owner who comes out with that answer, the only way is up. In other words, it's the absolute ground-state of any business. Every successful business is successful because of the marketing systems they have in place to drive sales.

There are no exceptions to this.

Sure, you might occasionally find a business enjoying short-lived success because of some fad or fashion, but once the moment has passed, if there's no marketing system in place to keep sales going, then the business is doomed.

So if a business owner answers, "I don't know", then it means anything they do is going to be better than what they're doing now, because what they're doing now is nothing at best and randomly dabbling with it at worst.

So What About the First Two?

Remember?

"They can't afford it", and "They don't want to"?

Believe it or not lack of money never stopped *anyone* buying *anything* they *wanted*. Never. Not since we crawled out of the slime a few hundred million years ago.

Oh yeah, people will tell you they have no money to pay for the essentials and the debts they've incurred, but you can wager the soul of your firstborn they always manage to find the money for beer, cigarettes, junk food, *big* TVs, and piles and piles of shoddy but expensive shit for the kids at Christmas. I remember reading an interview with a family who claimed to be "hard up", and they brazenly told the interviewer they "had" to spend £2,000 at Christmas on the kids. Go figure. They're not short of money — they're short of smarts.

Anyway, my point is this: no one is really interested in spending money on what they *need*. But they'll spend any amount of money on what they *want* if you *ask* them to. There's an important lesson in that sentence. I'll come back to it further on when we talk about selling.

So the second answer, "They don't want to".

You think?

I think you'd be surprised to discover how willing they really are to spend money with you… *if* you give them a reason to.

A client of mine runs a gym and had an email list of a few hundred people, and his occasional emails to this list made him maybe €200 or €300 every month.

Until I… well, let him tell you in his own words:

> *When I first joined Jon's list I nearly unsubscribed, I got pissed off. But then I realised I got pissed off cuz I wasn't doing what he was telling me. So I stayed on his list and started to like his style of marketing. I signed up to Email Supremacy and in 6 days of sending regular emails (10 to be exact) I made €3,000. Now this was to a list I was normally making at most 2-300 quid a month from. Not only*

*that but the life time value of these clients was worth far more than just 3 grand ~ **John O'Connell, SF Fitness, Dublin***

That's a 1,000% or more increase in sales to his list simply because he bothered to reach out to them by email, using some simple methods I shared with him on the programme he mentions.

Now, my point in sharing this with you is not to blow my own horn, but to demonstrate a point I'm about to make: the reason your customers and clients don't buy more from you is…

You're Just Not Asking Them To

What it really boils down to is lack of follow-up. You know — you get an enquiry or even make a sale, and then you never reach out to that person again, and instead "hope" they'll remember you and come back.

Good luck with that, because you're going to need it.

Why?

Well, here are some scary numbers for you:

- 48% of sales people never follow-up with a prospect
- 25% of sales people make a second contact and stop
- 12% of sales people only make three contacts and stop
- It's a staggering discovery, but only 10 % of businesses make more than three contacts with a prospective customer or client.

So what does this mean? Well, it means they're losing a small fortune. Because…

- 2% of sales are made on the first contact
- 3% of sales are made on the second contact

- 5% of sales are made on the third contact
- 10% of sales are made on the fourth contact
- 80% of sales are made on the fifth to twelfth contact

So if you're like almost half of all businesses and make no more than one follow-up to your prospects... you're leaving 98% of your income on the table for someone else to come along and pick up.

If that wasn't bad enough, here's why it's even worse than you think. Look at these eye-opening statistics about why people stop buying from businesses:

- 1% die.
- 3% move away.
- 5% follow a friend's or relative's recommendation.
- 9% find an alternative they perceive to be better quality or value.
- 14% are dissatisfied with the products or services.
- And a massive 68% of people leave a business because of... your indifference to them.

Ouch.

So that's the problem, and as you can see it all stems from one small way of doing business virtually everyone follows: trying to make the sale immediately.

But what's the solution?

Relentless Follow-Up

And you keep doing it until they buy, die, or scream for mercy and beg you to stop.

Now, I just want to be clear here: I am not advocating bullying, browbeating, harrying, harassing, and haranguing them into the sale. That's "hard sell", and you won't make yourself many friends with it.

Sure, you'll make a few sales to people, but you'll not sell to them more than once because they'll be sick and tired of you. And, as we've seen, the real profits in your business are always in the long term relationship you have with your customers and clients, just as it is in mine.

No, I'm talking about a gentle, softly-softly approach where you treat them to a constant stream of informative, interesting, engaging, entertaining, and *useful* messages by any number of different methods. The easiest and quickest by far is email, but that doesn't rule out postcards and other direct mail, fax, and even the telephone.

But as I say, email is the easiest so let's take that one as an example. Just bear in mind when I say "email", this could also be write, telephone or however it is you reach out to your market. It's all just follow-up really.

If Regular Follow-Up Brings in More Business… Why Don't More Business Owners Do It?

Here's one reason: most people fear prospects and customers will object to being followed up. They mistakenly believe people don't enjoy being sold to in the right way and, in any case, *their* prospects, customers, and clients are far too sophisticated, worldly-wise, and intelligent to fall for these silly marketing gimmicks. It's certainly true *some* people won't like it; but you won't lose business because the people who object were never going to buy from you anyway.

A second reason is they send the wrong kind of follow-up and get poor results, which discourages them from sending any more[23]. As I said above, you've got to *ask* them to buy things. There are ways of doing this... and then there are ways of doing this.

I prefer the gentle approach and I find it works much better than the typical "Buy My Stuff <u>NOW</u>" nonsense screamed out by all those sad and desperate Internet marketing "gurus" with the Brylcreemed hair and the glassy eyes.

Constant and relentless follow-up works, and it works fabulously. In fact, if you're not actually working your list by following up and making offers, you might as well not have it in the first place. Not following up with them in case they object and unsubscribe is like holding your breath to conserve oxygen.

But...

Of course, you need to get your visitors' email addresses and names or other contact details in the first place... which takes us full circle back to lead-generation marketing again.

Fancy that, eh?

How Do You Know Your Marketing Is Working?

To be worth anything at all your marketing has to be bringing in more money than it's costing you. This is "square one" on the Snakes and Ladders board of business life. And you're not getting off this square for any length of time until you really grok this.

Marketing is about making a profit, and every business has to make a profit on sales — even non-profits (because they have to cover their running costs plus the costs of the

---

23. Some people even let themselves get discouraged and dissuaded by the occasional unpleasant messages they get from people they've followed up. Nothing to be done about this except grow a thick skin and remember when someone is unpleasant and nasty for no good reason, it's something going on with them and nothing to do with you.

Effective Marketing Made (Dead) Easy

products and services they supply). And the chances are your own business's marketing efforts are falling short of what you know they should be achieving, because otherwise you'd be out there busy making heaps of money instead of reading this book.

But there's a catch: how do you know your marketing is profitable or not?

As far as I'm aware, there's only one way: you have to measure and track everything you're doing and crunch the numbers. Not the most entertaining thing to be doing of an evening, but it's absolutely necessary[24]. But most business owners not only do not know how to do it, but they don't realise how important it is in the first place. This is why we see business owners spending a fortune on everything from Adwords to Yellow Pages, and SEO to direct mail without a proper framework for testing and measuring response. And they pay a heavy price for this.

One old client of mine dropped £10,000 or so on sending a direct mailing to an untested list, and didn't make a single sale[25]. A smarter thing to do would have been to test the list first, with, say, 1,000 names. Sure, he'd have lost that money, but he'd have saved himself a fortune in the long run.

The lesson to take away from this is a simple one: if you don't know whether a given marketing strategy is going to be profitable or not, then you must find a way to measure it. If you can't find a way to measure it, then don't do it until you can.

This is often easier said than done, because emotionally it can be comforting to be doing something — anything —

---

24. But you'll be surprised how much fun it really is when you start seeing the improvements you're making and how your profits are growing. We'll say more about this later in this book.

25. This was before I came on the scene, I hasten to add.

---

rather than nothing. And it can be a blow to your ego to find your favourite and comfortable marketing strategy doesn't actually make you any money. But if you're following a particular marketing strategy and you don't know and cannot tell if it's making you money, then it might be costing you money... and if your purpose in doing it is an urgent one because you need the cash, then you could well be running yourself even faster into the ground.

Food for thought, eh?

Testing (How Not to Lose Your Shirt With Crap Marketing)

It might seem strange to be calling "testing and measuring" a marketing strategy, but I assure you it is.

Because, as we've already seen, marketing has one purpose and one purpose only — to make you money. If it's not doing that, then it's not just a waste of time, but it's *costing* you money, too.

And the only way you'll know whether a marketing strategy is working or not is by measuring it and crunching the numbers. Then, the only way to *improve* it is to test alternatives and see which one works the best.

See, most business owners just throw an ad into the local paper or drop a postcard in the mail and then wait to see what happens. And what usually happens is business just goes on as usual: customers come in, visitors hit the website, the phone rings... and sometimes they might fancy they detect an increase in business, and sometimes not.

This is woefully inadequate and deeply unscientific.

To be worthy of the name, your direct response marketing must be trackable to the point where you can tell with very high probability *exactly* where every sale came from. You'll never get a 100% record on this because you'll find the oddest coincidences and events conspiring to bring you traffic and customers, but anything is better than nothing, and so long as you build the notion of testing and measuring into your marketing you'll soon be able to track the vast majority of it.

Why Do We Test?

We test because unless we do, we won't know if something works or not when we put it in front of our target market.

I am forever being asked about specific strategies and tactics, and invariably the business owner wants to know, "will this work?".

And I don't know. I can tell you with a high degree of confidence if something *won't* work, at least most of the time; but saying if something *will* work is almost impossible.

Why?

Because even if you do everything "right" the capriciousness of the random factor — luck — means on any given occasion things might go horribly wrong.

Back in 1997 one very smart and wealthy direct response marketer had a tested and almost-certain-to-succeed campaign set to run over one weekend in the Summer. Unfortunately that was the weekend of 31st August, when Princess Diana died. That weekend no one was interested in his ads, even if they actually ran. This is a classic example of how Fate can intervene to nuke your tried and tested plans.

Why Do We Measure?

We measure so we know what results our tests are getting us. If they're making us money, then we know we're onto something; if they don't then we know we have to think again. If we neither test nor measure, then we simply don't have a clue what's going on (which accurately sums up most of your competitors).

How Do We Test?

We think of an idea, we bounce it off knowledgeable people in case we've made a really dumb mistake and missed it, and then we try it.

There's no point in over-analysing any of this and going into endless "what if" scenarios. Most of the time you're looking for certainty and a guarantee neither I nor anyone else can give you. And by the time you've asked around until someone gives you the answer you want to hear, tacit "permission" to do what you wanted to do in the first place, a simple test would have given you the answer already (and it's the *only* correct answer you'll ever get — reality is immutable like that).

So, after the "sanity check" just try it.

The classic test is called the A/B Split, where you get a list of a size big enough to give you statistically significant results, and then split it randomly into two sub-lists. Then you create two different marketing pieces (say two postcards, identical except for the headline), and send them out.

Then you wait for the results, and when they're in you count up how many were from postcard A, and how many were from postcard B. If you're lucky to get enough results back, you can start to gain some confidence in which is the better piece[26].

Then repeat the test a few times to make sure the results are consistent before ditching the *worst* performing of the

---

26. If you're sending emails or direct mail, to get some kind of statistical confidence you need to be testing 500 to 1000 pieces, and to be getting maybe 50 results. Sending 10 letters and getting one response is nice, but not statistically significant

two and test the *best* performing one against a new postcard and try to beat it. By doing this you will, by a process of incremental improvements, build a formidable marketing machine that'll pay you back handsomely for years to come. Your best performing piece of the moment is called your "control". And the better your controls get, the harder they'll be to beat. Some controls have been out there making money for literally decades.

The important thing to remember when you're testing one version of the same piece against another is to have only *one* difference between them, such as two different headlines or a different coloured envelope. If you have more than one thing different, say you change the headline *and* the envelope, you won't know which one of the two is responsible for the difference in results.

A powerful strategy for zooming in quickly on the most effective piece we can get is first to try radically different pieces, say a DVD and a long-copy sales letter, and see which one wins consistently, and then switch to tweaking small things in similar but different versions of the same format.

So you might run a half-dozen tests between DVDs and long-copy sales letters, and find the DVDs win every time. You'd then take your best-performing DVD and see if you can beat it with a different DVD, say one with a different coloured print on the front, or a less "formal" video.

Repeat this process enough times and you'll very quickly have an awesome business with profits to match.

How Do We Measure?

In essence, we count how many people take the action we've asked them to take in our call to action. Ultimately we measure the *success* of the thing by how much money it makes us.

We can track all this using Google Analytics or another service like GetClicky online; and for offline marketing we can use unique phone numbers, landing-page URLs, and coupon-codes, just for starters. To do the maths you need nothing more complicated than an Excel spreadsheet and someone who's reasonably competent at creating them.

What Can We Test?

Anything and everything, from the words you use and the font you write them in, to the size, colour and material of the clothes your sales people wear.

Here are a few examples just off the top of my head, both offline and online:

- Postcard versus long copy
- CD versus a DVD
- Online video versus plain copy
- The colour of the font on your pages
- The clothes you wear in your videos
- The location you record them in
- Sales letters versus tearsheets
- Sales letters versus CDs and DVDs
- Different telephone scripts
- Different sizes of ad in newspapers
- Colour or black and white
- Different fonts for your body copy
- Different coloured envelopes for your direct mail
- Different sizes of postcard
- Different headlines

- Different offers
- Different guarantees

And the list goes on forever. This is, incidentally, why it annoys the fuck out of me when people claim to know the "best" way to do these things. They can't possibly know that because there is an *infinite* number of tests and combinations they would need to try before making such a claim, and most of them are basing their certainty on extremely narrow experience.

As I you can see, testing is a wide topic and one we can't do justice to in a book like this. But don't let that get to you. What you have in your hands is a manual for *best practice*, and remember *no one can see the future.*

So just pick something, run a "sanity check" on it, and have a go.

The Burning Stupid of Marketing Budgets

Finally, testing allows us to dispense with marketing budgets altogether. The only reason they exist at all is the people setting them don't understand how marketing works. If they did, they'd not be so stupid.

Think about it this way: the ideal marketing system makes you, say, two Groats for every Groat you put into it. And, since this is how properly constructed marketing systems are put together, this return on investment (or ROI) is predictable and consistent within certain statistical parameters of error. You know this because you've been testing and measuring[27].

So the question is this: knowing your ROI is both predictable and consistent and every Groat invested returns a Groat in profit... why would you limit the amount of money

---

27. Haven't you, hmm?

---

you put into it to some arbitrary amount?

The answer is… a sane and intelligent person wouldn't.

A sane and intelligent business owner would keep cranking the handle of what is effectively a printing press able to turn out brand new bazillion-Groat notes until his arm dropped off.

So that's a very important thing to understand, and I've mentioned it several times already: marketing should never be a *cost*[28].

It's an investment.

Selling

I don't know who said it first, but one of the big clichés in sales is, "nothing happens until someone sells something". And it being a cliché doesn't make it untrue.

Because you can have the best product or service in the world, and the most eager and raving fans who love the idea of what you do… but if you don't actually sell anything to anyone, then you don't have a business. This is all self-evident, but still it causes massive problems for business owners… because, in the main, they simply don't like selling. They'll make all manner of excuses for it, from claiming their product or service is somehow "above" being sold, to their particular market doesn't like being sold to. And it's all nonsense.

What it *really* comes down to is timidity and squeamishness at asking for the sale. And this causes Hell and all problems because your prospects have this funny tendency to buy when they're ready to buy, and not when you're ready to sell. Which means if you don't Do Something to get them ready

---

28. Except when you're testing something new, in which case then it's *research*.

to buy, you're probably going to wait a long time[29].

And that "something" is *selling*.

I'm sitting in my office right now with two bookcases: one to my left and one right in front of me. In the hall outside my office door there are another three or four bookcases. There are two more in the living room, and even one in the kitchen. Upstairs on the landing there are three more, and there's at least one in each bedroom. All told we have 16 of them about the place. And on them I have maybe 20 or 30 books on sales, plus a half-dozen CD programmes on the same topic. In other words, there's no way I can even begin to do justice to the topic in this book, even if I dedicated the entire tome to it.

So all I'm going to say is you need to do three things.

First, you're simply going to have to get used to the idea of selling, and then actually do it. I know lots of successful business owners, and I know lots of people who are squeamish about selling. But I don't know anyone who's in both groups at the same time.

I can feel you tensing up already.

Relax.

It's not as bad as all that, because I'm not for a moment suggesting you learn hundreds of "closes" by rote and dive headlong into the hard sell. Make no mistake: that approach does work, but as you've seen already, we're in this for the long haul and the lifetime customer and client value.

My own style of selling is very low key and I do it over *time* with my daily emails and other relationship-building activities. As a consequence my conversion rate to sales is very high and there are people on my list who have been buying from me for years and buy everything I offer to them.

---

29. And possibly die of starvation in the meantime.

Effective Marketing Made (Dead) Easy

Mrs. EBG has a similar experience and her list converts at up to 47% on ebooks because of the relationship she's nurtured with them over time, and not because of the sales letter I wrote for her (it's only 360 words long!). You'll learn how I do this "relationship" thing in the upcoming sections on *Premier Positioning* and *Email Marketing*.

Secondly, you've got to learn how to ask for the sale. There are ways of asking and there are ways of asking. More to the point, you've also got to get over the reluctance to ask because you don't want to be told "no". A "no" is rarely a "no never", and even if it is, it then allows you to move on. You'll cover this in Appendix I.

And finally, understand people do *not* object to being sold to if you're solving their problems. Being sold to is actually a pleasant experience when it's done well. A little while ago I bought a new bike from a bike shop rather than online. The bloke didn't have to sell me anything, because I was already ready to buy. Probably not that often an Evil Bald Genius walks in off the street and drops almost €1,000 on a bike, with no salesmanship required. But while the service was pretty good, I still found myself vaguely disappointed and wondering about my own boyhood dream of owning my own bike shop. I mean, the bar is so low at the moment and it would be so easy to dominate the market.

Disappointed?

Yeah, disappointed. Because while he did manage to upsell me from the Ridgeback Flight 02 to the Flight 03, on the grounds the Flight 03 has a stronger set of wheels and more robust bearings and gears (they all get a lot of punishment on the broken and gritty roads of West Cork), and he managed to get me to take a new pair of mudguards, the truth is he had a whole shop full of goodies he could have sold me had he just taken the time. For example, my old Altura jacket was still serviceable, but torn and I could really have done with a new one. But that close to Spring? Nah, I was happy to wait until October, all other things being equal. Yet if he'd bothered to ask Sir if Sir needed anything else, a nice new jacket, perhaps, to go with his new bike... then it would not have been a tricky sale at all. And... my old fingerless gloves have seen better days, too. And my white jersey. And my old GAP baseball cap (and while I don't wear a cycling helmet, it's not impossible he could have talked me into one). Oh, and those old tracksuit bottoms? Would Sir like to look at these fine leggings? It would have been simplicity itself for this fellow to turn the €959 sale into a €1,559 sale, if only he'd asked and taken the time to get to know me and my cycling habits. What's more it would not only have been more pleasant for me because I wanted to enjoy the experience of being sold stuff I love to buy and own (Lord... I sound like such a bloody girl), but his profit margin would have been truly gigantic, since his already tiny cost of sale had already been laid out. In other words, it would have been "free money"[30].

Fact is, selling isn't hard, not when you do it the right way, and sell to people who have already bought from you or have come to you asking for your help, knowledge, and assistance. No one likes the hard sell... but once we're "in", we're easy meat.

Bottom line: learn how to sell, and sell with pride, because when it comes down to it, it's nothing more than finding out what people want and then giving it to them.

---

30. Money he's definitely missed out on now, because since then I've bought *all* of these items — and more — from an online retailer who keeps sending me emails. There's a lesson right there for you if you care to learn it. And I've yet to receive *any* marketing from him. I've never had even so much as an email.

Effective Marketing Made (Dead) Easy

Summary of Chapter 3

1. **Effective marketing is simple.** It's a matter of putting the right message in front of the right person, at the right time, and in the right way.

2. **Lead generation marketing is almost always more profitable than selling "off the page".** Begin your relationships with your customers and clients by *giving*.

3. **The key to successful selling over time is follow up.** Most business never follow up on leads all; and almost none of them follow up enough. You should follow up until they buy, die, or beg you to stop.

4. **Testing and measuring are essential.** Profitable marketing systems do not spring into being overnight. They are always the result of constant and continuous testing and measuring to see what works and what doesn't.

5. **Nothing happens until you sell something.** If you are squeamish about selling, then you need to change this. Otherwise you'll die poor and hungry.

Chapter 4

Your Message

Your Message is what you say to your market to get the people in it to buy from you, and it comprises two parts.

First is the *explicit message*, what you actually say in the words you use in your marketing pieces, in your sales presentations, and in everything you explicitly put out there with the intention of selling.

And secondly, there's your *implicit message*, what people perceive about you, your business, and your products and services from your ongoing actions and the dialogue you have with them.

Now, in both cases you need to tailor your message to your target market, and, obviously, the more accurately and precisely you can define your target market, the more accurately and precisely you can target your message.

The more accurately and precisely you target your message, the more you'll sell, the less your marketing is going to cost because you've got less wastage, meaning your ROI will dramatically increase.

So what does it mean to "target your message"?

Well, quite simply it means you say what you've got to

say in a way to resonate in the minds of the people in your market.

For example, if you're, say, marketing gym membership to women in their 40s, you'd use very different language, for example, from the language you'd use if you were selling the same thing to young studs in their 20s.

The former are probably more interested in losing the flab around their middle and being able to fit into that hot little black number hanging in the back of the wardrobe without looking like 10lb of spuds in a 5lb bag; and the latter are more likely to be swayed by the kind of language implying they're going to look like Adonis and have women throwing their knickers at them.

In my own case I have a very particular kind of business owner in mind for my products and services, and everything I say or do is aimed at attracting those people and driving the others away. I'll say more about this in the next chapter.

Your Explicit Message

The explicit message you give out is all the stuff you say in your marketing materials. Since this changes from day to day in the detail, we can usefully think of this as your *tactical* message.

At the very base level it's the actual structure and content of your sales letters, postcards, web-pages, emails, and everything else you put out there on a day-to-day basis. I'm not going to go into detail about copywriting and direct response design here, but I give them a full treatment in Appendix I.

For now, it's just important we understand a few vital concepts, beginning with the important question…

Why Do People Buy?

There's only one reason anyone buys anything, ever: to solve a problem.

What those problems are vary from individual to individual and even vary for the same individual over time. For example, I have spent the last thirty years or more blissfully unaware of all but the vaguest idea of who my dentist is. I know that sounds strange, but it's true, nonetheless. I've been a couple of times recently, but before that I didn't go for at least ten years.

Why?

Because I've got great teeth[31].

They don't *look* great, but they're strong, and my old dentist told me decades ago I wouldn't have any problems until I reached late middle-age, and likely not even then... and so far he's been right. But here's something: you can bet your left kidney if the one filling I have[32] fell out, then finding an emergency dentist would very quickly be A Big Problem for me. Although for some unfortunate folks, who can't even look at a sugarlump without their teeth falling out of their head, the dentist thing is indeed an ongoing problem.

Here's another example for you: nothing to do with golf will ever be a "problem" for me unless you're trying to hit me with a golf club, simply because I can't stand the game; but a golf-nut will be equally bemused by and incredulous of my obsession with all things bicycles.

You want to catch my attention, then start talking to me about disc brakes that'll stop me on a sixpence when I'm haring down a wet and muddy lane in West Cork, go flying

---

31. Fascinating evolutionary fact: bones are adapted teeth thanks to the long process of evolution.

32. The legacy of a schoolboy fight when I was 13 or so.

---

around a blind bend, and come face-to-arse with a cow just ahead of me.

That's a problem for me, right there — disappearing headfirst up the back-end of a cow is not something I want to do, if I'm perfectly frank. So being able to stop in the wet and hold my wheel right on the point of locking so I've effectively got myself a set of anti-lock brakes is of utmost importance to me.

So what?

Where are we going with all this?

Well, the point I'm making here is how we define something as a "problem" is utterly subjective.

And if you really get your head around what I'm about to share with you, then just that one thing, in and of itself, is going to make a huge difference to the way you market your business.

Ready?

OK... here it comes...

No one is interested in buying anything from you for any other reason than to solve their problems.

They don't care about:

- You
- Your name
- Your logo
- Your products
- Your services
- How great you think you are
- What your mission statement is
- What you want
- What your dreams and passions are

Your Message

- Your brand
- How long you've been in business
- How many shades of pink your widgets come in
- How many widgets you sell every week
- How much you need or deserve the cash

You might think this is all very obvious and wonder why I'm sharing it with you. But before you go too far down that road, just think about how most businesses present themselves. The ads they put in the Golden Pages, Yellow Pages, other business directories, and newspapers are usually nothing but oversized and very expensive business cards.

They typically comprise the company-name or logo followed by a list of stuff they do, with some half-hearted plea for you to "come in and see us some time". It's the same with websites, sales letters, postcards, emails, and all those other things we throw into the marketing mix hoping they'll bring in some business. They all so often start like this:

"Hi, and welcome to my boring website. My name's Billy Boring, and I love bikes. I've been riding them for years, so I thought I'd open my own bike shop, Billy Boring's Bikes. I do bikes, tandems, biking clothes, and all the other stuff people who love bikes need.

We sell all the best brands, too. Loads of them! Trek, Ridgeback, Scott, Raleigh… you name the brand, and we've probably got one for you.

My mission is to give you the best bikes and all the other cycling stuff you need at the lowest prices possible.

We're different from all the other bike shops out there,

because, well, we say so. And we give great service.
So why not give us a call — we'd love to hear from
you and maybe sell you a bike."

Now, that's an exaggeration, but not much of one, to be sure. The big problems with it are it's all about *them*, *their* products and services, and what *they* do, and the best promises they can come up with are they give "great service" and a "low price".

Well, I've got news for you: "great service" is a *minimum requirement* and nothing to write home about; and a "low price" is a terrible thing to be selling on for all sorts of reasons we'll come to shortly. See, no one cares what you do; they care only what you can do *for them* by way of solving their problems. Because of this they don't even care much about low price, at least not the kinds of customers and clients you actually *want* in your business. In other words, I don't care about your bike shop, your brakes or your discs: I care only about their ability to bring me quickly and safely to a halt and stop me from disappearing up a cow's arse at high speed.

Why Do People Buy From **YOU**?

We know people do buy stuff, and now we know *why* they do so. But that's no use to us if they're buying from our competitors. So the question, and it's often an unspoken one held unconsciously in your prospective customer's or client's mind, but a question you must answer nevertheless is "why out of all the available options should I buy from you instead of from your competitors?".

This is probably the most important question you can ask yourself about your business, and until you have the answer, I strongly urge you to stop all of your marketing activities and set your mind to purpose in answering it.

Your Message

Your Unique Selling Point

The abstract answer to that question we just asked is often called your *Unique Selling Point, Unique Selling Proposition,* or just USP. It's what makes you not just different but also *better* than your competitors for that particular product or service.

Here's an important point: anyone can say they're different, and most people do. One particular ad I saw some years ago springs to mind. It was a bunch of penguins with one purple one in the middle, and the caption said something like, "we're different". As I recall it was advertising some professional service or other — a full page, full colour ad in a professional trade-magazine and probably cost an arm and a flipper.

My question is this: how on Earth is any of that supposed to answer the most important question?[33] Not only is that a terrible ad in its execution, but the concept is fatally flawed: saying you're "different" is easy. But *what's* different and *why* should I, the reader and prospective client, care? Merely being different isn't enough: to secure the business, to answer that all-important question, you've got to be *better*, too.

This is where your USP comes in, because it's an explicit or implicit promise to be just that — better. It's the answer to that question we saw a few minutes ago.

An explicit USP is something like the one Domino's Pizza used: "You get fresh, hot pizza delivered to your door in 30 minutes or less — or it's free!" It's a clear and unambiguous promise aimed at a very specific target market: people who want fresh, hot pizza and who want it *now*. Another example is the Remington Razor USP: "Shaves as close as a blade or

---

33. I can just imagine the design team sitting around tossing about ideas trying to decide on the exact shade of purple for the fucking penguin.

Your Message

your money back". A third example is from Ross Jeffries, the seduction "guru", who says, "If you don't get laid, I don't get paid."[34]

Your USP is not the same as a strapline, which is usually just a catchy phrase that doesn't actually mean anything. It drives me nuts when arty and "creative" people talk about the need for "catchy straplines". There's no point in being able to *remember* these things if they don't bring up an association with the business they relate to *and* answer that big question.

Your USP is the answer to that big question, remember, so saying something like "Boring Bill's Bikes... We're Wheely Good" isn't a USP.

Secrets to a Compelling USP

Crafting a compelling USP is a matter of sitting down with a pencil and paper and coming up with a whole load of ideas, starting with the premise your customers and clients need you to answer that all important question.

A simple and effective place to start is to think of all the things your target market hates about your industry. Don't be offended when I say this, because no matter what business you're in there are "pet hates", and you and your colleagues are going to be tarred with the same noxious brush.

For example, some common perceptions:

- Lawyers are slippery and charge a fortune for sending letters they didn't need to send ("Dear Client, nothing further to report. We'll write to you again next week to let you know if we have nothing to tell you. That's another 25 Groats, please.").

---

34. An important thing to note here is these USPs I've mentioned are not about the promise of something for free. What they actually are is guarantees of performance and they serve to take away the risk of buying.

- Estate agents (Realtors) lie, exaggerate, and will say anything to sell a house.

- Plumbers do shoddy work, overcharge, and even charge for work they didn't *need* to do (and often for work they didn't *actually* do).

- Car Mechanics (see plumbers).

- Builders (see Car Mechanics).

- Banks... 'nuff said.

- Delivery men don't turn up. When they do, they expect your 97yo granny to carry a wardrobe upstairs on her own because they're "not insured".

- Salespeople of all kinds are full of shit.

- And not to leave myself out of this... marketing professionals will say anything to sell you a product or service and when it doesn't work, they strangely are hard to get hold of to call on their guarantees.

I stress: I am not claiming the above are necessarily true, and I'm certainly not pointing the finger at any individuals... but none of it will come as a surprise to you, I'm sure.

And so creating a powerful USP, or at least a good starting point, is to figure out what people hate about *your* niche and then promise not to do it, *and make sure you make and keep that promise consistently*. Just note you can have more than one USP if you offer different products and services, especially if they have different target markets.

Now, if you can have a simple, snappy USP encapsulating your core business principle, all the better. But often this isn't the case. I don't have one, for example, and nor do many of the other big players in my industry.

So does this mean we don't have a USP?

Nope.

Here's why: my own USP is in my *implicit message*. It's the picture of me, my "positioning", my image, if you like, emerging from everything I say and do.

In my case I'm particularly well known for my blunt and often coarse language and attitude, lack of tolerance for fools, as well as my integrity and unswerving honesty. If I had to sum it up in a single idea or concept, it's *I am trustworthy*[35].

How to Get Trust with Guarantees

Of all the things standing between you and your prospect and the sale is trust, or, rather, the lack of it. Think of it this way: in any transaction or exchange of value, there is always a risk of things going wrong.

From the buyer's side the worry is the product or service won't be delivered, or won't do what it's supposed to do. And it's not just the worry about the money, either. There's all the associated hassle and frustration of having to get your money back and then go through the whole buying process again, and all the time you've *still* got the problem. And even worse, perhaps, for some purchases there's also the worry of ridicule and embarrassment. Imagine you've just bought into the weight-loss fad doing the rounds: if it doesn't work, you're not only out of pocket and still overweight, but you also look a bit of a chump. That hurts.

From the seller's side there's also a risk: the risk the customer or client won't pay or will prove to be an utter pain

---

35. I'm even honest and upfront about *why* you can trust me: it's not because I'm a nice guy, necessarily, but rather it's because it's in my own rational self interests to be. Like everyone else on the planet, I'm looking out for No. 1, and you can definitely trust me on that without having to second guess my motives for saying it. And... my business can be successful only if I help make my clients' businesses successful, and I won't do that by lying to them or selling them crap. This is a message I send out both explicitly and implicitly in everything I do. And it works very well for me.

Your Message

in the arse and then demand his money back.

The problem for us as business owners is the two sides are not equal: there are almost always more sellers than buyers and *usually* we want their money more than they want our products and services.

The upshot is the buyer really holds all the cards. So this is where guarantees come in, offering what Jay Abraham called "risk reversal". What it means is you offer a (usually) unconditional guarantee your products and services will do the job they're supposed to do else your customer or client can have a full refund.

So, remove that last stumbling block and offer risk reversal. Say to them, "I want you to have this. Try it. If it doesn't work, I'll give you your money back. No questions asked." You can't do this safely all the time or with everything. For instance, I wouldn't write a sales letter and offer to give all their money back if it didn't work because there are so many other things that conspire to derail even the most carefully planned and expertly executed marketing campaign. If I was going to offer that kind of risk reversal, I would probably charge 10 times the fee because to me it's 10 times the risk, and I'd have all sorts of conditions in there to make sure they didn't change so much as a comma or a hyphen. But the guarantee I used to give was "if it doesn't work the first time, I'll rewrite it; and if it doesn't work the second time, I'll rewrite it again. If it doesn't work by then, obviously there is something fundamentally wrong and not just the sales letter because, I don't make that kind of mistake three times in a row".

And despite the irrational fears business owners have of them, people almost never, ever cheat you. One or two might, but imagine if you make 50 extra sales because of the guarantee and 10 of them cheat you. You still made a net profit on 40 extra sales you wouldn't have made before. The only thing that stops you letting those 10 lost sales go it is your righteous pigheadedness in chasing after the people who've cheated you. Forget about it and them, and enjoy the extra cash.

In general, the better the guarantee, the better the sale. Counter-intuitively, the longer your guarantee, the less often you're called on it. On Mrs. EBG's blog she gives a lifetime guarantee and her refund rate is less than 2%. It's about 1.5%. I know you could say you'll never know exactly how much it's going to be until she's dead because it's a lifetime guarantee but, in practice, if they have not claimed their money back within a couple of months they're just never going to.

In my own business I have a product called *Profit Kickstart* — www.profitkickstart.com — and with it I offer the guarantee that if after 12 months it has not made you at least £10,000 in additional profits you can directly attribute to it, I'll refund every penny. You don't even have to send it back to me.

And no one has *ever* asked me for a refund.

Your Implicit Message I — Premier Positioning

The common wisdom tells us we start a business, work hard in the field of our choice for a depressingly long time — measured in years if not actually decades — and then at some point mysteriously and magically we get to ascend to Expert Status, most likely after a sprinkling of Expert-Fairy dust, grudgingly wafted our way by the incumbent experts in our chosen field.

Some years ago I was consulting with a client in my office and I asked her about her pricing. Her fees were probably half what they should be. "OK", I said, "don't tell me how you got that figure — let me read your mind".

So I put my fingers to my temples, closed my eyes and concentrated for a moment, then said "you looked at the range of fees charged by your competitors and picked somewhere in the middle". "Close", she admitted sheepishly, "I actually picked a price nearer the bottom". And it turned out she was going to do the whole tedious and laborious routine of climbing that big ol' Expert Mountain before charging more.

Think now how you set your own fees or prices. My guess is you've done something similar. Don't be shy about admitting it. Personally, I think that attitude sucks and it makes for a seriously crap life and business. Oh yes, I freely admit I did it myself... *at least, until I figured out I didn't have to!* I've done the whole "competitive pricing" thing, with one eye firmly fixed on my competitors, in the mistaken belief it actually matters what they get up to. But not for a *long* time; and never, *ever* again.

Best of all... *you* don't have to, either.

Not now, not ever.

One of the most dangerous ideas in business is that of the "going rate". It's entirely imaginary, yet it serves to keep business owners in line all charging roughly the same prices and fees as each other.

But the "going rate" is a chain that holds us only if we accept it. One client of mine is in the printing business in Watford in the UK, an area saturated by the printing trade. The average margin in his industry is 15%, but after following my advice, often lovingly administered with a sharp kick up the backside, his margins are now 65% — meaning his prices are vastly higher than the "going rate" charged by the 65 competing companies in his area. Better yet, he's suddenly attracting a much better class of client, including some "blue chip" companies, because he's presenting himself in a

Your Message

manner to make price irrelevant.

It might be hard for you to grok how this all might work right now, but it does, nevertheless. You will, I hope, come to understand it all by the time you've finished *Grow Your Business __FAST__*. I won't pretend it's always going to be easy and there will be times it seems far easier just to relax and go with the flow. In my experience, though, those are the times when it's even *more* important to keep a "stiff upper lip", straighten your back and soldier on.

It's worth it, I promise.

What Is "Positioning"?

In a nutshell we can say it's how we orientate ourselves, our image, our behaviour, and the messages we give out so the world sees us in a particular way.

And in our case, as business owners, we want to be perceived as high-end expert vendors of our products and services, rather than as the "hired help".

That's what I call *Premier Positioning* or *Expert Positioning*. It's about becoming the biggest fish in your pond, no matter how large or small that pond is, and it breaks down into three areas:

1. **Self-Positioning.** How you see yourself. Sounds very New-Age and woo-woo, but I can't help that. More in a moment.

2. **Market Positioning.** How your target market sees you. This includes your pricing, which I cover in the next section.

3. **Competitor Positioning.** How your competitors see you. I think this one is pretty much irrelevant and I don't propose to say much more about it. Do you care what the guy down the road thinks of your marketing?

No. Not unless you're a numpty.

Top, Middle and Bottom

In any industry or niche there's going to be a range of providers, from the low-end and in-betweeners to the high-end, with there being many more of the former than of the latter.

We all know this, but it's something we never really think about; worse than that we seem to assume the upper reaches of the scale are beyond us, or, at best, something we can aspire to only in time.

And it's not true.

Premier Positioning is essentially the art of leapfrogging the crowd and taking yourself right to the top of your industry without the bother and inconvenience of passing through the intermediate stages. I predicate this on one thing, of course: that you can and do actually deliver the goods.

I'm not one for passing moral judgement on others, and how you run your business is a matter for your own conscience. But if you're going to set yourself up as an expert and charge premium prices for your products and services, then unless you *do* deliver the goods you are quickly going to fall flat on your face. Remember this is about long-term income, not short-term rip-offs.

So, as a rough guide, if you can't pick ten topics in your area and speak intelligently about each of them for an hour, even if it's just in a Q&A format, you might want to think about learning more[36] or picking another line of work.

---

36. Go to Amazon, buy the top 25 titles on the topic and read them. You'll then know more about it than 99% of humanity.

Your Message

Self Positioning... an Unavoidable Slice of Personal Philosophy and Self Help

I really wanted to avoid writing about personal development and stuff, not because I don't think it's necessary and useful — it is, and one of these days I may well have more to say about it — but because there's so much crap out there and it's too easy to come over as happy-clappy. But I think it *is* unavoidable. So I promise I'll keep it as brief as I can.

The point is...

Premier Positioning Is an Inside Job

In other words, if you don't have your self-positioning sorted out first, then the rest is going to be exceedingly tough for you.

Why?

Because, to put even more use on a well-overused phrase, it means taking yourself well outside your comfort zone.

And in short, in this case it means if you want others to look upon you as the Big Cheese, you've got to look upon *yourself* as the Big Cheese, first.

Luckily, it's OK to fake it till you make it, so long as you *deliver on your promises*, and this approach does have merit because as science has shown us over and over again, our physiology not only reflects our neurology, but also our neurology reflects our physiology. In other words, act confident and you'll start to feel confident; act like a Big Cheese and you'll start to feel like a Big Cheese.

I'm going to share something with you now which at first glance might seem irrelevant. It's not. I'll call it the *Ultimate Coping Strategy* (UCS) for now.

There are loads of things in life we don't like, and some of these cause us real problems.

I have a dear friend and client who has a real problem with relationships. She dives headlong into the most unsuitable ones she can possibly find, spends months, sometimes years, deeply unhappy... and then is distraught when they implode, along with the rest of her life.

Lather, rinse, repeat.

Some time ago I did some one-on-one work with her and pointed out there are three things we can do in cases like this:

- **Avoid them.** Fine in theory, not always possible in practice. She doesn't even *want* to avoid them and do without emotional and physical intimacy. And as business owners we have our own uncomfortable situations we can't afford to avoid. For example, we can't easily avoid situations where we've got to sell ourselves in some way, not if we want to make money.

- **Change.** Which is always harder than it seems, and I'm not convinced permanent change is even *possible* for everyone. It requires eternal vigilance, just like freedom and my six-pack.

- **Accept them.** I suggested she save £10, £20, £50 a week, whatever, in a "disaster fund", cognizant of the fact the relationship will end and she will feel like shit... and when that happens the money will pay for a week in a swish hotel where she can get drunk and enjoy the self-pity. This is the Ultimate Coping Strategy, or the "fuck it" strategy as I sometimes call it. Another friend of mine was in a bad car accident. She wasn't hurt but it was pretty traumatic. She said to me, "I can't stop crying when I think about what happened". I said, "So stop trying". And the moment she stopped trying to force herself to feel a certain way, and simply accepted how she *did* feel, the whole thing got a lot easier.

My point with all this is... you don't *have* to change. If you find Premier Positioning uncomfortable then you don't have to fight yourself or re-engineer your psyche to make it comfortable.

You can just accept it's hard and create your own UCS. Apart from anything else, the moment you stop resisting it, it'll lose a lot of its power over you[37].

In other words, just give these things a try, watch the numbers, and bugger what friends, family, colleagues, and anyone who isn't a customer or a client says about it.

Market Positioning... How to Become King of the Hill

The actions you have to take are simple and they don't cost you anything. But it's not always easy to take them, as I hinted above.

So here's a plan for you. I'm not saying it's the only plan; I'm not saying it's even the best plan. But it's a plan that worked for me, it's worked for others, and I'm confident it'll work for you, too. You don't have to follow it slavishly, and you are free to take out what doesn't suit you, add in what does, and otherwise play around with it until you find something that works.

The point is it's a framework you can start with to create your own business philosophy to put you at the top of your profession.

---

37. But here's a curious thing. You'll find, most likely, after a while of behaving this way, even if you don't feel it, it becomes natural. In other words, you've effected a long-term change without really trying too hard to make it happen.

Your Message

Step 1: Choose

No matter what business you're in, someone is going to be top-dog.

- Someone is going to have the highest fees or prices.
- Someone is going to be on the TV, on the radio and in the newspapers.
- Someone is going to be the "go to" guy or gal.
- Someone is going to live in the "ivory tower" and be spoken of in hushed and reverent tones by their competitors.

Question: why should that someone not be you?

Because if it's not *you*, then it'll be *someone else*.

And the biggest obstacle standing between you and that exalted status is the *decision* to claim it for yourself.

I know, that sounds terribly success-guru like, but it's true.

I'm not aware of a single business in the free world where your fees are set by law, so there is nothing to stop you asking top-whack right now[38]. Moreover, it's not like hacking off a limb or jumping out of an aeroplane without a parachute. If you try something with a dozen potential clients and it doesn't work, then you can try something else.

In any case, the risk is so low it's almost zero. There will be a small and sometimes vocal minority of people who won't like what you're doing, but so long as you stay within the law and the rules of any professional body you *have* to belong to, then let them bleat like the miserable sheep they are.

It's almost like a law of nature: once you get to the top, there are an awful lot of people with "advice" and "opinions"

---

38. And if there are industries out there where this kind of unwarranted intrusion into your personal and business life is allowed, then you might want to think about doing something else for a living.

out there. You'll see this in particular on forums, but they'll probably email you, too. I *still* get people, even other aspiring copywriters working for peanuts, telling me "you might do better if you softened your tone". Fuck off. I don't care.

These people have no clue about me, my business, Premier Positioning, Premium Pricing, or *anything else*, come to that; and that's why my copywriting fees were an order of magnitude more than theirs will ever be, and why they're reading *my* stuff rather than the other way round.

So, you want to be top dog?

Then make the choice and then...

Step 2: Set Your OWN Boundaries

I am constantly amazed how so many business owners don't have their own internal set of rules by which they live their lives and run their businesses. It seems every decision they make is based on whim, necessity or expediency. And while these things might work tactically in the short term, as long-term strategies they are terrible. So don't skip over this step. It's probably one of the toughest yet most rewarding exercises you'll ever do.

Trust me on this.

Create a Set of Rules for Yourself

It sounds very square in these times to talk about "values" because you either sound like a religious fruitcake or a politician with an agenda to control people's lives, but they're important. This is key. It doesn't take long to build up a set of rules to make most areas of your life start to run themselves practically on autopilot.

I was talking with a client some time ago about this and suggested he write a "rule book" for all his staff, a set of values *everyone* bought into and *everyone* has to stick to. I suggest you do it for yourself and your own business, too. This doesn't have to be onerous and the rewards are immeasurable.

For example, I said, "have a minimum fee below which you won't take on a job, no matter what". By doing this, you save yourself a lot of time hemming and hawing over "borderline" cases. In fact, if you ever find yourself wondering if a certain rule applies... you already know it does. The longer and harder you wonder, the surer of this you can be.

Stick to the rules and it works.

Sure, you'll occasionally miss a good opportunity, but you'll massively offset this with all the crap you manage to avoid getting into.

One of my own rules, for instance, aside from a minimum fee, is I won't meet people in a business context unless they're paying me. Simple.

Lunch? Fine.

Drinks in the bar? Even better.

Kinky sex in a hotel room? Best of all (as long as she's really hot and asks me very nicely).

But meetings to "talk over proposals" and stuff?

No.

You want to get into that level of attention, and you're my client. If you're my client, it means you're paying me.

Another rule is clients don't just call me on the phone whenever they have a brainfart. If we need to speak we set a time. When we've set the time, that's when it happens. If you're more than a few minutes late, we re-schedule. Even my accountant, bank manager and solicitor don't just call me without an appointment.

Anyone can do this. It's your business and ultimately you set the rules about how it's going to run. Even if your business needs the phone to be answered, who says *you* have to be the one to answer it? Limiting access to yourself is a fabulous strategy for Premier Positioning. People love to jump through hoops, so when they do get to speak to you, or get on your client list, they feel they've achieved something.

And then, as well as having rules for your clients, have rules for your vendors and suppliers, too. Some years ago a guy from a certain well known and popular business directory wanted to meet me to "discuss" the "proposal". I didn't need or want no steenking meeting! All I wanted to know is how big, how much, in what format, and by when he needed the copy? I didn't want or need to speak to him on the phone, even. Email and fax was fine. But he kept bugging me about getting on the phone. Eventually, I had to lay it down in plain and simple English for him when he said, "well, 99.9% of businesses meet with us".

So what?

I'm not 99.9% of businesses, and 99.9% of businesses don't know Jack Shit about marketing or advertising. That's why they meet with wide-boys like him (and because they've got nothing better to do than go to meetings... and meetings are usually just "activity" and that isn't necessarily the same as "achievement"). More to the point, since *most* businesses barely scrape by, what *most* businesses do clearly isn't that smart or effective. What he *really* wanted me to do was try to sell me stuff I didn't want or need — useless whitespace with a logo on top, no doubt.

A great quote I heard some years ago was, "People are walking around with an umbilical cord in their hand, looking for somewhere to plug it in". Spot on. They *want* to be told what to do.

Bottom line is this: do it my way or you don't get my business.

Your Message

Be Honest

Most people are honest most of the time in most situations. And I'm not going to start moralising about there is never any time when telling a lie is acceptable. If someone comes knocking on my door saying he wants to beat my son up and asking if he's in the house, then of course I'm going to lie and say he's not[39]. But in the main I don't lie, even if it's for no other reason than it's too much effort to remember what's been said to whom.

Yet most people take a much more flexible attitude to the truth than that, especially when it comes to minor deceptions they make to save face or money. I used to do it myself until I figured out it really was far more effort and trouble than it was worth.

Just recently I was helping out at a marketing conference, and someone tried to get me to sit down with her and critique her website. But I'd been working hard all day and was now relaxing with some friends and clients. So she said, "I understand you're busy and can't help me right now". But that wasn't true and I made a point of making this clear to her: it wasn't a case of *can't*; it was a case of *won't*. To me it was important she and everyone else understood this because she was crossing my boundaries. It would have been easy to let the little face-saving, feelings-sparing white lie pass, but long-term that could do me and my business more harm than good.

In my experience being upfront with people saves a lot of time and effort down the line, and even if people don't necessarily like the answer you've given them, if they're worth knowing, then they'll respect you more for it.

---

39. Then I'm going to beat him to death with a pickaxe handle and feed the body to the dogs.

When I got my first big client, someone in the US who later went on to refer me to loads of his friends and colleagues and so was worth hundreds of thousands of Groats to me over the years, I remember making what at the time seemed like a *huge* error in a print ad I did for him. He had a marketing system for mortgage brokers he licenced for other brokers to use, with the restriction only one broker could use the system within a given area. And in the ad I was supposed to list all the cities already spoken for, along with the state they were in. Somehow, I managed to put a town in the wrong state and I didn't notice until it had gone to print.

Man, I got into a cold sweat about that one, but it was clear the right thing to do was to come clean and tell him what I'd done, and offer to make amends. So I told him, and offered to cover the cost of the ad in the publication, even though I really didn't have the money to do that. But he just came back with "OK, no worries", and that was that.

The temptation in situations like that is to say nothing and then, if it ever comes to light, play stupid or blame someone else — even the client, because you might say he should have checked it himself.

But that's no way to run a business, not really.

In the short term honesty can be difficult, expensive and very uncomfortable. But long term it pays, both in terms of income and your own self-esteem. No one feels comfortable knowing they're a liar, I'm sure.

If you're going to lie, really do save it for those times when in doing so you stop a much greater evil — don't do it just to save face, make a sale or a profit you're not really entitled to, or to make life easier for yourself.

There's also another reason I'm honest and why people are safe putting their trust in me. And it's simply because I always act in my own rational self interest. Everyone else does this, too, but the difference is I am completely open and upfront about it. Even people who claim they're altruistic and do good turns for others are acting in their own interests, because they get the reward of the good feelings resulting from what they do for others. The more people I help with their businesses, the better the world I get to live in because there's more wealth floating around in general, and there's more in *my* pocket in particular.

This is why I always say you can trust me — not just because I'm honest and a nice guy, but because it's not in my rational best interests to screw anyone over. I am highly suspicious of anyone who offers me something, especially in business, and claims it's just out of the goodness of his heart. It doesn't make any sense to be doing it, so from where I'm standing they're either nuts or lying to me — and in either case, I don't want to be associating with them.

You're in business to make money.

No one should begrudge you that, and if they do, then they're exactly the kind of person you ought to be going out of your way to avoid.

Cultivate Integrity

Integrity is one of the most important characteristics of anyone who seeks to be successful. Mark my words... if you don't have integrity, eventually it *will* come back and bite you in the arse.

And having integrity leads people to have a sense of *deservedness* as opposed to a sense of *entitlement*.

Deservedness is the sense of expectation of getting a just reward for your labours and your efforts. I believe I deserve to do well. I believe I've earned it. I expect it, and I'm almost never disappointed. It suits me well and it serves me right. I've worked hard on myself and I work hard for my clients.

I don't get it right every time, and when I don't I do my best to fix it. I don't expect something for nothing and I lay claim to the fruits of no one's labour but my own.

Entitlement, on the other hand, is a dirty, ugly thing. It's what an unemployed single mother might feel because she's perhaps made poor choices in life and sees other people getting ahead. It's the sense you get from men with families living in small, crappy assisted housing wanting to move to better places because they feel "entitled" to it — "hey, I've got kids! Think of my children!". It's the feeling people get when they see what others have and think somehow some of it "belongs" to them... or at least *should* do.

Don't misunderstand me — I make no judgement on anyone for their lifestyle choices, because their lives are their own. But in the same way as they have the freedom to make their own choices, they have the obligation of taking responsibility for them and the consequences that follow. What I *do* have a problem with is people who make poor choices and then feel entitled to be bailed out at others' expense. Unfortunately, this sense of entitlement is rife in our society. It's the sentiment behind the entire "redistribution of wealth" movement. But enough of that.

How do you cultivate a sense of deservedness and leave entitlement behind?

Easy: by working on your integrity and by sticking to your own rules.

Once you start practicing integrity —— saying what you're going to do and then doing it — it opens up all the doors you could ever want opened.

It's amazing the difference it makes to your entire life, never mind your business. So many things require no further thought because you're living according to a framework of rules you already have in your life. Just remember the old

Buddhist saying, "All things in moderation, including moderation itself". Meaning, be ready to re-evaluate your rules periodically.

Let me give you an example... I'd never work with or for a client who sold, say, cigarettes. I don't have anything against smoking, I'd never in any way seek to stop people smoking in any quantities they desired, but it's not my cup of tea. All the evidence demonstrates to my satisfaction it's addictive, unhealthy, and often a killer. I don't want anything to do with marketing something so destructive, so I wouldn't do it. End of. So back when I was writing copy for clients, if I was ever approached by someone to do work for this kind of business, I didn't have to stop and think about it. I didn't have to weigh up the fees, see if I could slot it into my schedule, bat it back and forth in my own head trying to convince myself it was "OK", and tell myself "maybe this time I can make an exception".

Because I'd *already* decided: I didn't "do" tobacco. Similarly, I didn't "do" gambling, the majority of weight-loss products or programmes, anything remotely connected with "The Secret", religion, or spirituality of any description.

I was not just a copywriting "gun for hire", available to anyone with a huge wedge of cash and a burning need for copy. I have principles, which are entirely my own, and integrity takes care of the rest.

Give it a whirl in your own business. You'll like it, and your market will respond to it like crazy. For best results, the values you create should come from inside. They should be *yours* and not be imposed from the outside by society, religion, or any other outside agency.

Why?

Because if they're *yours* you *own* them. They mean something to *you*. You'll stick to them because you truly believe in them. I'm honest because *I* feel it's right for *me*, not because people tell me so or because it's written in some holy book somewhere. So it's *easy* for me to be honest. I have integrity for the same reasons.

Finally, you don't need a huge pile of these rules, and you can add to them or take away from them as you go. You don't have to copy anyone else's or, once you have your list, seek anyone else's approval to make them your own. But I think it's essential you *do* have them... and then make sure everyone knows about them, and there's no question in anyone's mind about your sticking to them.

Step 3: Just Do it

We get our newly-minted King of the Hillness out there by communicating our values in everything we say and do. It's not just *in* our message... it *is* our message. To use an often overused phrase you start to "walk your walk" not just "talk your talk".

You make your way of doing business an integral part of your business and of your personality.

Let's see how we can do that.

Sending Out the Message

This is the easiest thing in the world. Once you stop shaking and crying for your mammy.

When I made up my mind to start doing this it was just after coming back from a Dan Kennedy SuperConference in the US. The very first thing I did was fire two of my only three clients. On the face of it, I couldn't afford to do that... but I really couldn't afford *not* to do it, either. And the next thing I did after firing those two pain-in-the-arse clients was change the "contact me" and "about me" pages on my website.

Your Message

Whereas before I had the usual stuff about "call me to discuss your project" and whatnot, along with my phone number and email address, I replaced it with a set of instructions about how they could contact me — and none of it was convenient or easy for anyone but *me*. I don't remember all the details, but it was essentially a set of hoops they had to jump through, beginning with sending me a *fax*, before they could expect to talk to me personally. The general rule I was following, and it's a rule I always recommend to anyone who seeks my advice on these things, was "I don't talk to people on the phone unless they are 90% of the way to giving me money, and the conversation I want to be having with them is 'when can you start?' not 'what can you do for me?'".

Over time this has evolved and developed to the point where I almost never, ever get on the phone with anyone, simply because I don't want to. Phone calls, especially unplanned ones, are a huge waste of everyone's time. Even if the call lasts just 10 minutes, the actual disruption to my work is probably three times that. It's the same with emails. Although I do have a contact email address on my website, it's not my personal one. I check it once a day and reply if a reply is necessary

All of this is *scary* when you first begin doing it because you're terrified you're going to lose business — that's just common sense, right? But common sense or not, it's not how it pans out. If you've positioned yourself correctly and you have the requisite expert status, then inaccessibility is *expected*.

If you're busy — too busy to take random, unplanned phone calls from any old Tom, Dick, or Harriet who decides to call you on a whim, kicking tyres to check your prices, or to squeeze as much free information and advice out of you as they can — then it says something about you. For one thing,

Your Message

it says you *are* busy. That means you must be successful and in demand. And that is *incredibly* attractive. There is nothing quite so powerful in making people want to do business with you than telling them they can't. It's a curious trait of human nature for us to want what we can't have, and to cling on to what we might lose. This is why the strategy of *scarcity* is so powerful in nudging people into taking action.

Only your own personal experience will convince you of this, but if you start making it harder for your prospects, customers, and clients to get direct access to you, then your desirability will skyrocket.

This is not the same as making it hard to do business with you. I'm not suggesting you leave phones to ring and emails and letters unanswered or acknowledged. But you don't have to jerk at the end of a string like a marionette every time someone gives it a tug. When I was actively looking for copywriting clients, for example, I made it clear I'd respond to enquiries within 48 business hours... and no matter how not-busy I was, that's how long I'd wait. It takes a certain kind of self-control to play it cool when you really *need* the work, and not respond instantly to an enquiry. When someone emails and says, "I'd love to talk to you about my project — call me", it's *very* hard not to grab the phone right there and then and do as you're told. If you do, you immediately put yourself at a disadvantage; and if you don't, you immeasurably strengthen your positioning and vastly increase your chances not only of getting the work but also of commanding a higher fee for it.

When people ask you to meet them to talk about their projects, tell them there's an upfront charge for it. Why should you give them your time for nothing? Your time is valuable. Why should they get something of value from you without the *quid pro quo* every business owner has a right to

Your Message

expect?

One reason business owners resist this kind of positioning is they're worried about what people — competitors, clients, customers, and even friends and family — might think about them, since it's been drummed into you since day one other people's opinions matter and strong positioning pisses people off no end. But, unless you're facing a jury, people's opinions don't matter. They're not even any of your business. Other people's opinions and criticisms have only the weight you, yourself, give to them.

And in terms of your business, the only people whose opinions matter are the opinions of the people giving you money, and even then it's contingent on them doing things your way[40].

If you strengthen your positioning and start changing the way you do business, you might reasonably argue your existing customers and clients might object to your new way of working. And this is possible. But if you take the time and trouble to explain it's going to enable you to be more effective and productive and to serve them better, and so give them better value for money, then there is no reason for them to complain or object, not if they are giving you the respect you deserve. After all, unless you have some kind of service agreement saying you're available 24/7 on the phone to jump up and bark like a good little doggie every time they whistle, why *should* you? If they want that level of service then they should expect to pay a stiff premium for it.

What about potential new customers and clients, those

---

40. This attitude is exemplified in this wonderfully amusing clip from Howard Stern's radio show when a paying subscriber and listener calls in to offer his "constructive criticism" of the show. Stern's positioning is beyond perfect and his income — a 500 *million* dollar contract reflects that. The clip is here www.jonmcculloch.com/gybf/howard-stern.

you're still courting? Won't inaccessibility put them off?

And the answer is no, not usually. If you send an email detailing your new rules to your list and 40 people unsubscribe from it, but you also make 5,000 Groats in sales to new customers and clients who are drawn to your new positioning, why would you care about the 40 whiners? Yes, some of the people who unsubscribed might *eventually* have become buyers or clients. But would you really *want* their business, especially now you realise you can and should be very choosy and particular about the people you work with?

Remember the 80/20 Principle: 80% of your hassles and headaches are going to come from 20% of your list.

Good news: you just got rid of a bunch of them.

Pushmi-Pullyu Positioning

I often write about something called *polarisation*, and it's something you don't usually hear being discussed by the "gurus", chiefly, I think, because they have no idea what it is.

Let me give you an example of what I mean. That's the best way to explain it.

Occasionally I send a particularly acerbic and politically incorrect email to my list with an invitation for people to unsubscribe if they don't like it. Mrs. EBG does it with her list, too.

Why?

After all sending email is free, so why would anyone want to go out of their way to get rid of people? It's not like you have to put up with their carping, because you can use email block lists and filters.

So what's going on?

Polarisation, that's what's going on.

See, for every strong and unpopular opinion you express you'll get the *Marmite Reaction*: your readers will love it... or they will hate it.

Some of the ones who hate it will quietly unsubscribe; some email and tell you they've unsubscribed; some email and tell you they are going to unsubscribe if you don't mend your ways; and some email and complain... but then end up being your most responsive buyers.

But for every person you push away, you pull another towards you. More than that, everyone who gets an email saying, in effect, "If you don't like the way I do things around here, go away", and yet chooses to stay, is reinforcing the commitment they've already made in their own minds. So getting your message out there is as simple as writing your message to your values.

We cover copywriting and all the specific "how to" of this in Appendix I, but in outline it's as simple as I just said: tell them what your values are, make sure they're everywhere in everything you write, and then stick to them. Again, this will polarise people. Some people — maybe most of them — won't share your values. In my own case, I'm a libertarian atheist, as you know, and I know a good many people who really don't like that. As if I care — because enough people either have no strong feelings about it, or think along the same lines, to provide me with a very good living in return for the service I render. Similarly, while many people don't appreciate my lack of Political Correctness, enough people *do* appreciate it.

The bottom line is this: if you stand for something you're going to attract a certain type of person. But if you stand for nothing, then the chances are you'll attract no one of any particular consequence, and anyone you do attract is likely to be the wrong kind of person for your business anyway — and you're just going to end up with a lacklustre business with a commensurate income.

Your Message

You cannot be all things to all men and women. If you try, you'll just end up not being anything to anyone.

Finally, I'm not saying you have to copy me and have the same values, talk the same tough talk, shave your head and pump iron.

Be yourself.

Be authentic and you're likely to enjoy the same kind of experience I've had, but in your *own* niche and according to your *own* rules.

Your Implicit Message II — Premium Pricing

If you're selling at premium prices, then that is a Premier Positioning strategy in and of itself; moreover, if you have your Positioning down pat, then people expect you to be charging premium prices.

You know it's true, and you have to look no further than your local Rolls Royce dealer to *see* it's true. No one expects a discount on a Rolls... and no one thinks a Rolls is anything less than *quality*, even it they're not to your personal taste.

So, with Premier Positioning and Premium Pricing, one begets the other, which is marvellous news for us as entrepreneurs.

And the best thing of all is... it's all so very easy.

The biggest and most easily corrected mistake people make is failing to realise two things:

- You don't need anyone's permission to adopt Premier Positioning.
- You don't need anyone's permission to start charging higher prices.

The perception is, though, in today's troubled economy everyone is scratching to make a living. It seems like no one is buying, and everyone wants the best deal: "Money's tight", you'll hear them say as they check out the prices on your goods, and with a wistful look they'll be off down the street to buy from your competitors.

Or will they?

Well... the sad truth is, yes, they probably will.

And do you know why?

Because you've become *commoditised*.

It's because whatever you're selling — products, services, whatever — are indistinguishable from the products and services of your competitors.

The Pain of Commoditisation

The indistinguishable nature of your business from your competitors' is a blow to the ego, and a sad and unpalatable truth... but it's a truth, nevertheless. Yet when I point it out to business owners they usually object and come back with all sorts of "reasons" they think their business is a better choice than their competitors', things like "but we give great service"; or "we've got a bigger selection and choice"; or "we've been in the business longer than anyone around here, so we know the ropes better than anyone".

All these things might be true, of course, but given what we know about customers and buyers buying only to solve their problems and caring only about themselves, none of these reasons mean anything to anyone but you, the business owner. In any event, giving great service isn't a selling point — it's a minimum requirement.

When you boil it all down and cut through the bluster and the bullshit, it usually comes down to businesses competing on one of two things: location and price. And neither of these is anything but a disaster in the making. And it's a disaster of your *own* making and one you can *easily* avoid.

The "Location" Fallacy

Yes, a good location is better than a bad one, most of the time. The downside is you usually pay more for it, and with your marketing done right... it's frequently no big advantage.

Ultimately, location is not what makes or breaks any business. Think about your own experiences... when is the only time you ever went into any kind of shop *just because* it was in the right place. I suspect it's going to be only those times when you've wanted something that was a *commodity*. A pint of milk, a box of sticking plasters, aspirin, cigarettes... all of these are *commodities*. Just think for a few minutes and I expect you can think of a dozen times you just "dropped in" to a store to buy something you could have bought anywhere, but the location at that moment was convenient to you.

And now think of your favourite restaurant or butcher or any place, in fact, where you *prefer* to go for whatever it is. Honestly now, did your favourite restaurant become your favourite restaurant just because of where it *is*?

I suspect not.

In fact, I'll hazard a guess the only time you choose a restaurant because of its location is when you're on a trip and a handy McDonald's comes over the horizon just in time to stop the kids complaining! Any business owner who thinks location is the only reason for their not getting the sales they want is sadly mistaken.

So what about the second thing you think you have to compete on, *price*?

Price is a strange and sensitive subject among all business owners, and it's one so often misunderstood. In a moment, I'll share with you some very powerful insights about pricing, although first, I just want to invite you to consider looking at

Your Message

price cuts and discounts in a rather unique way.

If you're like most business owners, you have a marketing budget[41], and the purpose of the marketing budget is to invest in relationships with customers and clients. Think about it: that's exactly what marketing is — investing in relationships with customers and clients.

So when you cut price in an effort to bring in more customers, what you're actually doing is spending your marketing budget. And instead of spending it on bringing in more relationships or nurturing the ones you already have, you're actually buying yourself a huge amount of trouble.

The Deadliness of Low Prices

Competing on price leads to a slow, painful death for a business. Not only does it mean you're working much harder than you need to for far less money than you can make otherwise, but it also means you're going to attract the worst possible customers and clients and often will be lucky if you get paid anything at all. In my experience, "price buyers" are the quickest to complain and the slowest to pay. What's more, they have precious little respect and no loyalty — because the moment they perceive your products and services can be replaced by something or someone cheaper, they're gone.

When I was working with clients, writing sales copy, I adopted a very strict attitude to my fees, other than making sure they were eye-wateringly high, that is.

I had a "three strikes" rule.

The way it usually played out was a prospective client would ask me about working on a project and would invariably ask me "how much?" even before I'd had a chance to look at it properly, or even look at it at all.

---

41. Idiotic though having a marketing budget is, as we've seen.

Of course, that's a question I couldn't answer, because until I knew what their project was all about, I couldn't even begin to suggest a plan of action; and if I didn't know what the plan of action was, I had no idea how much work or what *kind* of work was needed; and if I didn't know *that* how could I possibly know how much it was going to cost? I'd explain it to them using the "doctor metaphor": you don't go to the doctor and ask him to prescribe your treatment until he's examined you and made his diagnosis, do you? And fixing someone's marketing is just the same.

So I'd patiently explain this to them; and invariably a short while later they'd ask the same question, only to get the same answer, only a little more forcefully put and with "if you're focused on the cost of this rather than the benefits and potential profits, then it suggests you don't understand the value of what I can do for you" tagged on the end of it.

And if they then asked a third time, they were gone — fired before they got fully through the door.

Why?

Because I knew from experience they would be *murder* to work with.

I had a very similar hard-line to anyone who came to me with the old "I'm talking to another two copywriters about this project, so be realistic with your price". That immediately told me they were price-buying, and I wanted no part of it — so I would always and without exception send them packing.

The point here is price buyers are a curse upon your business and will bleed you dry if you invite them through your door. This is why you *need* Idiot Filters like I had to stop them getting through.

Let me now show you why this is so important.

Your Message

The Uncomfortable Truth About Your Prices

How often have you heard people say this: "I had to cut my prices! The competition *made* me do it!"?

More important: how many times have you said it *yourself*? The truth, unpleasant though it may be, is no-one *makes* you do it, in the same way as no one *makes* you angry or happy or sad or hungry. Your feelings always from within. Quite simply: *price cuts are always a self-inflicted wound*. Full stop. Unfortunately, as you will see below, like any wound, a price-cut can be fatal.

So how does this wound happen? And why? What kicks off the whole process? How dangerous is it? And what can we do about it?

I'm not sure what the roots of it are but it's endemic in our society. We are constantly bombarded with countless marketing messages from a tiresome procession of "discount stores" and cheap supermarkets, budget DIY shops, cheap clothing stores... the list is practically endless. Yet the shocking truth — and it truly is shocking — is there is no historical evidence to suggest these discount stores have any long-term future. In my local town of Clonakilty I see store after store with windows displaying signs advertising discounts of 50% and even 75%; many of them also promise they "won't be beaten on price".

Many businesses try to win using massive discounting as a strategy.

But, historically, all ultimately fail.

You may ask "what about places like Wal-Mart, Asda, B&Q and all those other firms?". What about them?

Well, if you have deep enough pockets you can sustain a haemorrhage of cash for a long time... but history is littered with the bones of heavy discounters. Look at the number of airlines that went to the wall in the US after deregulation. Look at Ansett in Australia, Freddy Laker, EOS and others in the UK.

There are exceptions, of course, and the most obvious of these in Ireland is Ryanair, whose CEO, Michael O'Leary has taken the company firmly down the route of low prices/high volume. But all is not what is seems with this model, and Ryanair make up for what they lose in fares by savagely cutting costs and by making money on extras, as well as ancillary services and sales[42].

Who Buys on Price?

It's a common misconception to think people always and only buy on price. But it's actually so rare, it almost never happens. People will *tell* you they buy on price alone and they may even believe it.

But they almost never do. And nor do you.

And I can prove it very simply: do you wear the very cheapest clothes you could possibly have bought? Do you have the cheapest food in your cupboards at home? Did you have the cheapest wedding you could scrape together? Do you take the cheapest option with your kids at Christmas and birthdays?

No.

Now, it *does* happen occasionally. There *are* some people who will buy on price only. Maybe one in a few million. And there are times when we *all* buy the cheapest *because* it's the cheapest. If I want cheap paper for my printed "roughs" in

---

42. For a detailed examination of this I recommend O'Leary's biography *A Life in Full Flight* by Alan Ruddock. Read it and you'll see why this kind of business is not one for the timid and faint of heart, nor one to be taken up lightly. And low-prices notwithstanding, Ryanair *still* have incredibly strong positioning in the industry.

Your Message

my office, I'll buy the cheapest I can get... yet even then I won't cross the street to save a few cents: I'll buy the cheapest I have available to me at the instant I want it. Furthermore, there are times when buying on price is mandated by law (as, I believe, in the case of the tendering laws enforced upon us by the European Parliament). But even then, businesses routinely get round it by drafting the invitations to tender in such as way only the preferred supplier actually meets the requirements and so is the lowest price by default.

I'll explain why people don't actually buy on price alone in a minute, but just for a moment, I invite you to take my statement at face-value and just act "as if" it were true. Next time a customer or client says to you something like "I don't care about anything else, I just want the best price!", imagine what might happen if you were to tell them they can have it in eighteen months' time, or you'll sell them the "quality rejects". From my own experience and the experience of my clients, you'll mostly get the answer "I can't wait that long!" or "No, they've got to be good enough quality!".

So what they *really* mean is they either want top-quality, top-service, and a low price; or, worse, they want *your* quality and service at your competitors' prices. Makes sense, doesn't it? And the only sane and rational answer to that, of course, is something like "If you want a low-price, you get a low-price quality and service; if you want premium quality and service, you pay the premium price". It's a safe bet to do this because if he really could get exactly the same thing from someone else at a lower price and that was all he cared about, then he wouldn't be arguing with you about it — he'd be off down the street buying it.

If you're in a situation where you really want the business as part of your long-term strategy or you can see a good reason for doing the deal — other than fear of losing a sale

— you can do this: "OK, here's my best price. It's for this quantity and it's good for the next five minutes. Here's the pen. Sign."

Scary, eh?

Bet you don't often talk to your clients like that, do you? I used to, all the time, and they loved it. People like to be told the way things are going to be — it saves them having to think.

In any case, you'll see shortly why it's a pretty safe bet to do this when a client is haggling with you over price.

Is Discounting Always Evil?

No.

There might be times when the situation merits it, when spending your marketing Groats in that way is a legitimate strategy. But they're rare and you should think very carefully before doing it.

Sometimes it can be worth doing to impress a particularly juicy client, but even then I think it's a strategy fraught with problems.

Better than a discount is a BOGOF or similar.

Why?

Because if you sell a 100 Groat widget at 50 Groats, you attract 50-Groat-mindset buyers. But if you sell two 100 Groat widgets for 100 Groats (which is 50 Groats apiece) you attract 100-Groat-mindset buyers.

Think about it, and you'll see it makes sense.

But, discounting is almost always unnecessary because people simply do not buy on price.

Here's Why People Do Not Buy on Price

Price makes a statement about quality.

It might not be a true statement but it's one widely

believed. A low price almost invariably confers an image of lower quality than a higher-priced similar item. And people usually value quality and service above low price. There are times when price is the only determinant, but those cases are very rare, as we've already seen.

Let me tell you a true story.

Many years ago I used to work with Graham. And Graham wanted to be Gillian. Indeed, Graham *became* Gillian. After a fashion. Anyway, some way into his hormone therapy I changed jobs and didn't see him for ages.

Some while later I was walking through the town when I spied Graham/Gillian coming towards me. We spoke for a while and he told me he'd taken early redundancy and was using a part of his wedge to pay for The Op.

"Oh", I said.

"Yes", he said. "I'm going to Amsterdam to have it done".

"Ah. OK... why Amsterdam specifically?"

"Because it's cheap!"

Hmm. Now perhaps this is just my own small minded prejudice here, a kind of surgical price-snobbery... but I can't help but think if I'm going to have all that... stuff... hacked about, then I want *quality* not low price.

Think about it — doesn't price here say something about the perceived quality of this operation? Didn't the thought of going to have your genitals sliced and diced by one surgeon rather than another just because it was "cheap" fill you with horror?

I know this story seems like it's contradicting what I've just said about price, but think about your own reaction... Graham was definitely in the minority — he really was the exception that proved the rule.

I mean, would you shop around and automatically go for the lowest-priced dentist, cosmetic surgeon, or paediatric heart-surgeon to operate on your 5 year-old daughter?

I hope not.

If you take the trouble to go out and ask your clients and customers the single more aggravating thing their vendors or suppliers can do to annoy them beyond all sane and rational limits, nine times out of ten you'll get this reply: "delivery problems!", where things are delivered late, incomplete, or even not delivered at all.

Don't believe me?

Just think back to your own experiences of rearranging your entire life to wait in for a plumber to come fix a leaky tap, or for a washing-machine to be delivered and the guy doesn't turn up. Maybe it's just me, but when people do that, I could cheerfully eviscerate them and feed their entrails to the dog. And if I didn't have a dog, I'd take the trouble to go out and buy one especially for the purpose.

Look at it any way you can, any way you choose, and you'll see it's true: almost no-one ever buys on low-price alone. You certainly don't, and you're no different from anyone else.

Here's Why Sellers Sell on Price

Fear.

Sellers fear losing sales to price-buyers so they keep prices low, either consciously or unconsciously — typically to the same level as their competitors. And this phenomenon is almost universal. It's classic herd-mentality: one store lowers its prices, and all of a sudden everyone else is doing it, too. It's called a "price war", I recall. But it's one of those wars where everyone loses, a true Pyrrhic victory.

Because... no one ever wins a price war!

Most people look for three things when making a purchase: the finest quality, the best service, and the lowest price. But I haven't found a company yet that could provide the finest quality and the best service for the lowest price. I can't do it. And neither can you. So when you do sell yourself cheap, you don't do anyone any favours. You cheat yourself out of a decent income and you ultimately end up cheating your customers and clients out of the quality and service they deserve.

In my work with health professionals from various different disciplines, including dentistry and chiropractic, I've observed the same thing over and over again: a patient who pays a high fee is more likely to comply with instructions and attend therapy and follow-up sessions necessary for their recovery and improvement than someone paying low fees.

The same improvement in compliance occurs in many other industries, too, including my own — meaning a client who's paid me 50,000 Groats for a sales letter and a marketing package is far more likely to *follow* my advice than if he'd paid me 1,500 Groats or even got it for free.

I'll leave you with a comment from a very good friend of mine, Carlos Alvarez, of TelEvolve in Arizona — www.televolve.com:

> *"In almost every service business, lower prices will get you the lowest denominator of clients. It took me until around the late 90s to realize that raising my prices only got rid of my worst clients, raised my income, and I worked fewer hours. Which then was a net benefit to my top clients because I had more time to pursue additional education and spend time contemplating how to solve customer issues.*
>
> *These days if a customer even suggests that price is an issue, I will nearly get up and walk away. They only get one chance to understand 'the price is the price and based on value, I don't negotiate or discount.'*

Your Message

> *We've proven repeatedly that the discounted customers are the worst customers, by giving discounting a try. Never again."*

Answering the Price Objection

So what happens when a client or prospect challenges you on price? What do you say in response to statements like "What?! I'm not paying that! Your prices are higher than so-and-so down the road! I can get the same thing from him for less money!"

First, the best response you can make is this: "So?" This does a number of things. It acknowledges your price is higher. It's an observable fact and no less than the truth. It's a strong statement of where you are. You're not justifying, apologising, or explaining. Apart from anything else, trying to "hide" objections your prospects have just isn't going to work. Believe me, if there's a genuine objection, they'll ferret it out. But if you bring it up first, then you control it.

Secondly, it puts the ball firmly back into his court. Because he's then got to come back at you, accept the price, or walk out. And in truth, it's only the first of these we need to worry about.

Why?

Because if he accepts the price, you've made a sale; and if he walks out, you never were going to make the sale at a price giving you a decent profit and securing you a decent client. And that's why you're in business, right? Remember: if he could get exactly the same thing at a lower price and the price was all he cared about he'd be down the road buying it and not arguing the toss with you.

So what happens if he comes back at you?

The chances are it will be with something like "Well what

makes you think I'm going to pay those prices?", or "Why should I pay that much?".

And these are excellent questions — because they then give you the opportunity to say "Well, I'm glad you asked me that because here's how we're different from our competitors", or some similar sales presentation that's engineered to position you as the only logical vendor.

And do you notice something about this?

How often do you find it hard to get the prospect to listen to the long list of benefits of your services and products?

And why is this?

Because they're not interested... yet.

But when he's asking those kinds of questions he's giving you *permission*; nay, he's *asking* you to present it to him.

Just How Much Damage Can a Price Cut Do?

This is where you really want to be sitting down while you read because it's not pleasant. Bear in mind also that the same scenario below occurs when you don't increase prices and your *costs* are increasing through inflation, increased taxes, and your vendors raising *their* prices.

Many business owners take the line they can cut prices and make up for it in volume. I bet you've done this. But I bet you don't know how insanely, incredibly, and amazingly dangerous it is. Never mind the fact that your profits plummet (as you'll see below) but even if your volume does increase massively, can you cope with the demand?

What frequently happens is either demand increases to the point where you end up unable to meet deliveries or maintain quality, so you lose your customers anyway; or your competitors also cut *their* prices to match, keep their market share, and the *status quo* changes not one iota. You're all back where you started except you're working harder and your profits have just taken a nose-dive. Even the customers and clients don't really benefit from this because they're typically getting lower quality and inferior service[43]. More to the point, as we saw, one way of viewing the money you're losing in cutting your prices is spending your marketing budget — for no gain and with no imagination!

However, with that aside, let's imagine you want to match your competitors and drop your prices by a mere 10%. Just bear in mind these calculations are a little simplistic because they don't explicitly distinguish between fixed and variable costs — but the difference in the results is tiny, and it's really the *principle* I want to drive home to you.

Industries differ, but we're not a mile out if we take a broad margin of 35% being typical. This is about right for most businesses in most industries. Yours might be lower or higher and you can plug in the numbers yourself. Just be aware, the smaller your margin the more drastic will be the results of a price cut.

So let's say you're selling widgets at 135 Groats with a margin of 35%. This means your cost of supply is 100 Groats, and you make 35 Groats on each sale.

Now let's cut the price by 10%, so you're selling widgets for 121.50 Groats, meaning your profit on each one is now just 21.50 Groats. In other words that 10% price-cut has slashed your profits to just:

$$21.50/35 = 0.6143 = 61.43\%$$

Of their previous level.

To put it another way you just *cut* your profits by 38.57%.

This means cutting gross selling price hoping to "make it up in volume" means you're working a hell of a lot harder just

---

43. Say... why not cut prices and make up for your lost profits in even more volume, eh? What a great idea!

to make the same money (then remember your competitors will also cut *their* prices to match yours, so you're all back where you started, only working for less money). And the lower your margin, the more vicious and deadly these price cuts are.

The Magic of a 10% Price Increase

So if cutting prices is so dangerous, how beneficial is raising them? Increasing your prices by 10% increases your profits by a massive 39% or so on the same volume of sales. Another way of putting it is that you can *increase your prices by 10% and have your sales fall by a huge amount and still make the same amount of money.*

Is it just me or is working only until late morning on Thursday for the same amount of money as a full week actually A Really Good Thing?

Let's see how.

Your 135 Groat widgets are now 148.50 Groats with a margin of 48.5%. This means your cost of supply is 100 Groats, and you make 48.50 Groats on each sale. Your profits have now jumped to:

$$48.50/35 = 1.39 = 139\%$$

Times their previous level.

To put it another way you just *increased* your profits by 39%. For no extra work!

How To Make More Money From Less Work... Starting Right Now!

So, what happens if you increase your prices?

You *may* lose *some* customers.

However, first, you'll lose a lot fewer than you think; and

secondly, you don't want to be dealing with those customers anyway. Invariably my worst clients have always been quick to complain about price and slow to pay. Another thing is the quality of your whole business, your products, and your services as perceived by your customers and prospects goes up.

Sounds good, eh?

So, here are three ways to sell your products and services at higher prices than your competitors and not lose any sales:

Embrace Premier Positioning

It won't be easy, necessarily, especially at first. But it will pay you back enormous dividends — and will begin to do so immediately. And the more you do it and the more you experience the results the easier it's going to get.

And there's nothing quite like results to give you motivation.

Adopt Premium Pricing

It's that simple. Just raise your prices and see what happens next. The hardest thing about it is getting the confidence to ask higher prices than your competitors and then stick to them.

Giving your customers and clients that *wow* factor is not hard — it might take a little extra thought and then some investment in time and money, but the rewards are way out of proportion to the extra trouble.

And *keep raising them*. Wait a month or so then do it again.

And again.

And again.

When you eventually find demand starts to drop off, you have a choice: throttle back to the last step before demand fell, or enjoy the extra free time you have.

Your Message

Increase your prices by 10% just three times on a sale price of 100 Groats with a markup of 50 Groats (not untypical for many businesses, especially in service industries) and you'll double your profits and be only 25% more expensive than your competitors.

And making up for that 25% difference with excellent marketing, Premier Positioning, and service is not hard.

Go Upmarket

No matter what you're selling there's a market for a high-end and deluxe version of it. You have only to look around you to see this is true.

One of my Inner Circle Members is an optician and he sells his hand-made spectacles at around £1,500 a time. Even an eye-test is £200 or more. But you don't have to look far to get these things for a tenth of the price on any high-street.

Or maybe a massage is your thing? You can probably get a quickie for a few tens of Groats in any large town; or you can go large and settle for the Fantasy Island Luxury Massage, a three-day weekend on a private tropical island with three of your best friends and 12 stunning masseuses on call to cater to your every erotic whim, all for a cool £1,000,000.

But perhaps you'd rather just play it safe and have a night in watching the TV, in which case you can get something cheap and cheerful for a few quid from Dunnes; or you can go upmarket and pay $2.26 million for a Stuart Hughes' PrestigeHD Supreme Rose Edition TV.

The point is this: regardless of your market and industry there is a very small percentage of people who will pay insane prices for top-end products and services.

All you have to do is find them. And that's easier than you think because if you have a list of past and existing customers and clients, some of the people on that list are almost certain to be in this exclusive category. To find out who they are and serve them all you have to do is offer them the high-end and deluxe versions of the products and services you sell. It really is that easy.

Here's a very mundane example for you: imagine you're a painter & decorator and you offer the usual stuff all painters & decorators offer. On top of that, though, you *also* offer the Ultimate Home Transformation Experience where you don't just completely revamp the entire house and all its contents, but you send your clients away for a fabulous weekend in a luxury hotel in Paris to get them out of the way while you do your thing. This would cost you nothing to offer and yet when you got someone to take you up on it, your profit margins would be enormous.

You'd not get a huge number of people taking you up on this offer, but once it's there, it's there, and you don't need many takers before your profits are heading for the stratosphere.

Any business can create this kind of ultra high-end offering, and every business should.

Summary of Chapter 4

1. **People buy because they have problems they need solving.** They never, ever buy for any other reason.

2. **To get them to buy from *you*, you have to answer the most important question you can ever ask yourself.** It's simply this: "why would anyone choose to buy from me rather than from my competitors?". Stop marketing until you know the answer to this question and can articulate it.

3. **Someone is going to be "King" in your niche or industry, charge the highest fees, and get the best customers and clients.** The focus of your marketing should be to ensure that person is *you*.

4. **You don't need permission or approval to appoint yourself the expert in your niche.** But you *do* have to be able to deliver on your promises.

5. **You don't need permission or approval to charge premium prices.** All you need is the balls to ask for them. It can be tough but the financial and emotional rewards are immense.

Chapter 5

Your Market

These are the people you want to sell to. And this is the area most business owners get terribly wrong, assuming they "get" it any way at all — because most business owners don't even know they have a "market", let alone that they should seek to refine, hone, and target their marketing in a way to get it in front of as many of these people as possible.

Some years ago I was working with a client and I took him through an exercise beginning with the question, "Who is your ideal customer or client? Describe him or her to me."

And his answer was, "anyone with a credit card". I can't tell you how depressing that was to hear. I mean, the guy who's just stolen your mother's handbag now has a credit card, but you probably wouldn't want to do business with him, right?

The mistake this fellow was making — and it's a mistake the vast majority of business owners make, so don't get feeling all smug or depressed, whichever way your own approach to this has fallen — is he didn't realise how important knowing who his "ideal customer or client" was. And yet virtually every business owner will, if you ask, be able to describe for

you very accurately the kind of people they serve the most...
yet they do absolutely nothing with this valuable information.

Valuable?

Yes, because once you know exactly whom you're selling
to, then you can do two things: first, you can more effectively
create your "marketing messages" so they appeal to these
people; and secondly, you can start thinking of all the different
ways of getting that message in front of them.

We call this "stuff", this information about the people in
your target market, the *demographics* of your target market,
and it encompasses everything from their age, employment
status and sexual orientation, to shoe-size, hair-colour, and
eating habits, and everything imaginable in between. Golden
Rule: you can never, ever know too much about the people
you are selling to or want to sell to.

The Power of Knowing Your Market

Here's a real life example for you.

Some years ago there was a guy in the US who had a
"Russian Brides" website. Because it was a competitive
market, he was constrained in his pricing by the "going rate".

His service was a commodity, in other words.

And then one day he decided to look at the kinds of people
his client-base comprised. To his surprise and wonder he
found something like 70% of them were truckers. We can
theorise all we like about why this was the case, but the facts
remained: 70% of the people on his books were truckers.
What that then allowed him to do was to scrap all his existing
marketing and then to reinvent his entire business and become
the "go-to guy for truckers who want Russian brides". As
a consequence he was easily able to raise his fees from the
industry norm — some $39 a year or so — to a staggering

$8,000 or more. That's 200-times the going rate. This was possible only because he figured out who his "ideal client" was and could then tailor his entire marketing strategy to fit.

More recently a client of mine in Dublin, a gym owner, trawled his membership data and discovered most of his clients are women in the age range 34 to 55. This means it's now possible for him to aim his marketing directly at women in this age group — meaning anything he sends to them will be more relevant to them and thus will get a better response and so give him a higher ROI.

Never Mind the Facts

Here's something else you'd do well to understand and embrace: people buy for emotional reasons and not logical ones. Real-time FMRI scans have shown what marketers have known to be true for a long time: we decide things emotionally and then back-rationalise the logical reasons for making the decision. It happens pretty quickly; so quickly, in fact, we fool ourselves into thinking we came up with the logical justification first and then made the decision.

And that's just not how it happens.

Why does this matter?

Well, it matters because when it comes to constructing our message to resonate with our market — telling them we can solve their problems, in other words — we're going to get a much better response if we sell on emotions rather than if we sell on logic. It's the old "you don't buy the drill, you buy the hole in the wall thing", kind of.

But even that doesn't go far enough, because it's more like you buy the drill for the warm and fuzzy feeling you get when you look at your daughter's photograph at her graduation you just hung on the wall.

Your Market

Now, most people will deny this happens. Most people will tell you marketing doesn't work on them and they make their decisions on logic and logic only.

That's cool.

That's how it *feels* for me, too.

But the fact is, if you're a human being rather than some alien who's evolved in an entirely different way and you don't have a limbic system, I'm afraid you make your decisions emotionally[44].

We say a lot more about this and how it affects the way we create our marketing messages in Appendix I.

For now, just take my word for it: once you know whom you're talking to, it becomes so much easier to figure out what motivates and moves them and so construct your messages to suit.

The Gold Lurking Within Your Business

Knowing your external market is one thing... but perhaps even more important is knowing your *internal* market.

Let me explain...

We've already seen how your easiest and most profitable sales are made to your existing customers and clients, and we've also seen how the greater part of your profits is always to be found in your long-term relationship with them. But what we've not really looked at yet is the subtle differences between the people who buy from us.

The immediate and most obvious thing to think about is how the 80/20 Principle applies here: if you take the list of the people you've done business with over the past year

---

44. Maybe you'd like to be introduced to the same aliens some business owners think comprise their own customers and clients. And you can choose not to believe this if you wish, of course. Just be aware it's your profits that'll suffer, not mine.

---

you'll likely find 80% of your sales have gone to just 20% of the people on your list. That broadly tells you who your best buyers are. Look closer and you'll probably identify a small percentage of them, perhaps just 1% but maybe as many as 5%, who buy *everything* you offer to them, regardless of what it is. We touched on this briefly at the end of the last chapter.

Those people are your "hyper-responders" and I guarantee you have them on your list. I have them on mine, for sure, and I know most of them personally because I make it my *business* to know them. There's very little I won't do for them because they are so valuable to me.

You need to identify these hyper-responders, as well as your most profitable 20% and reserve your best offers and services for them.

How effective is this?

To give you an example, one client of mine regularly hosts large meetings and seminars in London, for anything from 500 to 1,000 people at a time. As you can imagine, not only is there an enormous cost in setting up and running these events, but actually getting people to them is a mammoth task. Filling an event or a seminar is one of the toughest challenges for any marketer or copywriter.

Until fairly recently his approach was to send everyone on his list all the same stuff, so every letter, postcard, brochure, lumpy mail, and other direct mail piece would be sent out to more than 30,000 people.

That ain't cheap.

More recently though, he's changed his strategy somewhat and now focuses this costly direct mail on only the top 40% of his best customers.

The result?

He fills up the events just as quickly but does so with a lot less work and at a saving of 60% off his marketing costs.

Your Market

Given the numbers, that's a *lot* of cash and it's all going right back to his bottom line.

Segmentation, Segmentation, Segmentation

But we can go far beyond this simple idea of selling only to the best buyers by segmenting our list into the *categories* of things they've bought or showed interest in.

For example, my own business covers a wide range of topics including copywriting, advertising, direct mail, email marketing, Google Adwords, PR, telemarketing, radio and TV advertising, sales techniques, and then there are all of the different ways I have of sharing my knowledge of these topics with the people who want to acquire it.

In other words it's highly unlikely everyone on my list, even the people who have bought from me before, are going to be interested to the same degree in everything I have to offer, and even if they are they won't all be interested at the same time.

There's an important point here...

All Customers and Clients Are NOT Equal

The obvious consequence of this is you should target your marketing at the people most likely to respond to it. That not only means *buyers* in general but also buyers of *specific products and services*. In my own business I have people I know who are particularly interested in email marketing, say, and so if I was going to do a promotion of my email marketing product, *Email Supremacy*, with expensive direct mail, I'd send it only to those people, and not to everyone on my list.

The second and less obvious but very much more uncomfortable conclusion is in how you should treat your customers and clients. Quite simply, the guy who's spending 100,000 Groats a year with me on services deserves more of my time and energy than someone who's invested in a 47 Groat CD set and manual and then wants me to answer his marketing challenges by sending me a string of questions by email.

Don't misunderstand me: they are equally deserving of *respect* as people and we're not making a judgement of their worth or value as human beings; but what we *are* doing is judging their worth *to our business*. That not only makes sense to us as business owners, but it's also *fair* on the customers and clients who *are* spending a lot of money with us. I'm fairly frequently asked to do "special deals" with people[45], and I always turn them down.

Why?

Because not only do I know from experience things don't work out the way my wannabe clients think they will (for all sorts of reasons), but also because it's unfair on anyone paying me top-whack.

Alex and Chris — The Two Stooges

Alex and Chris are special people, because they're actually not people at all. No, they're figments of my imagination and they exist only on paper and in my head. Better yet... they're neither male nor female, yet both at the same time or one or the other as best suits my mood.

On the following pages you'll see the current Stooge Descriptions I have. These are not "finished" and never will be because they evolve over time and become more accurate.

---

45. Which, however they choose to phrase it, comes down either to them wanting a discount, or wanting me to work with them for free upfront with a promise of a hefty share in future profits.

Your Market

So, why have I done this?

Well... they're my Stooges. I made them up to represent two kinds of people:

1. **Chris.** The kind of person I want to do business with.
2. **Alex.** The kind of person I'd rather dig out my left kidney with a blunt spoon than do business with.

They're not based on any one person, but rather they're a composite of the good and bad clients and prospects I've encountered over the years. You may even recognise aspects of yourselves in Chris, because if you were a lot like Alex you'd not have read even this far.

Why is this all so important?

Because every time I put finger to keyboard I am talking to Chris and Alex. I am pulling Chris towards me and driving Alex away. I want a life full of Chrisses and totally bereft of Alexes.

But wait... there's more: in one of my long-copy lead-generation pages on my website I even used the Stooges as you see them written over the page. And... it works. The optin *rate* is lower than I can get with different copy — but the *quality* of the person in terms of the fit with my business is exceptionally good.

I'm doing the "Pushmi-Pullyu" thing where I'm saying whom I want and whom I don't want.

But wait... there's more: if you're observant you'll notice something: "Chris" is very much like The EBG in many ways.

Coincidence?

Not a bit of it.

See, believe it or not, I am as human as the next man. And I like to do business with people who are like me. It doesn't mean we're identical, but it does mean we share some very important values. These are very subjective, of course, but objectively it means we're going to tend to get along, which makes for a better experience for both of us. Anyone recognising themselves in Chris is going to be drawn to respond to messages and then, as they get to know me, realise I'm a Chris, too.

But wait... there's more: if you're almost at EBG levels of awesomeness you'll realise the most powerful thing about all of this... I'm polarising them.

Anyone reading a long-copy lead-generation page, which is really a long-copy sales letter with the "sale" being them giving me their details in return for something of value is affirming they are a Chris and not an Alex — so when I start selling to them in a way a Chris would respond to, commitment to and consistency with the identity they have accepted as being representative of themselves is going to prompt them to say "yes".

There's nothing underhand about this at all, by the way. It's simply an incredibly effective and powerful filter to ensure I get only extremely highly qualified people wanting to do business with me.

Chris

Chris is a hard-working, libertarian-leaning (even if he doesn't know it) Entrepreneur who isn't afraid to roll his sleeves up and get his hands dirty doing what needs to be done to get where he wants to go.

He's usually a family man with older children, and generally between 35 and 55. Often he's done his stint as an employee but this is usually some time ago. His business is doing fair to middling but he knows it could be a lot better and he's frustrated at the lack of results he's getting.

Your Market

He's not driven by money alone but has no problem being wealthy so long as he becomes so honestly and with integrity. He's been exposed to the "success peddlers" and has found, often the hard way, they're selling rubbish. He knows there are ways to succeed, and the "gurus" have some of the answers but he's finally realised it's 90% perspiration and *work*.

He's willing to invest in expert guidance and realises the price of marketing advice, mentoring, and education is irrelevant unless considered in terms of the Return on Investment it yields. He's willing to pay a lot for the right information from the right person.

He takes responsibility for his life and work and is slow to lay blame even though it's tempting at times. He's a strong believer in justice and believes in absolute freedom of speech and expression, because he knows that's the freedom from which all other freedoms spring. He might not always like what you say, but he'll fight tooth and nail for your right to say it.

He's capable of great focus and is driven... but sometimes he needs a kick up the arse to keep him moving in the right direction, and just wants to be left alone to get on with his life and business — and he's content to leave others alone, too.

He's a live and let live, plain-speaking fellow. He's typically not especially religious but if he is he's perfectly comfortable with the idea I myself am not. He doesn't see *his* beliefs as a reason to make *me* follow his religion's rules for living.

Chris is also a masculine kind of guy. He's not a "new man" who thinks the way to interact with women is to be effeminate around them. He's got a soft spot for kids, animals and women, but he's also a firm believer in "tough love". Life can be tough and we don't do anyone any favours by mollycoddling them or pretending the world is other than it really is.

He's comfortable with his masculinity and while he loves and even adores and worships women he doesn't pretend to understand them, want to be one, or think he has to be anything but himself in his efforts not to offend the women he comes into contact with. He treats women with respect and is perhaps even a little old-fashioned in opening doors for them and being chivalrous. He laughs at women who take offence at this and thinks they should lighten up a bit.

If Chris is a woman, she's a feminist but not the man-hating kind. She, like me, believes in equality, but doesn't pretend men and women are or should be the same. She's comfortable for two people to disagree without it being personal. She's feminine and even a "girly-girl" but not a simpering idiot with it. She's aware of her femininity and embraces it and at least tolerates if not actively enjoys men's attempts at chivalry.

She's not offended by bad language and is more likely to roll her eyes at the things I come out with.

When it comes to business, Chris knows things go wrong and there are no guarantees, but that's OK. He knows one day he'll be dead, which puts all other problems in perspective and he also knows a rut is just a grave with the ends kicked out.

Alex

Alex... well... Alex is different. Special. So's his business, to hear him talk about it.

Alex has a hazy notion that the "market" owes him a living and his products and services ought to sell because that's "fair". He thinks "brand" and "image" are important and finds the idea of "selling" tacky and faintly distasteful.

He's convinced websites and emails need to look

"professional" and the most important thing on the planet is an integrated multi-platform Social Media Marketing campaign. He's fixated with counting how many "likes" his Facebook posts get and whenever he sends an email to his list, he brags about his open rate and click-through rate but is suspiciously quiet when it comes to saying how many sales he's made.

He leans to the left *or* the right and is happy for the government to use force against others when it suits him and they're doing something he doesn't approve of, whether it's watching porn if he's conservative, or living in a big house if he's a liberal.

He believes in justice except if someone is accused of something really bad like killing children, in which case they ought to be hanged immediately without the inconvenience of a trial. He's often to be found posting "hang the bastard NOW" on those interminable Facebook posts that appear whenever someone is arrested for a particularly nasty crime.

He also supports freedom of speech... unless you're saying something really icky he doesn't like or you want to watch a film he believes ought to be banned because he doesn't like it.

He's quietly envious of others' success and while he doesn't necessarily begrudge them it, he believes deep down it's all down to "luck" or some bright and shiny thing they somehow stumbled across. He believes vaguely in things being "fair" so long as any redistribution of success or money is coming his way. When it comes to the "haves" being forced to give to the "have nots" at the point of a government gun, he always manages to convince himself he's in the "have not" group.

He flits from "guru" to "guru" and strategy to strategy, never staying long enough with any one of them to make substantial progress. He knows hard work can get him where he wants to go... but he'd rather find an easier way.

Your Market

He comes away from seminars feeling all fired up, but then finds he needs to attend another one to keep the emotional charge high. When it comes to paying for advice he likes to cut corners and is forever downloading free stuff *because* it's free but never does anything with it.

When he hears marketing advice he doesn't like, he'll imagine reasons not to implement it based on nothing more than "feelings". The most common words out of his mouth when given advice are "Yes, but...". He wants certainty and rarely gets round to implementing or testing anything because he cannot bear the thought of making a mistake. He's going to start "doing" as soon as the right moment comes (which it never does).

He has very strange notions of how the universe works and while he might, say, think organised religion is silly, he's happy to believe in, say, *The Secret* and can't see how dumb that is. He's nice to everyone's face all the time so you never really know where you stand with him. You know at some point he's hiding something, but you can't tell when or what. He thinks he's a Special Little Flower, and gets peevish when the universe doesn't agree.

Take him on, and he turns out to be the Client from Hell.

Summary of Chapter 5

1. **If you can't describe your ideal customer or client, you don't have a viable business.** Knowing whom you're selling to is vital because you can then focus your marketing efforts with laserlike precision.

2. **If you can't describe your "client from hell", you're almost certainly going to attract the bad 'uns as well as the good 'uns.** Knowing and clearly stating whom you *don't* want to do business with is as important as saying whom you *do* want to do business with.

3. **You can never know too much about your target market.** The more you know the better you can craft your message and pick your media.

4. **Not all customers and clients are equal.** All deserve respect; but they don't all deserve equal treatment.

5. **Lurking in your customer list there *are* vast and untapped profits.** Your job is to segment and categorise your list so you can pinpoint your "hyper-responders" and make them high-ticket offers they cannot refuse.

Chapter 6

The Medium

The medium is the means by which you get your message in front of your market.

And it's perhaps where all the trouble really starts. You see, because most business owners don't know about this "three-legged stool" thing, they choose their media completely arbitrarily. The usual way it works is they'll get a well-timed call from some ad rep or other at the local paper or perhaps working for one of the popular business directories, and find themselves being talked into dropping a few hundred Groats on some advertising. After all, they know they need more business, and advertising reps obviously know all about advertising and marketing, don't they? Um, no. As it happens they don't.

What most advertising reps actually know about is selling advertising space and the associated creative services, because that's the business they're in — selling advertising. They are master salesmen and saleswomen, expert at extracting cash from business owners' wallets. A useful analogy is to think about a car salesman and imagine he knows as much about fixing cars as does the mechanic in the garage. Doesn't happen, does it?

Unfortunately, choosing your marketing or advertising medium *before* you've identified your target market and crafted your message is entirely the wrong way to go about it. It's putting the cart before the horse. I mean, how can you possibly know the best medium to use to get your message to your target market unless you know who they are and what you want to say to them? In other words, the media you choose should be guided by the audience you want to reach and the message you want to send to it. Sure, it's often an iterative process, and it's always worth testing a new and unknown medium if you can afford to lose the money, but the place to start is always with your market and your message.

And the range of media you have to choose from is vast. Don't be fooled into thinking everything has to be online these days. It's true every business should probably have a website, but to conflate this with the idea that means every business should also focus its marketing efforts online is a huge mistake.

A good example is the current fad for Social Media Marketing. It seems everyone and his uncle is pouring good money after bad into it, without any hard data on whether or not it's actually making them any money. I've even come across business owners who have stopped perfectly good and effective[46] marketing strategies and diverted the marketing Groats saved into Social Media Marketing — because, apparently, "that's where all the action is".

Well, yes. There is a lot of *activity* among Social Media Marketing consultants, bigwigs and gurus, I'll give you that. But I see little or no evidence anyone but these people are making money from it.

46. That means "profitable", remember?

The Medium

I'm not saying Social Media Marketing doesn't or cannot work, not a bit of it. No, what I'm saying is it's utter folly to *assume* it's going to work for your business and to dive in headfirst without testing it and measuring the ROI; and the folly is compounded if you neglect currently profitable marketing strategies in search of the Next Bright Shiny Object.

You should always choose your media very carefully and test it to see what response you get. And there are so many to choose from:

- Print advertising
- Direct mail
- Referrals
- Search-based Pay-per-click (Adwords, Facebook advertising, LinkedIn Advertising, and so on)
- Banner advertising
- PR
- Writing in the media
- Radio advertising
- TV advertising
- Flyers
- Article marketing
- Public speaking
- Trade fairs
- Stands in malls, stores and other places where you get lots of foot-traffic
- SMS marketing
- Search engine marketing
- Booths in garden centres, malls, and the like

The Medium

- And many, many more.

The list I've just given you is just the tip of the proverbial iceberg and comes straight of the top of my bald head. There are literally *hundreds* of different ways to generate leads and sales for your business both online and offline, and, indeed, using a combination of both. We'll revisit some of them later[47].

And the inevitable question, which one is best? The answer is… the ones you find make you the most money.

Every marketing guru and his uncle has his favourite marketing medium and swears blind his way is *The One True Way*. But this is nonsense. Not every medium works the same way for every business and for some businesses some media may not work at all (but work fabulously for the business next door). And this is, of course, why you have to test, test, and then test some more. For example, some people say Google Adwords is the last word in lead-generation marketing, but this is predicated on the false assumption people are searching on Google for a solution to the problem your products and services solve. If they're not, then Google Adwords simply isn't going to work for you.

Finally, be very careful not to rely on just one medium, no matter how effective and lucrative it is. We'll dig into this a little deeper later on, but for now just realise if you're reliant on one medium for all of your business, and that medium

---

47. In particular, there are some very good reasons for doing the offline-to-online lead-generation thing.

The Medium

stops working or is taken away from you[48], then your business is dead in the water.

Online Marketing

I think it's fairly safe to say every business should have a website nowadays, even if it's no more than a place-holder.

Why?

Because it's expected and these days virtually everyone is online in one form or another. We can draw a parallel with the telephone if we go back far enough — there would have been a time when a business having a telephone was unusual, then optional, and then, ultimately pretty much mandatory if they wanted to be taken seriously.

So even as recently as a few years ago you could probably get away without a website.

Today?

A much more difficult proposition, although possible with correct positioning.

This has been good news for website designers, even in the recession, because it's meant they've had a steady flow of business, often from beleaguered and struggling businesses who imagine their salvation lies in having a website and tapping in to the vast riches promised by the Internet Marketing "gurus".

A nice thought... but an ultimately fanciful one.

---

48. It happens. In the US one business owner had an umpty-million dollar business underpinned by relentless fax marketing... and then the US government effectively make it illegal, which meant he had no effective means of getting new business. More recently, hundreds, perhaps thousands of website owners have found their visitor numbers and thus their income plummet by 90% or more in response to the implacable and inevitable march of Google progress (and let's not even start on the Google-slaps meted out to many an Adwords advertiser for reasons no one is ever quite able to divine).

The Medium

There are many reasons the dream fails to materialise, but three really come to the fore.

The first is unrealistic expectations. The allure of effortless and fast millions made online is a powerful one, which is why there are so many snake-oil salesmen out there promising the Earth and delivering nothing much of substance. I've helped Mrs. EBG build a business online from scratch, a blog, so I *know* what's involved. I've also helped many of my clients do the same. In other words I know what I'm talking about and you can take it from me, the "Internet laptop lifestyle"[49] is a myth. None of the rich and successful entrepreneurs I've helped over the years is sitting on the beach with a laptop making effortless millions while some hot native chick pushes her tits in his face and serves up pina colada. That ain't the way it works, and anyone suggesting otherwise is someone to avoid because they're either fucking stupid, utterly deluded, or just lying bastards.

The second reason is flawed perception of what a website should be. Most businesses' websites are really nothing more than online catalogues, the Internet equivalent of glossy brochures that *tell* but do not *sell*.

An effective business website does two things: it sells the business's products and services, and acts as a kind of Concierge, allowing prospects, customers, and clients to interact with it.

Exactly how the sales are made and what the interaction consists of depends on the business, but it's important for you to understand technology and society are now at a point where your website should be an integrated part of your entire sales and marketing and not just an add-on, or afterthought. Indeed, for some businesses, the website *is* the business.

---

49. Yes, there are lowlifes out there peddling this nonsense, even as you read.

The Medium

Although, the chances are your website designer is a menace, and your website is likely doing more harm than good to your business. I always get complaints from people when I talk about this, even to the extent of one lady telling me rather huffily how offended she was and how it was "unprofessional" of me not to value these designers. But that's OK, because if you're offending people you know you're serving up some unpalatable truths, and we all know unpalatable truths have a habit of being left to rot and fester.

Nevertheless, let me be clear about something: I don't have anything against website designers. I think there's a definite need for their services and it's a skilled job they do, especially fiddling with all that newfangled technology most of us don't have a clue about.

But the problem is most website designers are very often graphic designers who have added another string to their business bow. And there's no shame in that... *except* when they present themselves as marketing professionals, which is something they do implicitly and explicitly. And business owners quite reasonably take their claims of creating websites that "stand out from the crowd" and "get results" at face value and sink thousands of Groats into websites that simply aren't fit for purpose.

Sure, they *look* great.

But as I already pointed out, they're the online equivalent of glossy online brochures and they suffer from the same problem: they *tell* but they don't *sell*. Something you can probably relate to is your website going live amid a big emotional high... and the expected and sometimes even promised results simply don't materialise.

A simple way to tell if your website designer or graphic designer is a competent marketer or not is to listen to what they ask you about the work you want doing. If they ask you how you want it to *look* before they ask you what you want it to *do* find someone else. Form follows function and once you know what a website or other piece is supposed to do, that will dictate to a large extent how it looks.

The Two Things Your Website Needs to Do

Success with online marketing all boils down to two simple things:

1. Getting visitors to your website — traffic, in other words.

2. Selling stuff to them.

But this simplicity also hides a lot of complexity and detail, and it's all stuff your non-marketing-savvy website designer simply doesn't know.

To this day I *still* see website designers turning out websites designed primarily to gain high rankings in the Search Engines because someone, somehow, has sold them on the idea this is *The Way To Get Traffic*. As you'll see shortly, Search Engine traffic is getting ever harder to come by, and, more important, is becoming less and less valuable[50].

In this section we're going to look at different ways to get visitors to your website, either for lead-generation or for sales.

We look at the mechanics of how to make your websites sell in Appendix I, because that's really to do with copywriting and page-design, and those principles apply to both online

---

50. In selling website design primarily on their Search Engine Optimisation skills, website designers are sending me the message they know fuck all about marketing

---

The Medium

and offline selling[51].

The Four Sources of Website Traffic

Getting visitors to your website is easy. There are loads of ways of doing it and we're going to cover some of the main ones here. But the thing to bear in mind is gross visitor numbers are not the be-all and end-all. Far more important than sheer volume of traffic is the *quality* of that traffic — and traffic quality depends on many things and varies enormously, depending on the source.

This is one reason paid traffic is almost always better quality and ultimately more profitable than so-called "free traffic" — because it's generally much more controllable.

But your traffic comes from four broad sources:

1. Paid online advertising (PPC, banner ads, etc.).

2. "Free traffic" as referrals from other websites (including articles, forums, Social Media sites, Search Engines, etc.).

3. Offline sources (such as direct mail, exposure in the press, etc.).

4. Links in emails (obviously your own, but also from other people who recommend your site to their own email list).

For reasons you'll see shortly, I'm not going to spend a lot of time on the second category of sources, chiefly because they are beyond your control, hard to measure, and so damned unreliable.

But we'll look at the other three in some detail, because if

---

51. People who claim copywriting for the web is somehow "different" are idiots.

you get them right, they're the keys to the treasury.

Pay Per Click (PPC)

First, let's look at paid online advertising which we most often see in the form of Pay Per Click[52]. Although it appears in various forms and can be complex in implementation (if you want to make money with it), PPC is simple in principle: your ad gets shown on specified websites, and when someone clicks on it, they get taken to a web page you've specified, and you pay the advertising network a fee for the privilege. It's called "Pay Per Click", because it's free to advertise and you pay the fee only when someone clicks on your ads.

Generally this fee ranges from a few pence or cents to a few Groats, but in some cases it can be tens, even hundreds of Groats[53]. But you can stop panicking now: these cases are rare, and in any case, the cost of a click isn't relevant unless you look at it in the context of the ROI you get from them over large numbers. Who cares if you buy a thousand 100-Groat clicks if they make you 1,000,000 Groats in sales?

When PPC first came on the scene back in 2004 it changed the online business landscape forever, and has had enormous repercussions in both the online and offline worlds.

Never before had it been possible for literally anyone with an Internet connection to put an ad for their products and services in front of hundreds of millions of people and not

---

52. The same networks running PPC fee-structures also tend to run CPM fee-structures, where you pay not for clicks but for "impressions". CPM stands for "cost per mille", where a "mille" is a thousand impressions. So if your ad is shown 2,000 times and it's cost you two Groats, then your CPM is one Groat. In this book we'll be sticking with PPC, but just bear in mind there are other options.

53. Just to give you an idea... the cost for a click for a Google Adwords ad showing for the searches on the keyword "mesothelioma settlement" was $142.67 in November 2012.

The Medium

pay a single penny for the privilege until someone responded to it.

Compare that with the typical model of advertising where you pay a newspaper hundreds of Groats to place an ad and then wait... and wait... and wait for a response... and if none comes, then that's just hard luck. You've spent the money and that's that.

Pay Per Click has changed the way we do business forever.

Google Adwords and Bing

Google Adwords is the paid advertising option for Google search. Bing Advertising is essentially the same, only it's owned by Microsoft and is run in alliance with Yahoo. The two systems are very similar but there's no denying Bing is a long way behind Google in terms of size, sophistication, and polish.

That said, I think this can be a good thing, especially if you're new to the whole concept of PPC, because Bing is easier to use and thus getting to grips with some of the fundamental principles is quicker and less frustrating. From my experience and the experience of others I've spoken to, the clicks are cheaper, the traffic quality is generally higher, and the Bing support people are definitely a lot easier to get hold of and talk to than the Google people. It also seems like Bing are a lot less strict with their landing pages than Google are[54]. So just bear these things in mind as we go through how the systems work. I'll be talking primarily about Google, but anything I say will apply pretty much equally to Bing.

On the following page you can see images of a typical Google Search Engine Results Page (SERP) with the

---

54. If you've heard the stories of people having their accounts banned forever because they've sent traffic to landing pages Google don't like... they're true. I know people this has happened to.

The Medium

Adwords ads highlighted, and below it an almost identical one from Bing.

As you can see the ads on both platforms (sometimes called "sponsored listings") look very similar to the free listings (which is why some people don't realise they *are* paid ads. Even business owners, who really should).

You'll also notice they come in two flavours: the ones in the right-hand column and the ones at the top in the left-hand column. I'll say more about this later, but for now it's enough to realise they're essentially the same and the difference is just in the way they're presented, with the ones at the top being more desirable a place to be in from the advertiser's point of view.

Sometimes a similar set of ads appears at the bottom, but they're not shown in these images:

The Medium

A close up of an Adwords ad or a Bing ad shows they're made up of four parts, but how these are displayed depends on where they are on the page:

Each ad comprises a headline, two lines of descriptive text, and a display URL. The one above is from Bing Advertising, but it's virtually identical to Google Adwords.

This is how it works:

- Searcher goes to Google and searches for something. In the case above it was "marketing for small businesses".

- Google goes away, snouts around in their index and delivers the SERPs. They are the "free listings" you can see.

- At the same time they look into their Adwords database and see which advertisers have said they want their ads to show for these keywords. How they do this is complex, but the important thing to understand is you tell Google which keywords you want to "trigger" your ads.

- A small proportion of searchers will click on one or other of the ads and will then be taken through to the web page specified by the advertiser. At this point Google charges the advertiser for that click (often called a "click through"; and the percentage of people who click on your ad having seen it is called your Click-Through Rate, or CTR). Exactly how much you pay for a click, your Cost Per Click or CPC, depends on many factors.

Now, the obvious question at this point is how do Google decide where to place your ad on the page, and what, if anything, can you do to influence their choice?

And the obvious answer is to offer to pay them more for each click. But it's wrong, because while it's one factor in the calculation, it's not the only one and not even the most important. Neither Google nor Bing sell higher places in the ad listings as a straightforward auction. Both of them have what they call a *Quality Score* and the price you've said you're willing to pay for a click, called your *bid,* is only one of several factors.

Other factors affecting your Quality Score are:

- Your Click-Through Rate.
- The quality of your landing page.
- Your "history" and results from past Campaigns and ads.

At all times it's going to pay you to remember Google's stated aim of providing searchers with the best possible search experience, because it also carries over into their Adwords system. Bing seem to be less strident about this, but in the end, they're going to have much the same agenda.

The watchword is "relevance". The more relevant your ads are to your topic, the better results you're going to get — more click-throughs, lower CPC, better conversion rate on your landing page, and, eventually, higher sales. All of which add up to more profits.

If I may be bold and sum it all up in a vastly oversimplified nutshell, success with Adwords and Bing Advertising is about reducing your CPC and increasing your ROI, and *that* all hinges on having lots of carefully chosen and targeted keywords paired with highly relevant landing pages. So, when you start out your costs can be high and your payback low. But the secret of any amazingly powerful, effective, and profitable marketing system is in the stepwise refinement: you test something and get a result. You then change something and test again, seeking constantly to improve your CTR, lower your CPC, and increase your ROI.

Over time you ratchet up your results until you have a highly efficient and effective marketing machine churning out profits like I don't know what. Thing is, it takes time and it takes effort — time and effort most business owners aren't willing to put in, even if they know enough to know this is what they ought to be doing. Most dabble with it, maybe get a smidgeon of a bloody nose, and then walk away in a huff. But if you stick with it you will succeed, in the same way as if you keep putting one foot in front of the other, you cannot but help climb the highest mountain or complete the longest journey. Unless you die, of course; and the obvious analogy is you don't want to spend all your money at the beginning so you go bankrupt and end up living in a shop-doorway eating dead rat.

So the trick is to start with a budget and not spend more than you can afford to lose. It's also utterly necessary for you to track and measure what's going on because otherwise you'll never know what's working and what's not.

The good news is Google make this easy for you with their awesomely powerful Analytics tools[55].

The bad news is you've got to keep your eye on the ball here and go in at least once a day (at least in the early days) to make sure you're not throwing money away. The idea you can stick a few Adwords up there and waltz away a billionaire is just a fantasy (but a surprisingly common one, it has to be said).

Always remember Google is a company and the purpose of a company is to make money for the shareholders (actually a legal obligation for publicly listed ones). So if you set things up wrongly, then Google will happily take all your money. They provide some amazingly powerful tools for you and

55. One major difference between Google and Bing is their analytics. Bing's is primitive by comparison. Fortunately, you can use Google Analytics with Bing advertising if you set things up correctly, or you can use any one of a number of alternatives, such as GetClicky, which is my own preference.

The Medium

you can make a lot of money putting them to work in your business... but like many other powerful tools, it's easy to do yourself some serious damage if you don't use it properly.

Now, I've mentioned keywords in passing but I haven't given them much attention yet. But the truth is the quality of your keywords is what is ultimately going to determine your success or failure with search-based PPC. All the tweaking and the testing is important, but my point is none of that is going to be profitable if you haven't done your keyword research right.

What Are Keywords?

Quite simply they are whatever the searcher typed into the Google search box[56].

And the reason they are so important is they represent what's in the searcher's mind when he is searching for information online... and no one looks for a solution unless they have a problem to solve, either. Meaning, when people are online typing stuff into search engines, their minds are focused on what they are looking for, and nothing else. It's vital you understand this because it's why we generally split keywords into two classes: Head and Long Tail.

- **The Head is the main keyword, and is typically one or two words long.** — For example, "internet marketing", "marketing", "online dating", "dogs" and "dog training" are all Head keywords.

- **The Long Tail comprises keywords three or more words long.** Keywords like "internet marketing for

---

56. Keyphrases are just several words typed in at once e.g. "clothes" is a keyword and "children's clothes" is a keyphrase. We tend to use them interchangeably and synonymously.

The Medium

dentists", "marketing for small businesses", "online dating in Seattle", "dogs suitable to have around small children", and "dog training classes in Cork" are all Long Tail keywords.

Here's a tip to make you a lot of money if you pay attention to it: the money is always in the Long Tail.

Why?

Because while the search volume is low, the *intention* is very specific. You can see, for example, how if you run dog training classes in Cork, then someone typing in "dog training classes in Cork" is as good as sold. Which means the most successful Adwords advertisers tend to have hundreds and sometimes thousands of Ad Groups with each one being targeted at a long tail keyword.

The Personalisation Analogy

Think of it this way: if you send the same generic direct mail to a thousand people, what kind of results are you going to get? As you can imagine you have to be somewhat general and non-specific, because you're trying to talk to everyone at the same time and hope something you say resonates with each individual. This is necessarily going to suppress response.

Now look at the other extreme: you painstakingly research all 1,000 people and not only personalise the letter with their name, but write it specifically for them, all 1,000 letters, one at a time.

With the second approach you are going to get a much higher response, all other things being equal. But the price you pay for response is sitting down to write 1,000 letters. At some point between those two there is going to be an optimum trade-off for whichever criterion you are concerned

The Medium

about. You can look at your keywords in a similar fashion. If you target Head keywords you're effectively trying to talk to everyone at once. That's going to decrease your CTR, increase your CPC, and decrease your ROI.

But if you have umpty-thousand Long-Tail keywords each with its own Ad Group, ads, and bespoke landing pages, each with a very specific message, then you're going to get a much better CTR, lower CPC, and higher ROI.

The trade-off is you have to find those keywords, and write, measure, test, and tweak all those ads. The extreme is one keyword per Ad Group, and that's the model I use myself. Each Ad Group might only get a few clicks a week, but if you have 1,000 of them, then it adds up to substantial and highly qualified traffic, which in turn leads to profits.

Understanding Keywords Is Critical to Your PPC Success

And I am afraid there are no real shortcuts to finding them.

It comes down to:

- Your experience.
- Knowledge of your market.
- A bit of educated guessing.
- Data from your website (existing Analytics and new data from your Adwords and Bing ads).
- Keyword research from one of the many available tools (e.g. the free Google tool; Wordtracker; Market Samurai, and others. I use the Google tool exclusively now, because it's much improved over the past year or two).

Not too comforting, perhaps, but the point I want you to take away is this: even in very competitive niches, like marketing, weight loss, sex-toys, and fetishes, there are dozens, if not hundreds of unexploited keywords you can take advantage of. And almost every other niche you could possibly think of is going to be less competitive than these four. Ecommerce sites have a particular advantage in that they frequently have lots of products each of which is a very specific and targeted long-tail keyword in its own right. Sure, getting all those ads up there is a lot of work, but it's work that pays off in the long run.

Banner Advertising

Banner advertising has a terrible reputation, and one historically well deserved. Back in the dot-com boom website owners were selling advertising space at frankly stupidly large prices and equally stupid marketing departments were happily burning through their budgets hoping to get a slice of the largely mythical "action". I remember doing some myself and paying over £1,000 to have my banner at the top of a specific site for a month or so. The less said about that the better, I think. Even The EBG can be stupid on occasion. Since then the market has crashed and banner advertising is pretty much off the radar for most business owners, who think it's either too expensive or ineffective, or both.

But things have changed.

It should come as no surprise to discover the Big G has its fingers in many pies and has built itself a huge network of partner sites. They call this the *Display Network*, and it includes websites from all over the world, such as *The Independent* newspaper, *The Metro*, YouTube, and so on, meaning you can be advertising on some very prestigious and high-traffic sites, no matter how big or small your business is. Better yet, you can now do your banner advertising on a PPC basis rather than paying a gigantic fee upfront and

The Medium

then crossing your fingers and hoping for a result. In the screenshot above there's an example of what banner ads look like. This one is from the Irish Independent website. The ads in this case are for The Lotto, and they're not exactly subtle.

Banner advertising is different from Adwords in that it's not search related[57], and your ad-design is not constrained by the same text limits you get with Adwords. Google[58] have figured out a range of allowable sizes and partner sites sign up to the ones they want to run. For that reason you often

---

57. Although you can add keywords to your campaign specification so your ads can be targeted better on the various partner sites.
58. Bing also let you run banner ads in much the same way.

The Medium

have to create essentially the same ad in a number of different shapes and sizes, although Google's Ad Builder helps.

The same logic about the CPC applies to banner ads as applies to Adwords ads: it all comes down to ROI, and your CPC depends on a number of things, including your Quality Score, which is calculated in much the same way as it is for Adwords. The first thing you'll notice when you start running banner ads is the CTR is very low — typically under one tenth of one percent. Normally it would be around 0.1% and maybe even as high as 0.18%. But these are still very low compared with the 8% or more of a good Adwords ad.

Why is this?

Well, it's because of the mindset of the person seeing the ad. When they're *searching* their mind is on the topic they're searching for, as we've seen before. But here we're interrupting them — we're putting an ad up there in the hope we can deliver a virtual slap around the head to them and get them to notice us *and* click on our ad. No mean feat.

But these low numbers don't really matter because while the CTR is perhaps two orders of magnitude smaller than it is for Adwords, the ad is being seen by vastly more people, and we can still use the selection options in the system to ensure we're still targeting the right audiences. This makes banner advertising incredibly powerful. Google have also upped the ante by adding some extremely cool and powerful functionality to their advertising placement engine. The first is you can select which sites you want to advertise on. Nothing too astounding there, since you'd probably expect that as a minimum requirement. You can also use keywords to help automatically narrow the focus of your ads on the relevant pages. In Google's own words, "Choosing keywords for a Display Network campaign is like playing matchmaker for your friend: You want to pick keywords, or potential mates,

The Medium

that best fit your campaign, or picky friend. For example, if your friend likes to hike, you might pair her with someone who enjoys the outdoors."

This allows you to select which type of partner sites your ads appear on; you can also select partner sites individually and by topic in your Google Adwords dashboard.

Google collects a *lot* of data. They know more about you than you'd believe. I'm not going to argue the rights or wrongs of that, but I am going to tell you what they know about other people can make you a lot of money.

So here's where it starts to get super-cool:

1. **You can select on demographics.** Yup, you can decide whom to show your ads to based on age and sex. Google doesn't know these details about everyone, to be sure, but where they do, they can target your ads at them.

2. **You can select on interests.** Not only does the Big G know what kind of genitals you have, but they can infer from your *behaviour* the kinds of things you're interested in.

   Take me for example. From my online behaviour, Google will pretty quickly be able to infer I am a business owner and interested in all things business and marketing.

   They've done this kind of jiggery-pokery for a whole load of areas and offer you the chance to target your ads at people who have certain interests.

   This is not the same as *placing* your ads on partner sites about these topics. That's also possible, of course, with the placement options, but this is different: this is showing ads to visitors depending on how Google have divined their interests based on their past behaviour.

3.   **And the ultra-coolest thing of all is...** Well think about this, first: using all the data Google collect for you on click-throughs, audiences, ads, and whatnot, I hope you can see how trawling through it all to optimise your CTR and so minimise your CPC and maximise your ROI is a simple — if laborious and boring — process.

But Google have now excelled themselves with the *Display Network Optimizer*. What this does, in essence, is do all the hard work for you. It tracks and monitors your ads, clicks, costs and ROI and over time will show the right ads to the right people on the right sites and at the right times — all the stuff you'd do manually, in other words.

To start using it you need to have done the manual process for long enough to have 15 conversions, but then you can just switch it on and let it do its magic. Just remember to keep your eyes on it because it's not perfect and it doesn't always get things quite right.

Perhaps the best thing about banner advertising is the opportunity it offers us as business owners. Right now it's still in its infancy in its current form and only a very small proportion of business owners are using it. It's like the good old days of Google Adwords.

This situation won't last forever and it's estimated banner advertising will eclipse Adwords and search-based advertising in the next two or three years, so the time to get on board is right now, *before* your competitors do.

The Medium

Facebook Advertising

I read something really stupid a while ago on a blog I was directed to from an email by a fellow copywriter (he seemed to agree with it, which really tells me he has no clue about any of this, which then tells me why he's still struggling and charging low fees).

It starts like this:

> *"A few weeks ago, Mark Cuban caught dissension from all over the Internet for calling Facebook a 'Time Waster'. The purpose of this article is to point out the simple fact that for Businesses, he could not have been more correct. If you run a business, and you are looking to make money through driving people from Facebook to your products or services, Facebook is very likely not in any way worth the amount of time or expense required. For Advertisers, we believe Facebook is a complete waste of time."*

I've heard some bullshit in my time, but this has to be one of the biggest bovine-turds ever. The article is probably worth reading because it's instructive: it shows you how people can revel in very strongly held opinions based on incorrect assumptions. For example they mention the low CTR of just 0.051% and from this conclude the advertising isn't effective.

Hmm.

Last time I checked, CTR isn't important other than how it can influence your CPC. Because now we know the important thing is ROI since that tells us how much we make on average per click and so how much we're prepared to pay for one.

Let me give you an example, again from my own

experience[59].

With my best-performing Facebook ads in my last test I paid €622.32 for 917 clicks, an average of 68c per click. My optin rate was 14.76% on a long-copy optin page. So for €622.32 I got 92 optins, for an investment of €6.76 per optin. Given that *on average* 5% of optins convert to my Inner Circle, *Business Supremacy*, each Member was costing me €135.29, which was slightly higher than I'd ideally have liked it to be because I wasn't quite in profit when they paid their second month's dues.

Is this a Bad Thing?

No.

First, my "in profit on the second payment" is purely arbitrary — there's an 85% chance people stay for a whole 12 months. I can think of only a couple of people who have left before the third month.

And secondly, on the thank-you page after they confirmed their optin there was an upsell to a €47 product which converted at almost exactly 10%. The profit from these upsells paid for a substantial portion of the clicks, meaning I was actually in profit by the second month of their Membership.

Given these kinds of numbers, unless something unexpected comes out of the woodwork to derail things in subsequent larger-scale tests, there's no reason on Earth for me not to run these kinds of ads forever and pump in as much money as Facebook will allow me to spend.

Why?

Because I know my numbers.

And if you know *your* numbers you can do much the same thing. You can also be sure your competitors won't be doing it.

---

59. I love it when pontificating idiots get trumped by hard data.

The Medium

In principle Facebook advertising is just the same as any other PPC advertising: you put the ad up for free, people see it, some click on it, and when they do you get charged for the privilege and they get sent to your website or a "page" within Facebook itself. You can even choose to promote a post you've made rather than a "page" or an external website (and expect all this to change and grow on a pretty much daily basis).

Which is best?

I don't know, and you'll have to test. All the "gurus" strut around telling us the *One True Way* is to send them to a Facebook page because you get better click-throughs and cheaper clicks (the premise of this latter claim being Facebook reward you for not sending people off their site).

And this almost universal advice, dished out with utter certainty is great, except for one thing: it's *wrong*. Sometimes you do, sometimes you don't. In my own testing sending them to my own site gets a better optin rate and a much better ROI in the end, every single time

Moral of the story: test.

Facebook are continually fiddling around with their advertising system because it's the only way for the site to make money. One problem they have is their users are accessing the site more and more frequently from mobile devices like tablets and smartphones, and this makes the advertising much more challenging.

On a desktop, laptop, or tablet with a full browser, Facebook

The Medium

advertising looks like this[60]:

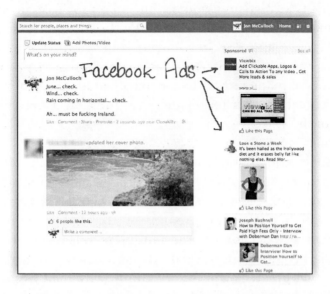

Obviously on the much narrower screen of a smartphone and the sometimes limited browsers on tablets, this kind of display isn't possible.

So now sometimes you'll also notice ads appearing right in your newsfeed, something they've added for those mobile users and then have also extended to everyone else for certain ads. How effective this is I don't know, and monetising traffic from mobile devices is a real thorn in all the big advertisers' sides, Google included (they've made lots of sweeping changes to their Adwords system in the past few months for the same reason: they need to monetise mobile traffic). All I can say is watch this space and assume whatever you expect will happen probably won't.

But all that aside, the key to success with Facebook

---

60. Today. When I wake up tomorrow, it might have changed.

The Medium

Advertising is... targeting. In fact, it's the key to all advertising as we've already seen.

Your Facebook ads are similar to Google and Bing banner ads, and the chief difference is you get to include some text as well as an image. They consist of three parts: the headline, the body copy and the image, and the image needs to be *eye catching*[61]. Of all the images I've tested simple ones like the one below have worked best, but I've also had pretty good results with faces (including mine, believe it or not):

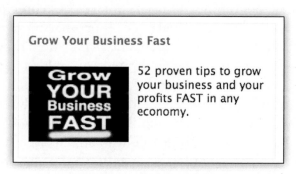

The trick is to make the ad specific. In this case it's specific to growing your business, and the headline, the image, the ad copy and the landing page are all based on that theme. For email marketing, say, everything would be based on that theme, and so on.

And then, of course, be careful how you choose your audience. Facebook Advertising is similar to newspaper advertising and Banner Advertising in that it's *interruption advertising*. This means it's shown to a wide audience who are engaged in doing something else, such as reading a newspaper or wasting precious hours of their lives on Facebook and you

---

61. This is one place where the image really does have to do (some of) the talking. Although images with text on them also do very well (at least, they worked for me).

---

hope some interested parties click on it.

But Facebook is so huge, with over a billion users, you can get an awful lot of so-so clicks that bring your ROI right down to zero and even less than that. The remedy to this is targeting — and Facebook allows you to target your ads with unprecedented accuracy. I can conclude only that the cretin who wrote that blog post I mentioned had no idea at all about the power of targeted ads.

So you can select your geographical preferences and your preferred demographic. This lets you select people based on location, and then sex, sexual persuasion, marital status, level of education, languages spoken, and even where they work.

Facebook have now started letting you upload lists of the details of your customers and if they have a match in their database of one billion email addresses, they'll show the ads only to those people who match. In other words you can start showing Facebook ads to people who already know you and have done business with you, even if you're not connected in any way on Facebook. This is incredibly powerful. The only downside is you have to use the Power Editor browser extension and you can run that only with Google Chrome. But it's a small price to pay for such amazing power and laser-like precision, methinks.

There are also a number of products and services now on the market designed to trawl Facebook and extract the user IDs of people belonging to and posting on groups relevant to your chosen subject. You then load those IDs into an ad campaign and only those users will see your ads. So, for example, if you were selling, say, carp fishing paraphernalia, you'd get your system to search for Facebook pages and groups about carp fishing, and when it found them it would return a list of the groups to you along with a list of the most recent and active members. You'd then load your carp-fishing-stuff ads into Facebook, press the magic button, and they'd then be shown only to those carp-fishing enthusiasts (once Facebook have approved your ad, of course).

In theory this is going to give you a very highly qualified audience. I haven't actually tried any of these so-called "stealth" systems myself yet, so I can't comment on how effective they are. My guess is you'll get a better response than from doing manual targeting and the comments and reports I'm seeing are encouraging. But you'll do well to remember the testimonials you see are going to be from their very best successes (and remember the 80/20 Principle is going to be active in their businesses, too, so don't make the mistake of thinking what you're seeing is going to be typical for the average user).

LinkedIn Advertising

LinkedIn is a business-orientated Social Media site, essentially "Facebook for Business Owners". As with any Social Media site there's lots of opportunity to create and join groups, and then spend most of your waking hours getting "brand awareness" or whatever it's called this week. Personally, I think that's all a waste of time unless you're a special kind of person who can stomach that kind of thing. I'll say more about Social Media Marketing in a moment.

But *advertising* on Social Media sites is a different thing altogether... and if you're selling your products and services to other business (commonly called "B2B"), then there's no doubt whatsoever about it: you should be at least testing LinkedIn Advertising. The biggest objection I get to LinkedIn Advertising (and it comes out immediately and with no actual thought whatsoever) is it's "too expensive".

Hmm.

It's true the clicks on LinkedIn come at a *minimum* of $2.

But only a fool would make any judgement about that at all without first looking at the *quality* of the traffic those clicks represent. And from my own experience, and the experience of my clients and colleagues, the traffic you can get from LinkedIn is incredibly highly qualified and responsive — meaning, in my case, they buy maybe ten times as frequently as other traffic and tend to spend more with me when they do. For example, if I do an optin for a free report and then direct them straight to an upsell page once they confirm their email address, from, say, search-based PPC traffic I might get 1% of them take me up on the offer; but if I do the same with LinkedIn, then it's more like 10%[62].

LinkedIn Advertising is also similar to Facebook Advertising, in that you get to include some text as well as an image. Below you can see a typical example of some LinkedIn ads on a random page from the site:

As with any form of advertising, your success or failure with it comes down to your ROI and that in turn comes

---

62. And 10% conversion rates to effectively "cold" traffic is just insane.

The Medium

down to how well you manage to target your ads.

And this is where I think LinkedIn excels: the level of targeting you can achieve is incredible. You can narrow down your choice of audience to individual companies, job-titles, where they went to school, and so on. This makes it possible to create lots of very highly-focused ads which necessarily increases response and thus boosts the ROI. I was told recently one brave fellow was able to focus his ads so precisely he proposed to his girlfriend with a LinkedIn ad only she would get to see.

One downside (well, not really a downside, just an irritation) is the volume of traffic you'll get tends to be very small, meaning it takes longer to grow that coveted highly qualified list. But the time will pass anyway, and it doesn't cost you anything to run the ads, so you may as well get them up there and leave them ticking along. Several of my clients have reported they've picked up some very profitable big, long-term contracts from LinkedIn Advertising, and the traffic I get myself is very profitable.

Remarketing

Remarketing is one of the coolest innovations ever to hit the Internet. It's a relatively new thing from Google (and others) and while it's extremely powerful the basic idea is very simple: someone visits your website and you somehow use this as an opportunity to keep tabs on them and show them more of your stuff as they surf around the Internet.

Sounds like science fiction, I know. But it's not. It's here, it's real, and while the details of the technology are probably quite complex, at the front end where we see it, it's dead simple. It's also extremely easy to get started. With Google, it's simply a case of accessing the Remarketing lists in your

Adwords account[63].

This is how it works in principle:

1. **You put a short snippet of code on the pages of your website you want people to track.** This code connects back to Google[64] where they have all their smarty-pants software.

2. **As you randomly flit around the 'net, you'll inevitably end up on a site owned by or partnered with the Google Display Network.** Then... Google stores a number in your browser using a "cookie" to remember the visit. This number uniquely identifies your web browser on a specific computer, and not you as a person.

   Just to clear something up: a cookie is just a string of text stored in your browser. Some people get into a tizzy about them, but that's all they are: text. And if you don't like them, you can turn them off. Doing this is going to cause you lots of problems on many websites because they're really useful for storing information about what you are doing (such as login tokens for websites, so you don't have to keep logging in every time you revisit them or change pages).

3. **From that point on whenever someone using that browser visits another Remarketing-enabled site, the Google code snipped thereon reads back this number.** So, imagine someone visits

---

63. I'm not going to go into details about how to do this, because interfaces change frequently.

64. Other firms offer this, too, but Google is the biggest so we'll stick with them. Alas, Bing don't offer it (yet) but there's nothing to stop you using Google Remarketing with Bing Advertising.

The Medium

jonmcculloch.com. If the cookie is already set, then the fact of the visit is logged somewhere deep inside Google's innards; if it's not been set, then Google will kindly set it as I described and then log the visit in the same way.

4. **Next, they leave my site and wend their way to I know not where...** until they land upon a page hosted by one of Google's advertising partners rather than an *advertiser*, like me[65].

    At this point the Google code snippet on that site reads the cookie and sends the unique identifier back to home base where the clever computers there say, in effect, "Hey, this guy has been to jonmcculloch.com!", and then serves up one of my ads to show the visitor.

So... imagine this... the Evil Bald Genius is sending traffic to his *Buy My Evil Stuff* pages from his daily emails (although the traffic could be coming from anywhere, of course, which allows you to stalk your PPC and SEO visitors across the 'net like an evil weird creepy person).

But my victim doesn't buy, and instead toddles off on his daily surfing of the 'net and in her travels he hits, say, *The Daily Groan*, the website of a national newspaper.

And he's reading the most recent and terribly important gossip about Johnny Depp's left nut and he suddenly realises he's also looking at an ad for the Evil Bald Genius's Evil Stuff.

"What?!", he says to himself, "The Evil Bald Genius is advertising on a national newspaper's website? Oh my... there must be more to this funny little bald man than meets

---

65. Advertising partners are the people who own the websites running the ads, and advertisers are people like me who run the ads on them.

the eye... I need to have another look at this Evil Stuff..."

So he clicks on the ad and lo!

He's back on my sales page.

And so it goes.

What's happened, of course, is when he originally visited my "Buy My Evil Stuff" page, the Google code I added to my site set a cookie in his browser if it wasn't already set, and then updated the Google database with the fact he'd been on my site. Then, when he hits a partner site, in this case the site of *The Daily Groan*, the code there reads the cookie and checks the database, and Google says to itself, "aha... this person has visited the Evil Bald Genius's Evil Stuff sales page... and that means we need to show him this ad to send him right back again if he clicks on it". So Google shows the ad in the relevant spot on *The Daily Groan*'s website.

This is *incredibly* powerful because it means any business — and I mean *any* business — can advertise itself on any participating website with amazing accuracy. See, even if *The Daily Groan*'s site is a national site, I can configure my Remarketing campaign to show my ads to my erstwhile visitors only if they are in my local area. In other words, if I am a hairdresser in Halifax, I can configure my ads to appear on the website of *The Daily Groan if and only if* the visitor is also from Halifax; if I'm a butcher from Birmingham, only visitors from Birmingham will see my ads on *The Daily Groan*'s website; and if I'm a... you get the picture, I'm sure.

I use Remarketing myself, of course, and I'm always tickled by the number of emails I get from people telling me they've seen my ads on these extremely prestigious sites. My Inner Circle Members realise, of course, it's my Remarketing, but others generally don't, and they seem amazed at how much online advertising I'm doing and wonder how much it must be costing. The truth is they are the only ones seeing my

The Medium

ads... but they are seeing them everywhere they go.

Here's what it looks like when you're on the receiving end. This was sent to me by a client:

Blimey! Me and the famous Paul Weller hobnobbing it on the same page of the Daily Mail. I bet Paul was chuffed.

But wait... there's more!

Not only can you pick and choose the areas your ads are shown in and the websites they're shown on, but you can selectively redirect people from ads you're displaying to any landing page of your choice.

In principle you can mix and match and slice and dice, and send anyone who's visited any one of your pages to any other page from any ad.

So, for example the Evil Bald Genius could send people who landed on the Evil Stuff sales page but didn't buy back to the same page for another go; or maybe send them to a downsell page. And yet people who *did* buy could be sent to an upsell page for higher-ticket options.

The thing is you can get arbitrarily complex with Remarketing using *Custom Combinations*. If you take the time and make the effort and *structure* everything accordingly right from the word "go" then while it's a lot of work, it's just repetitive and not complicated or difficult. With a bit of thought you can create a complete funnel where you move people around from list to list according to their behaviour[66]. In combination with an email autoresponder like OfficeAutopilot, you become like a fucking marketing Terminator[67]:

For example, imagine the following scenarios:

- **Visitor hits your site and opts in to your email list.** You send them to an upsell page but they don't buy.

  So you then begin showing them Remarketing ads sending them back to a *different* page where they get an improved offer for the same thing. If they visit *that* page and still don't buy, you log this fact and remove them from the list so they don't get the offer again.

- **Visitor hits your site, opts in and confirms, and**

---

66. In effect. In reality you wouldn't be removing anyone from any list but would be *adding* them to lists and then *excluding* those lists from new combinations. I know... it might be hard to get your head around all of this, but trust the EBG: it's going to be worth it.

67. "Listen. Understand. That Terminator is out there. It can't be reasoned with, it can't be bargained with. It doesn't feel pity or remorse or fear and it absolutely will not stop. Ever. Until you are dead." Classic. And you get the picture, right?

The Medium

then goes away happy with his or her free report. You then stalk them with an offer to give them the same information in a different form for a small fee (say on a CD or printed). This is similar to the last scenario but likely to get fewer objections at the front end. It's just one alternative to offering an immediate upsell.

• **You send your email list to a video which gives them some useful information on the topic at hand.** Right after they click the link they automatically get an email saying, "if you liked the video here's how you can...". If they click on the link in the email they get to a sales page.

If they buy, they go on to one Remarketing list where you follow them around with an upsell to the offer (this is where you might want a short-duration list for scarcity), and if they don't buy you follow them around with ads sending them to an improved offer over the original.

And if they watch the video but don't click the email link... why, you can figure that one out with Remarketing Custom Combinations, too, and show ads to them to get them to watch the bloody video!

I hope by now you can see how awesomely powerful this can be if you're prepared to get stuck into it.

Getting Started

You access the Remarketing functions from your Adwords dashboard. Like Adwords, it's free until someone clicks on an ad, and you don't have to be using Adwords to test Remarketing.

It seems confusing at first, but it's worth putting in the time and effort to get to grips with it.

The Lie of Free Traffic

There is no such thing as "free traffic" when it comes to SEO, Social Media, or even Article Marketing, because even if it's free at the point of delivery, so to speak, there is an upfront investment required. Whether that's an investment of time taken to do it yourself or money in paying someone else to do it, is irrelevant.

The *fact* is you *don't* get it for free.

And the sooner you accept and embrace this idea, the happier you are going to be. Because then you'll realise the value of traffic is its Return On Investment — ROI — and not how much of it you can get for as little as you have to invest in getting it.

So a better measure of traffic than the cost of it is the ROI it brings, because it makes no sense to talk about the "cost" of traffic without factoring in the benefits it brings in terms of sales.

Search Engine Optimisation (SEO)

I'm now going to commit Internet marketing heresy and tell you that for most business owners SEO is a waste of time and money, and you are almost always going to be better off investing your time, energy, and money into different ways of generating traffic to your website.

Last year I was dragged up on stage in London to sit in front of 500 or so people and tell them SEO was likely to be a waste of their time and money.

This wasn't what they expected. More to the point, it wasn't what I'd planned to say. In fact, I hadn't *planned* to say anything because I wasn't given more than an hour's notice, which is probably why I was so blunt.

Now, before I get into the details I want to be clear on one thing: I am *not* telling anyone to stop doing SEO. What I *am* saying, though, is test and measure the quality of the traffic you're getting from it before you do any more of it. If it's working for you, then that's great. But don't get complacent and rely on it for all or even most of your traffic. The reason I say this is my recent experience has been SE traffic is not only becoming harder and harder to get, but the quality is low and getting lower — what's more it's going to continue getting lower for some time to come.

There is a long-held assumption and belief, one cherished to the point where it's unquestioned and axiomatic, that a high Google ranking means lots of traffic and lots of traffic is the same as making lots of sales. This is a non-sequitur, as I'll show you in a moment. Moreover, there are some other very good reasons for focusing your efforts on different ways of getting traffic to your website.

First, though, let's look at SEO and what's changed since early 2011.

The Woes of SEO

There's no denying SEO has been something of a gravy train this past decade or so. There was a time when a high ranking in the SERPs frequently meant a lot of highly qualified traffic; what's more, because of the relative ease with which you could get those high rankings, it was possible to get them with pages you'd optimised for optins and sales rather than a great user experience.

This has now changed drastically, and the gravy train has left the station with very few people aboard. It's always been changing because, if nothing else, competition has grown, but the Search Engines themselves have changed, too[68], and certainly in the last year or two that change has accelerated and been more dramatic. And it's only going to get worse.

That said, no one should be surprised by it, because Google have plainly stated their intention is to give the *searcher* the best experience possible and deliver the most relevant and engaging results they can. In other words, they are not interested in *you* as a website owner at all.

A lot of people piss and moan about this, but Google are looking out for themselves, which is entirely right and proper for a business to do. If you have been so short-sighted as to base your business model on the good will of a mind-bogglingly powerful and wealthy corporation with aims and goals very different to your own, then you are nuts.

Incidentally, I'll extend this comment to include Social Media platforms like Facebook and Twitter, and even LinkedIn to perhaps a lesser degree. All of these companies are concerned with themselves, and their product is the user base.

Now, some people wonder why I don't wax lyrical about Social Media Marketing in my work. Well, it's because I think it's mostly a waste of time. And even if I'm wrong and it isn't, I don't see any easy or reliable way of measuring it — meaning anyone claiming Social Media Marketing "works" has to provide evidence to support their claim if they expect to be taken seriously.

As it is... I'm still waiting.

Oh, sure, you might get the odd one or two "bites" from your efforts, as I'm sure I have done myself, but in terms of ROI it's appalling and definitely right down there in the

---

68. Google is the big one, but form follows function and they're all more or less going the same way.

The Medium

lowly 80% of activities responsible for a paltry 20% of my results.

If you dangle enough carrots in front of enough equines you're bound to get the odd donkey or two from time to time; but it's much easier to go to the Donkey Sanctuary and pick one up that's already looking for a home, right?

Right.

Hard Data

OK, back to the apparent futility of SEO and what's happened at Chez EBG with Mrs. EBG's blog. Search Engine traffic has now stabilised at just 23% of what it was before things went South in September 2012; in other words, 77% of the traffic we were getting from search engines has vanished. Historically, most, but not all of that was from Google. I have not bothered to see if traffic from other search engines has also been affected (I simply don't care enough, for reasons I'll share with you in a moment).

The inescapable conclusion is in our case Search Engine traffic is not worth very much. And a similar picture emerges with my own website and the websites of several other people I've spoken to about this: Search Engine traffic is down, optins are pretty much OK.

Do you really think it's a coincidence I'm getting a *massive* increase in unsolicited emails from SEO professionals who are increasingly desperate for work because their little cash-cow has been made into Google burgers? One would be amusing; two would be a coincidence; the million I've had... an indication something is terribly wrong with their businesses.

Let Me Be Clear About What I am NOT Saying

I am not telling you "SEO is dead".

The Medium

I am not telling you not to do SEO.

I am not even saying visitors you get from the Search Engines are worthless.

No, what I am saying is this: Search Engine traffic has long been considered valuable and thus a high Google ranking has been the Holy Grail for business owners. But this is not necessarily true and there are lots of counterexamples showing SE traffic *can* be and often *is* worthless.

Consider Mrs. EBG's "dilemma": does she work like hell to get the Search Engine traffic back she's lost (which would mean increasing the *current* traffic levels by a factor of more than *four*); or do we put the time and energy into increasing the optin rate by a mere 18%?

I hope you can see that's a no brainer[69].

Nothing we've done in the past has been "wrong", by the way. The SEO strategies I've shared with my clients before have worked in the past and to great effect — Mrs. EBG's blog dominated the free Google listings in her niche for well over two years before it got hit.

The fact is, though, things have changed.

Deal with it.

One Exception I Am Aware Of

It does seem some sites are doing OK when they send traffic to vendors like Amazon and Ebay. The general business model is you set up a very tightly niched site with a long-tail keyword as the main focus and then forward your visitors to the vendors where you then take a cut from any sales. That's it in a nutshell, and I do know some people who tell me they

---

69. In fact, we are working to increase the optin rate, adding more articles, because we get great traffic from them, and we're improving the sales-funnels, too. We don't mess around, you know.

The Medium

are making reliable profits from it.

Personally I think there are better ways to exploit niches nowadays (like the Kindle store) but some of that of course is my personal preference for writing. It won't suit everyone. What would concern me if I was in this niche business, though, is they are still gaming Google to some extent. For example the vast majority of these sites are hosted on Wordpress. Well, Matt Cutts of Google has already hinted they're going to be taking a longer look at Wordpress sites when they come across them. I can't help but think these people are living in something of a fool's paradise. Google's noose ever tightens — this we know for sure.

Let's pretend Search Engine traffic comes to us easily and at no cost... and see why we'd still be a few sandwiches short of a picnic to base our business model upon it.

1. **No control.** Your traffic comes in quantities and of a quality determined by someone else.

   No matter how hard you try to match your pages' content with the mindset and psychology of the searcher and visitor, you are depending on Google to deliver the kind of person you expect.

2. **Unreliable.** No one knows what Google's algorithms are, except Google themselves, and they ain't sayin'.

   This means your traffic source — the primary way your business gets new customers and clients is completely unreliable. It can (and does) change at any time on a whim from the Big G. This is why we're now seeing people crying into their virtual beer on forums because they have lost 90% of their traffic.

   This makes it impossible to have a rational business plan predicated on sustainable and controlled growth.

- **Not scalable.** Search Engine traffic is finite and capped by the number of searches people are making for your topic, even assuming you are getting all of the traffic (and you're never going to do that).

  It's true this number can be very large but it will always be limited. Other traffic strategies don't suffer from this same limitation. They're still limited, of course, but the limit is vastly higher.

- **Low Quality.** While I cannot say this is universally true, it's true enough to be a general principle until disproven in a given case.

  The simple fact is, visitors from the Search Engines are of low quality — in other words, they are not often buyers.

  Worse: this is a trend we have seen increasing, for reasons we can really only speculate on. Even in the comparatively short time since my wife's blog has been running, SE traffic has been declining in quality. Over the 12-month period from September 2011 to September 2012, SE visitors numbers fell by just a few percent, but the *conversions* from these visitors were a stonking 78.67% higher in 2011 than they were in 2012.

  I think one contributing factor is people are simply getting more jaded by their experiences online. Even five years ago, the typical long-copy and scammy sales letter was new to most people. But now... we've all seen them, and probably seen them being slagged-off, dissected and lampooned on sites like Facebook. The world is a much smaller and better-connected place than it was.

The Medium

A second reason is Google is much less likely to put a page that's actually selling anything too overtly high in the Search Engine Results Pages (SERPs). If this is so, then we can only expect it to get worse.

And finally... the sites that *do* get highly ranked are (in theory) going to be higher quality generally, meaning the objective (as it can be) difference between the 10th position in the SERPs and the first is tiny.

Another way of looking at this is to say your marketplace for your potential buyers' attentions just got more crowded and more competitive.

But as I say, this is all just my musing. I could be wrong.

The Upshot

There are two Big Ideas to take away from what we've looked at so far.

First, SEO is not what it was and is going to get worse. Hitherto, one of the criteria you'd use when specifying and designing a website was all the SEO stuff — which often cost a lot of money to set up *and* was an ongoing investment. It's highly likely you can simply delete this from your shopping list if you're looking for a new website. A big, scary thought, but one you have to grapple with.

And secondly, just "traffic" is not what we want, because not all traffic is created equal. It's *qualified* traffic we want.

Please, don't have a stroke at the thought of losing all this "free" traffic. It was never free in the first place because *all* traffic is paid for one way or another. And it's not about the cost — it's about the ROI.

What it boils down to is this:

1. **If you have Search Engine traffic already and**

you have not dug deep into the numbers and proved it's worth having then stop any further SEO activities until you have done that digging. Don't be an arse and just "feel" the numbers must be OK. If you cannot tie sales to traffic — no matter where it's coming from — then continuing to solicit or send that traffic is not the act of a rational person because you don't know if your ROI is positive or negative.

2. **For too long the need for Search Engine traffic has been held as almost axiomatic.** And I'm telling you that's bullshit.

3. **If you don't have Search Engine traffic then don't bother with it unless you have time and money to throw away.** Because there are easier and better ways to get traffic even though you are explicitly paying for it

Social Media Marketing (SMM)

I'm now going to commit a second heresy and tell you that for most businesses Social Media Marketing is a waste of time.

The first flaw of Social Media Marketing is it's almost unmeasurable. Meaning, you can't tell if it's working or not. You might get loads of "interaction" on your page with people on your pages, and you might have a million Likes and Retweets to your name, but how much money are they making you? My guess is you don't know. And most of the time that's because you *can't* know. See, with very rare exception, no one is selling anything on the Social Media platforms. And to make a sale you have to get people off the Social Media websites and onto your own.

The Medium

So that should be your whole focus of Social Media Marketing. Likes, Retweets, Shares and all those things are means to an end not ends in themselves because they're practically worthless (I know one fairly big-name marketer who won't even take the time to Tweet to his 100,000 followers simply because it's not even worth the bother of writing just 140 characters).

In some ways there's a parallel here with SEO: in the same way as loads of visitors to your site is not the same as loads of sales, neither is loads of "interaction" on Social Media websites. There are staggeringly large numbers of business owners out there putting a lot of time, money and energy into Social Media Marketing and it simply isn't working (just to be clear: *advertising* on these sites is a different matter).

There's an interesting article on the USA Today website[70], titled *Social media a bust for small businesses* and in it you'll find such unsurprising[71] statistics as these:

1.   About 61% of small businesses don't see any return on investment on their social-media activities.

2.   Almost 50% say they've increased their time spent on social media.

3.   Only 7% have decreased their time.

Maybe it's just me, but these stats bespeak amazing stupidity from an awful lot of business owners.

Why do they do it?

My guess is it's because SMM is one of those comfortable and pleasant activities we can kid ourselves are equivalent to some kind of achievement and we can easily swallow the line

---

70.   http://www.usatoday.com/story/money/personalfinance/2013/04/16/small-business--social-media-facebook/2075123/

71.   To me and other people who actually know what we're talking about.

The Medium

from the 'gurus' that such things as testing and measuring are old fashioned and no longer relevant.

That said, if you absolutely *must* engage in Social Media Marketing because you have some strange compulsion, then what I'm about to share with you is probably the way you're most likely to get some kind of positive return. But I warn you: it's going to be very hard for you to measure the ROI on this, so use it at your peril. First, the obligatory diagram. I want to get this painful section out of the way and, fortunately for me, in this case a picture speaks a thousand words:

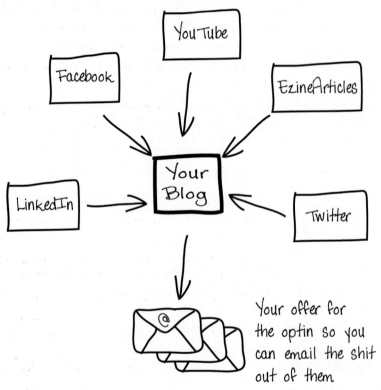

The Medium

Here's how it works:

1. **Pick a topic for the month.** For my business I might choose email marketing, for example.

2. **Write eight to 12 blog posts on different aspects of the topic.** So I might write about delivery, autoresponder companies, email sales strategies, and so on. I'd then schedule these to be posted on my blog two or three times a week, say, on Mondays, Wednesdays and Fridays.

3. **For each blog post create a load of posts, tweets, videos and articles on the same topic.** Each of these would be a *teaser* with a link back to the blog post and a call to action to get them to click on the link and read the whole post in detail.

4. **The blog post is really a sales letter.** And the sale is to get them to opt-in to your email list so you can market to them in earnest over time (see the next section).

What this is going to do is drive interested people to your blog where a proportion of them are going to opt-in to your email list.

There are two big differences between this method and the typical way of doing Social Media Marketing. The first is the topics are focused, so each month you're going to be attracting people interested in a very narrow area of interest instead of trying to appeal to the masses; and secondly, it's driving people to your own site and driving them for a specific purpose — to get the optin. Most people treat Social Media Marketing as a kind of fuzzy exercise in "engagement" with no rhyme, reason, or plan behind it.

Just to be clear: I don't do this myself. I simply don't have time because in true 80/20 style there are better ways for me to get traffic. But I'm not ruling it out and it's something I'll likely revisit in the future. In the meantime, I have other, more certain and profitable things to focus on.

Email Marketing

Email Marketing is, and will probably remain one of the most powerful and effective marketing channels you have available to you. It's not so much about getting traffic as the other online methods are, but is really about making the sale *over time*. It's virtually free and takes little more than an investment of your time and energy and a small amount for an autoresponder — yet it can increase your sales by over 1,600% when compared to the traditional model of selling over the Internet.

But your success is predicated on two things: doing it the right way; practicing until you get the hang of it.

The first I can help you with — and by the time you get to the end of this Section, my work there will be done.

The second is entirely down to you. I can encourage you and advise you, and even kick you from time to time... but I can't do it for you.

So read this Section from beginning to end at least twice, take (lots of) notes and then *take action*.

Email Marketing Myths

So, let's start right at the beginning: why bother with email marketing? I mean, it's old fashioned, clunky and doesn't work because it's been eclipsed by Social Media marketing, right?

Wrong.

Because when done the right way, Email Marketing is *insanely* profitable.

The Medium

Here are just a few examples of the kinds of results people are getting:

- **Mrs.** EBG, increased her sales by 114% in the first 30 days of Email Marketing the EBG Way... and they stayed there.

- **My own emails enrol people into my Business Supremacy Inner Circle...** at a rate of around 5%, which is excellent for a membership programme.

- **A couple of years ago, my dear friend and client, Angie Mattson of *Your Organized Guide* emailed her list every day for the first 15 days of December ...** and came away with six brand new shiny clients (at a time of year where the "gurus" tell you "no one is buying").

- **John O'Connell, Member of my Inner Circle, in 6 days of sending regular emails (10 emails to be exact) made €3,000.** Now this was to a list he was normally making at most 2-300 quid a month from. Not only that but the lifetime value of these clients was worth far more than just 3 grand.

- **Alison Stothard, at her wits' end, took my advice, knuckled down, and emailed her list four times over a Bank Holiday weekend...** and made more sales in those four days than she'd normally make in an entire month.

- **My emails for clients are legendary.** Some years ago I made one client $75,000 from just two emails, pitching an offer to a list they swore was "burned out". More recently I've routinely added a 25% bump to another client's seminar attendance figures as well as spanking the bottom of emails written by one of

Glazer-Kennedy's top copywriters.

I could go on, but there's little point: emails written the Evil Bald Genius Way make you money — heaps of it. And now I'm going to share with you exactly how I do it.

First, let's get the uninformed crap out of the way and bust a few popular but utterly incorrect Email Marketing Myths:

1. **Email marketing doesn't work any more.** Yes it does, as the results I've shared with you above demonstrate. What won't work is boring corporate-style "newsletter" emails of the type you get from all the big brands. For reasons we'll come to later in this section, those beautifully-designed emails that look gorgeous at your end look like a pile of dog's vomit at t'other. I'll fix that for you, so don't worry.

2. **People don't read emails any more.** Bullshit. They do. Email is actually one of the most popular forms of communication. Sure, many younger people might be leaning more towards the messaging systems provided by Facebook, *et al*, but email is still tops for one-to-one communication for vast numbers of people.

3. **People hate spam and will think I'm a spammer if I send them lots of emails.** Yes, people do hate spam. But they won't consider your emails spam if they've *asked* to receive them and when they do receive them get something interesting, enjoyable, informative, and fun that adds real value to their lives. More to the point, the more often you appear in someone's email inbox, the less likely they are to think you're a spammer.

4. **My customers are too smart and sophisticated to respond to EBG-style Emails.** Yeah, right. Listen, I

have all sorts of business owners who have responded to my emails, from lawyers and accountants, to cancer surgeons and gym-owners. And, more important, they have then gone on to use the same style of email marketing in their own businesses. Imagine: a lawyer sending emails like mine, even to the point of having one subject line set as "You Couldn't Make This Shit Up". Well, he sends 'em, and he has a *stack* of replies from people who love 'em.

5. **My customers don't like to be sold to.** That's possible. But if it's true, then it's because you haven't trained them to expect it or you've attracted the wrong kind of people in the first place. *Everyone* likes being sold to if it's done the right way. Being sold *at* is a different matter. No one likes the hard sell. But EBG Emails don't sell hard. They sell soft. But remember... even raindrops can wear down a mountain, given enough time.

6. **If I email my list...** they'll unsubscribe. Possibly. But if you don't email them... what does it matter if they stay? The point of having an email list is not to have a list. The point of having an email list is to make money.

Again, I could go on — but those are the main objections I get.

Here's what people really want: they want to receive emails from people, real human beings with warmth and personality. They don't want to receive bland, boring company brochures and other flavourless marketing dross. *That* is why so many people struggle to make Email Marketing work.

Now, much of what I share with you here is going to be

The Medium

counterintuitive, completely the reverse of what you've been told before, and it'll leave you feeling very uncomfortable. So uncomfortable, in fact, you'll likely be tempted to dismiss it or put it to one side until "later". If you do either of those things, you are making a big, Big, BIG mistake.

Fact: no one who has taken my advice and begun emailing the EBG Way has ever failed to increase their sales. One lady came close to not getting a bump, but we fixed her offer and it went *bananas*.

So I hope I've put your mind at rest — Email Marketing *works*. But only if you actually take action and start doing it.

So...

Get started by emailing your list.

Tell them you are going to be emailing them regular and frequent tips and updates they will find interesting, informative, entertaining and useful. Be sure to give them the option to unsubscribe right now, before you begin emailing them. Say something like, "... you can decide not to receive these emails at any time, or you can click the link below right now and opt out now, before I begin sending them. Just be aware if you do elect not to receive them, you'll also miss out on a whole load of special offers I reserve for my email readers only".

Email Structure for Maximum Response

So that was a quick overview of Email Marketing and we blew a few of the most pernicious myths out of the water.

And so now we're going to turn our attention to the structure of the emails we send. You might think this is a bit of an odd way to do it, because you've been told the content is more important than the structure, but that would be a mistake.

The Medium

Why Most People Are 'Sales Copy' Illiterate

Virtually everyone in the Western world leaves school able to read and write. A small proportion of them can write "well". And for reasons I won't go into here, this often leads them to the erroneous conclusion if they can write "well" they can write good sales copy.

This is probably the most expensive non-sequitur you'll ever swallow. Writing your own copy is a great idea and frequently a much better one than paying someone else to do it — with the caveat you must *first* learn how to write sales copy yourself (or at least what it looks like so you don't get sold a lemon). Simply writing "well" won't cut the mustard.

And not only does sales copy have content and style, but it has a structure, too.

Now, with a sales letter or postcard or web-page or whatever this is easy to see: headline, body copy, call-to-action at the bottom, all moulded around the AIDA formula (Attention, Interest, Desire, Action) and containing the four essential elements you need to have in there to make it all work: Pain, Commitment, Cure, and Reason to Believe.

The trouble with the kind of emails we send with Email Marketing is they tend to be shorter than typical long-copy sales pieces so we tend not to get this whole structure in and the whole way email works makes it slightly different for us because we sell through the ongoing dialogue we have with our readers.

The first thing to understand is while we want to stick to the structure as much as possible, it's not worth losing sleep over. I know people who have avoided sending emails because they were not "right". This is really dumb, because even if an email is somehow "perfect", if you don't send it, you won't make any money. That I can guarantee.

The Medium

So, here's a quick rundown of what needs to be in your emails and a guide to how to string them together, in the order of their importance.

First...

The 'From' Name.

Over time your name is much more important than your Subject line because if you're writing your emails the EBG Way, then your audience will be looking for your name in their inbox (and if you miss one or you're late with them you will get emails asking where they are and are you OK — this happens to me all the time).

Most people teaching email marketing tell you the Subject line is the most important thing in an email, but they're wrong[72]. If you have a good relationship with the people on your list, then your name is all important. I mean, imagine you fancied a hot chick or dude and you saw an email from her land in your inbox — you'd open it no matter what the Subject line said, right?

Right.

So your From name should be *your* name. Not your company name or anything else like that, even if you're writing from a company. Your name. I tell you — I am not a fan of the tax man at all, but you know what really gets me mad? Getting letters from them... without even the courtesy of a bloody name on them.

The Subject Line

Your Subject line is the next most important thing in your email. It's the second thing they'll see after your name, and

---

72. This is true only if the sender isn't well known to you and you're going for the immediate sale from someone with whom you have no real relationship

---

The Medium

often only thing they'll see giving them a clue to the content, unless they are using an email client where it shows a preview of the message (not all of them do, and often the user has this turned off, anyway).

So do spend some time on making your Subject lines "attention grabbers", because sometimes, especially if they are new to your list, your name might not be enough.

If you've read my own emails over time, you'll know I tend towards the risqué, crude, and frequently the bizarre. Sometimes I'll drop in a "how to" or whatever, but the relationship I have with my readers means they know me well enough to understand if I have a Subject line like "Kinky Marketing Secrets of the Pervy Fetish Enthusiasts" it *means* something and they are going to be rewarded by reading the rest of the email.

That's crucial: as with any headline (because that's what your Subject line is, if you think about it), you must be explicitly or implicitly promising a benefit to them taking the time and making the effort to read on.

First Few Lines

An important rule is to pay off your Subject line early — and the more risqué and awe-inspiring your Subject, the earlier you need to pay it off. Don't fall into the trap of using Subject lines that just get attention and have no follow-on in the email. You'll just leave your readers feeling tricked — meaning next time they won't open your email, perhaps.

I tend to make the first line of my emails short, just a few words. The second line is usually a little longer than that, and the third line longer still. This is all deliberate — because what I'm doing is easing them into reading my email. If the first line is a gigantic block of text, it's often enough to put people off.

The Medium

The trick with successful sales copy is first to *get* people reading and then *keep* them reading.

Body Copy

I say much more about this in Appendix I and even include a writing exercise where I will prove to you in just five minutes you can write conversational, informal, and profitable emails on demand.

But for now just think about being conversational, personal, and personable. Write like you speak and as if you were talking to a favoured aunt or uncle over a glass of sherry at Christmas.

Call to Action

This is the bit where most business owners chicken out, both in email and in other copy. But if you *wait* for people to buy in their own time, you'll be waiting for a very long time, in the main.

I have a simple rule that every email I send has *at least* one call to action: simply a link for them to click on, with the intention usually being they either buy something or somehow indicate interest in some niche where I'll sell them something further down the line.

There is a very specific pattern to how many links and where to put them we've identified empirically (and I share it with you in the Bonus Section) from lots and lots of testing, but just make sure you have at least one of them in there.

Exactly how you do this is up to you, but the important thing to understand is the "sale" in the email is usually (but not always) to get them to click the link and the product or service should be sold on the page they are landing on. A subtle but very important difference.

The Medium

Finally...

This all probably seems very complicated, but it's not. It seems that way because it's probably new to you, and like any learnable skill it will get easier and you will get better with practice. You won't become excellent at Email Marketing just by reading what I or anyone else has to say about it: you have to *do* it, just as you didn't learn to drive your car by reading a book about it. And once you've been writing regular and frequent emails for a while, you'll become so good at it, you'll do all of the stuff we've talked about unconsciously.

That, my friend, is a wonderful place to be.

Where DO You Get Your Ideas, EBG?

In Appendix I you'll see I share with you a very simple exercise to get yourself writing like a demon, and if you'd like to do it now, skip forward and just give it a go. I do want to stress I don't write my emails using that technique myself, in the same way I don't ride my bike with stabilisers or shuffle my hands around the steering wheel of my car when I drive. It's just a practice-technique, like the stabilisers and the shuffly-hand thing, to get you moving. After a short while you'll have burned some new neural pathways and writing will become much easier for you (but if it works and you want to continue with it, then by all means do). As I've taken great pains to point out before, I wasn't born a whizz with the old keyboard. I became an awesome world-class copywriter only because I was an awesomely crap copywriter who practiced, practiced, practiced, and eventually and painfully wrote himself better. There are no other alternatives and no real shortcuts.

But the sooner you start writing, the more quickly you're going to get better. Proof of this, if proof be needed, is my good friend Flor McCarthy, who is, of all things, a lawyer. Now, I'm sure you'd agree with me lawyers are not generally noted for their warmth or good humour and it's true he resisted the notion of sending informal and conversational daily emails to his clients at first.

But he tried it... and stuck with it and now he's an old hand... and he has a whole pile of emails from his clients telling him how much they enjoy and look forward to receiving his emails.

Needless to say, his business has improved, too.

The point is, if a lawyer in the smallest and most conservative of conservative small towns in rural Ireland can succeed with daily emails... then you can, too.

Anyway, let's move on.

Because now we have an inkling of how to write, the question is what do we write about? And the answer is... pretty much anything you like. In the original *Email Supremacy* teleclasses I shared a list of 31 different drop-dead-simple ideas for email topics, many of which could be effortlessly expanded into an almost infinitely long list of topics.

Here's a sample for you:

1. **A topical news piece.** I don't think I need to say a lot more about this, do I?

2. **Something about your day or weekend.** While talking about yourself all the time, especially in sales letters, is offputting for people, it's vital for growing and nurturing relationships, and relationships are the lynchpin of successful email marketing.

3. **Write about a habit you have now or have had in the past.** Good or bad. Makes no difference.

4. **Some big mistake you've made in the past.** Most

people make the error of only ever mentioning long-past mistakes in an effort to distance themselves from it. But the more recent the mistake you admit to, the more people will be drawn to you.

5. **Lists.** People LOVE lists. And you can make them as sensible or as daft as you like, from "7 Ways to Kill a Zombie" to "The 10 Most Painful Things I Ever Did". These are always entertaining.

6. **Something (good or bad) that's happened to you or someone you know in the past.**

7. **Your latest client.** You don't have to break client confidentiality, but there's nothing to stop you writing about the challenge they faced or the problem you're solving for them.

As I'm sure you can see, Nos. 4, 5 and especially 6 give you an almost unlimited range of choice. The thing is your topic does not have to be relevant to your niche, industry, product or service.

A while ago I wrote an email about my friend who used to walk — drunk — along the window-sill outside his long apartment window, 15 floors up. I'm going back a few years now, but so far as I know he's still alive. Here's the email as it went out:

        Hi Jon,

        Interesting email yesterday from someone who said, in effect, "I love the way you write your emails but I could never do that because my business is so boring and my readers aren't used to your kind of approach".

        Well... ummm... isn't this just another version of the old "but my business is different" thing?

Let me share something with you, but bear with me first.

It's over 25 years ago now, but way back then I used to hang out with a rum old crowd, and we spent most of our time smoking dope, fixing motorcycles and listening to Motorhead.

Anyway, things change, as they do, and we all moved on a little and, to be perfectly frank, some of us treated the drugs and stuff as the bit of fun they were meant to be... but others got a bit deeper into it all than they perhaps ought to have done.

As I recall, I was actually the only one holding down a steady job at the time; not only that but I also won a kind of 'scholarship' from my employer to go to university, get my degree, and come back as a Bigwig.

My brain wasn't QUITE so addled I didn't realise that was a fine opportunity, so I grabbed it with both hands.

The others were less fortunate. Some did get work and held down jobs, but others... well, they kind of spiralled down into one big messy shitpile.

So, at some point one of them, Tony, moved into a 15th floor flat on one of the crappier estates in Leicester. And believe me, those were then some seriously crap places to live. I don't now what they are like now, but then they were so rough even the trees grew in twos.

I didn't go there too often myself, unless I was scoring some blow, but one time I did drop in to see him I vividly remember him showing me his new trick (another time I went, one of his mates, Gus, was there drying his urine-soaked jeans with an iron -- oh, the perils of drinking so heavily you piss yourself while you're stupefied. The stench was unbelievable).

But that episode was not the worst of it, not by a long chalk (you might want to sit down

The Medium

while you read this, because it could make you feel slightly ill).

No, I was telling you about his new 'trick', wasn't I?

See, he had this bloody great big window in his flat, and at each end was a smaller one he could open. Gave a splendid view of the city from its vantage point of 150 feet or so above the sprawling mess of Highfields.

But Tony didn't use the window for looking out of; at least, not so far as I know.

Because what he used to do (I swear I am not making this up) was...

... open the window on the left...

... climb out...

... walk along the narrow and cambered window sill...

... and climb back in the window on the right.

You've seen trailers for 'Man on a Ledge"?

You've seen that old Twilight Zone feature?

Well, imagine that.

Only this is REAL.

And the guy is drunk, doped up to the eyeballs or on acid. He's giggling away and having a right old time of it. And then his "friends" occasionally would shut the windows and leave him out there for a while

Just for shits and grins, you know?

Did I tell you this was a 15th floor flat? I did, didn't I?

Jeeze. It sends me into a cold sweat just thinking about it. I'm not particularly bothered by heights, but there is no way on this or any other planet I'd shuffle along a 6in wide sloping ledge 150 feet in the air for "fun".

Same guy around the same time was caught

The Medium

stealing a bottle of whiskey from the Sainsbury's supermarket in the town centre.

The store detective chased him all the way through the city up to Victoria Park, where he managed to lock himself in the public toilets... and drink the entire bottle before Plod arrived.

So, what's the point I'm making here? What's the marketing message?

Well, there isn't one.

Nope. This email contain zero marketing content.

BUT it IS marketing in and of itself.

Let me explain...

If you've read this far you were probably caught up in the 'story'. You wanted to hear what happened next.

You kept reading because whatever emotions you were feeling -- curiosity, disgust, fear, excitement, incredulity, whatever -- had you gripped to the point you didn't want to stop.

And it had NOTHING to do with marketing or the services and products I offer.

The underlying point is this: anyone could do this in any industry and selling to any audience. Because it's storytelling, the finest kind of communication between humans there is.

The idea your market or audience is "too sophisticated" is a load of old tosh. No, not everyone will like it.

Some won't like the content; some won't like the delivery; some won't like the "unprofessionalism"; and some will decide they don't like YOU, personally.

But who cares?

Because by writing with your own personality weaving through the tale like a golden thread, you will attract people who DO like you -- and

The Medium

```
liking is a prerequisite to buying from you
(most of the time).

    If you've read this far (and you must have
done), then you have just experienced first-
hand the power of the kind of email marketing
I'm going to be sharing with you in Email
Supremacy:

    YOU, Fred, are exactly the kind of person I
want joining me.

    Warmly,

    Jon
```

See? No real marketing content at all. It wasn't about the "thing" I'm selling at all, really. But the point is that was the second most profitable email I ever sent and it had nothing to do with what I was selling. I say more about how to craft offers and calls in a moment, but for now just be aware you can make your call to action as simple as "and while I'm here...".

That's it.

So you can see there's no need to sweat any of this.

It's only one email of many you will be sending, and you're better off writing a so-so email and sending it than writing a perfect one and leaving it on your hard drive because you're a scaredy-cat.

How to Sell in Your Emails

We just looked at some very simple ways to get them ol' ideas flowing for your emails. One thing you'll come to learn is it's less important what you write about than it is that you *do* write regularly and frequently.

So now we're going to see how we can make these potentially whacky and off-the-wall emails relevant to our offers and launches.

And the secret is...

... you just fuggeddubaoudid.

It's really *not* that important.

Sure, often you'll find a way to tie your product or service into the topic of your email very neatly, and that's great. Do it when you can.

But if you can't, it really doesn't matter.

Your email does not have to be *about* the "thing" to *sell* the "thing". The simple thing about us humans is while we want a reason for something, that reason has to make only superficial sense. Meaning a simple "because" followed by the most inane and trivial of justifications will often be enough. So what that means is you can write something like this: "... by the way, while I'm here you really do need to get your act together and click that there link, because I have just a few more places left, and next time this widget sees the light of day, it'll be twice the price".

Dead easy, right?

And that could follow an email on *literally* any topic.

The thing is you're not selling like you'd traditionally be selling — one shot at the target so you're pulling every trick in the book to get them to buy. That's why we tend to write the long-copy sales letters and have salesmen and women giving well-prepared sales pitches.

But this way you're selling over time. And when someone does eventually buy from you it's because they've bought into you, thanks to the constant, conversational emails you've been sending them. Sure, I still write long-copy sales letters for myself, it's true. But that's because I *can*. It's easy for me, and fast, too. But Mrs. EBG regularly gets conversion rates of 47% or so and for her offers we use a simple and very formulaic 360-ish word sales letter.

Why does it work?

The Medium

Because of the *relationship* she has with her list.

Moreover, the repeated offers — like, repeated *daily*, over and over and over again ad nauseam in some cases — work because people buy when they are ready to buy, and not when you are ready to sell.

So you have to keep popping up in front of them so when that Special Day comes, you're right there waving at them with your offer. When they're ready to buy, there you are, ready to sell. And it works like a charm.

Finally, if you are launching a product or service with a deadline or some other form of scarcity, don't be shy. I'll typically email my list *seven* times on the last day of a launch, and while I lose maybe 1% of my list (who would never have been buyers anyway), I'll get maybe 80% of my sales in the last 20% of the promotion. Other business owners tell me they see much the same pattern.

And really finally finally... I get a lot of emails from people trying to divine the Higher Plan I have, working hard to figure out the deep meaning of the emails I send and the particular order and timing I send them.

Well... here's how I work it out.

I do a double integration based on the Wren-Davidson curve, cross-multiply it in Laplace Space with the size of my list and then apply the chi-squared statistical function and run it through a cost-matrix.

OK, that's a lie. It doesn't even make sense.

Truth is... I just make the bugger up as I go along. If feel like sending an email that's just occurred to me, then that's what I do. People who dig deep for the "real" meaning remind me of those pretentious types who try to analyse stories and make more of them than there really is.

I remember from my school days when my English teacher would read a passage from whatever book we were studying

The Medium

at the time and read into it some deep and profound meaning.

"The curtains were blue", she'd read, then raise her eyes from the book and tell us all, "the blue of the curtains is the author's way of communicating the deep depression of the protagonist as a result of his betrothed's infidelity".

Really?

How did she know?

Sometimes the curtains are just *blue*, and that's all the author wanted to say; and unless the author tells us differently, that's really what we have to assume.

The one exception to this is when I'm launching a new product or service — then there's a definite plan and a structure to the email sequence.

Otherwise they're just a more-or-less random ongoing monologue rather like a few chats down the pub of an evening, although I confess I will frequently place teasers in my emails hinting at things to come in a future email.

A classic example of this is the long and ongoing saga of me, my Jack Russell terrier puppy, Haggis, and the rats we've got living behind the house in the orchard. I usually play out these stories and sagas in the P.S.s of my emails and they keep people riveted. I've lost count of the emails I've had from my readers asking me what's coming next, or, if I haven't mentioned them for a while, how Haggis and the rats are getting on. Email marketing expert and creator of the excellent *Autoresponder Madness* programme, Andre Chaperon[73], describes this as a "soap opera sequence", or SOS. It works extremely well to keep people interested and engaged in your emails, and, if your SOS is about you and your life, then it creates massive "personality" in your emails.

---

73. You can (and should) find out more about Andre and his work on his website, http://andrechaperon.com

---

The Medium

Technical Horrors of Email Marketing

Now we need to look at some of the more technical nitty-gritty details of Email Marketing. And I warn you: while you might find this boring and something for the nerds to be taking care of, it's important you understand it because your web-designers almost certainly won't. You don't have to be a technical wizard but you *do* need to be aware of the problems and pitfalls. Because if you're not then your profits *will* suffer.

First, if you're tempted to use the "professionally designed" email newsletter templates that look like mini web-pages... don't. They are completely ineffective. Not only are "newsletters" often a waste of time (because mostly they "tell" rather than "sell") but all the fancy HTML formatting with tables and stuff is unlikely to be rendered correctly in many of your readers' email clients. Without getting too techy, although HTML is standardised everyone has his or her own interpretation of how things ought to look on the screen.

The upshot is my email client very likely makes the email look different from the bloke's next door, and both of them will be very different from the version you see when you write it. I generally go for either plain text or simple html — bold, underline, italics and a small amount of highlighting on occasion. I also justify the paragraphs and ensure the first line of each new paragraph is indented. The reason I, personally, use simple HTML as opposed to plain text is something of a compromise between best practice and automation.

Secondly, forget about using images for the most part. Again, to keep it simple, just understand images are usually hosted on a server and downloaded and displayed in the email on demand. Maybe only 40% of people will have their email

The Medium

clients set up to do this automatically (and they're insane if they do), so most people won't see your images at all.

Don't believe me?

Then look at the image below and be appalled: This is typically what more than half of your readers are seeing if you include remotely hosted images in your emails. What they *think* I see is on the left; what I *actually* see is on the right:

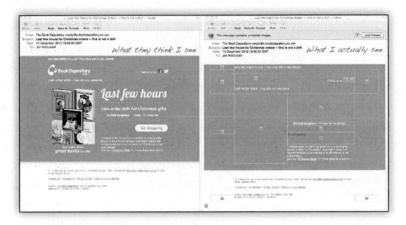

And thirdly, the same mechanism is used to calculate your open rates, which means they are horribly inaccurate (and who cares anyway? It's sales you want to be counting, not opens or click-throughs).

Open rates can be useful as a comparative measure in some circumstances, but mostly they're not worth your while even looking at. They're about as much use as a chocolate teapot or a Facebook "like".

What I've just shared with you is very important because if you don't get to grips with it all, then all your best efforts will come to naught because your marketing emails are likely to look like a dog's dinner by the time they get to the other end.

Why Email Marketing Works

I'm now going to share some insights with you into why I think emailing the EBG Way works[74]. It's not something based on science and all the information we've got is empirical.

So here are a few hypotheses to explain the facts we observe. I don't claim they're all necessarily correct, but they're reasonable and based on much of what we know to be true.

1. **You're there when they're ready to buy.** Consider: not everyone on your list is ready to buy all the time. For one reason and another their "buying temperature" goes up and down. Now, imagine they're in the mood to buy one day a week and you email once a month (which is still more frequently than most business owners email). The chances of your email landing in their inbox on the day they decide to buy, assuming both are independent and random, is approximately 1 in 900. But if you email every day, then you are certain to have an email in their inbox on the day they want to buy.

2. **You are top of consciousness.** Your having an email

---

74. Something you may have already figured out about me is I like to give you the why of things as well as the what and the how. And I do this because if you understand the why of something, you're much more likely to take action and put the strategies to work. Email Marketing done the EBG Way increases your sales. That's a fact. At least, I have never had anyone try it and not get a substantial boost in their sales and profits. This isn't to say it's impossible there's someone out there who won't. But the odds are insanely in your favour and businesses where this won't work are vanishingly rare. Consequently, the chances of your being a business where this won't work are very remote.

in their inbox on the Special Day won't guarantee they'll buy from you, but it vastly increases your chances. Why? Because you're the guy or gal they keep hearing from! When they think "widget!" your name immediately comes up. I mean it's likely very few people who read my emails would think of anyone but The Evil Bald Genius if they were pondering Premium Pricing.

3. **By writing conversational emails, written as you speak, you attract people who are like you.** This is not a trivial point and bears some explanation. But, in brief, we know we tend to like to do business with people who are like ourselves. And we tend to attract those people by writing naturally and conversationally. In other words, if you write like a stuffed-shirt, you'll attract stuffed-shirts for clients.

4. **Your emails are like the emails they get from friends.** When you get a nicely formatted 'newsletter' type email you know it's from a business, especially if that's the name in the From field. Immediately you know what follows is a pitch, no matter how gently it's put. But by sending emails the EBG Way, your emails look more like the kind of emails you send and receive for fun. Sure you know I'm selling but you also know there's no real hard sell and even if you don't buy anything you know you're going to get some value from reading it, even if it's just a giggle or two.

5. **You're selling not just telling.** Despite what I said above, if you write your emails the EBG Way, they will be sales emails. You'll be following the AIDA formula and structuring your emails with a proper call to action and each email will have a specific purpose

and one (and only one) thing to sell, rather than a meandering, boring brochure or catalogue of boring "stuff".

However it all *really* works we can but surmise, extrapolate, hypothesise and sometimes guess.

But the fact is... it does.

Now, here's the challenge for you: *doing it*. I know from experience most business owners resist Email Marketing the EBG Way for all sorts of reasons, from "it won't work with my market" and "they won't like it", to "I can't write" and "even if I could do it, I have nothing to write about". Well, I'll share a secret with you: some days I don't know what to write.

So you know what I do?

I just sit down and start writing about the fact I can't think of what to write. Pretty soon something comes out and I can go back and delete the first few paragraphs.

Job done.

Here's a slice of personal philosophy, based on a lot of observation and empirical data: I think most business owners invent reasons not to begin emailing their lists frequently and often simply because it feels uncomfortable and they want to rationalise their fears with bullshit excuses like the ones I've mentioned at the beginning of this section.

The Ultimate Link Strategy

It might come as a surprise to discover the number of links you have in an email *as well as where they are* can make a huge difference to response. It's not something I thought too much about since I'm very 80/20 focused and that kind of thing seemed to me to be most likely in the 80% of things that are not terribly important.

The Medium

But in a few cases this seems not to be so.

The back story is this... a client and I had something of a minor contretemps which meant I stopped writing emails for him for maybe eight months or so. We then met again at an event in London, and, not being one to hold a grudge, I made a point of speaking to him. Anyhow, long story short we made it up and I've since been writing his emails once more.

And when I first took up the reins again he sent me a load of stats he'd compiled because he found neither his own emails, nor those of the copywriter he'd hired from across the Pond (supposedly some A-list guy, but I've seen the emails he wrote and they were crap) could surpass mine.

So he'd been testing and tweaking and testing and tweaking desperate to find a way to beat my controls.

He never did manage to do that... but what he did find was one particular pattern of links consistently beat all the others.

Amazing, no?

And you know what?

I tested it myself and while I've not done any accurate measurements on it, it seems to hold true for both my emails *and* for Mrs. EBG's.

Here it is:

- Three links in the body.
- One link in the P.S.

We *seem* to get better results when one of the body-links is early in the email, but the bump we see is not statistically significant in the data we have. Not *yet* at any rate. But we have found emails with this pattern on average do 10% better than those without them. We've even split-tested the emails

---

The Medium

so they are identical in all but the links.

And still we get that bump.

Amazing, isn't it?

Now please, don't go off half-cocked and say, "The EBG says the *One True Way* is...", because that's not what I'm saying.

There are *lots* of other things it could be apart from the links themselves (for example, it could be that to get the three links in and have them make sense you have to write the copy in a certain way — which you do, in fact). But the point is *this is worth testing because it could make you a lot of money.*

I mean, what would an extra 10% in sales from your emails mean to you? To Mrs. EBG it makes a difference of $300 to $1,000 a month depending on what she's selling or whether she's doing a product launch. Not "guru numbers", but it's free money.

Well worth a try, eh?

But that's not all.

Because while we just touched on the technical aspects of Email Marketing (which I know has scared the living daylights out of some people) what we didn't look at yet is perhaps the most important technical consideration of all...

Deliverability

It's been likened, with some justification, I think, to "the war for your inbox".

The spammers have a lot to answer for because while SMTP is a very reliable protocol for delivering email, the constant stream of trashy emails from scams to offers of all sorts of weird and wonderful drugs, apparatus, and other questionable things to make your bodyparts longer, thicker, and more potent means there's a lot of stuff going on to stop your emails getting delivered to where you want and expect them to go.

Here are a bunch of reasons your emails might not be getting through, even when you're sending legitimate stuff people have asked to receive (and even gone through the double optin process):

1. **First there's the users and their email clients.** Many email clients (readers) come with spam-filtering built in. If the user hasn't gone out of his way to "whitelist" your email, it can get dropped into their spam folder right on their local machine. Imagine: it's got all the way to the other end and been stopped at the front door by a guard-dog the user probably isn't even aware he owns.

2. **Then there's the ISPs (Internet Service Providers).** They have to be *real* careful with spam. See, if someone is on their network and starts sending loads of emails and they even look just *suspicious* then the entire suite of your ISPs' servers can get blacklisted all over the Internet.

   What happens, simplistically, is all the IP addresses of dodgy spam-sending domains are stuck in a database, and MTU (Message Transfer Units) query this database to see if your domain is in there with them. If it is, you can kiss your emails goodbye pretty much until you've begged and whined and somehow convinced the nice people who own the databases it's all been a terrible misunderstanding.

   These people are private individuals and enterprises. You have no legal framework to help you, so it's a Really Good Idea not to get in their databases in the first place.

The Medium

This actually happened to a client of mine some years ago and the mess was *spectacular*.

This, then, is why sending bulk-emails from your own domain is really stupid *unless* you are certified as a legitimate sender by someone like Return Path — www.returnpath.com (previously Habeas). I know people who do this but I prefer to use an autoresponder with a good reputation (Aweber, OfficeAutopilot/ SendPepper, etc.) and let them deal with all this so I can focus on sending profitable emails.

3. **And let's remember the ESPs (Email Service Providers).** These are people like Gmail, Yahoo and Hotmail. They're really hot on spam, and what you might not realise is regardless of your not being in the spam databases above, if their own systems decide you're spamming their users, then they'll stop delivering your emails (and you'll never know).

Thing is, some of the criteria they use to decide this are not obvious or immediately intuitive. For example, if too many people at, say, Gmail don't open your emails then Gmail will slap your emails down for everyone you're sending emails to on that domain.

Thus, all your emails to Gmail users might be marked as spam just because some people aren't opening them. Good autoresponder outfits like OfficeAutopilot will stop sending your emails to people on your list who don't open them for a set period of time to protect your reputation with the ESP.

4. **Finally...** there's *you*. How you write and send your emails is vitally important. Some people think spam filtering is still like it used to be, when they'd check

for certain words.

But no. Like everything else, it's moved on. I use a commercial spam filtering service called SpamHero and they have a list of over two million "rules" they apply to emails — and the list grows daily.

Here are a few things to think about:

i.   Don't spam. Meaning, don't tell them they're getting a free report and then bombard them with crap they weren't expecting. When they opt-in make sure they know they're going to get regular and frequent emails and offers from you.

ii.   Don't buy lists or "gather" them from people. Email only people who have specifically asked you to and make sure you have a record of it. I always use double optin, too, so a new contact has to click a link to confirm the email address he's given be is functional *and* he's giving me permission to send him stuff. Single optin can work, too, but be careful how you to it and what you're selling. If you were selling, say, porn videos, then you'd be nuts to use single optin.

iii. Send from a dedicated IP address. If you're not using an autoresponder firm and your system is hosted on a shared IP address then the other people sharing your address can effectively get *your* emails blocked by sending spam. You all get tarred with the same brush.

iv.   Watch bounces. One red-flag to ISPs and ESPs is a lot of bounced emails from your list (many spammers blitz domains with millions of randomly generated email addresses, knowing some will find a working inbox).

v.   Don't use URLs as anchor text in your emails.
     For deep and subtle reasons this is bad. Just don't
     do it.

vi. Use standard HTML and use "clean" copy. In
     other words, don't copy from Word and other
     word processors straight into your email program
     because you'll include all sorts of control
     characters that make no sense to the system and
     look like you're trying to do naughty things.

vii. Encourage people to "whitelist" your email
     address. Not only will this mean your emails
     get through but it also positively enhances your
     reputation with the ESP and the ISP. Asking
     them to send an email to you from their email
     address can often be enough to do this (so I ask
     newly opted-in contacts to do it in my "welcome"
     emails).

Pay attention to what I've just said and you'll get much
better delivery rates — and that means you'll make more
sales. Better yet, use a reputable autoresponder firm and let
them take care of it all for you.

Offline Marketing

There's no doubting the fact the Internet has been a
Godsend for businesses. Indeed, not only has it made
it possible for a butcher in Basingstoke to sell steaks to
customers in Caracas with everything save the packing and
dispatch being handled by hands-off systems, but it has
actually created brand new businesses which simply didn't
exist before the Internet came along.

The Medium

Small wonder, then, business owners have latched onto it with all the tenacity and tunnel-vision of a drowning man clinging on to a lifebelt. In fact, I've heard more than one business owner say he or she has pretty much stopped any other marketing or promotional activity not based on the Internet. Not only is this incredibly short-sighted in terms of their missing out on potential profits, but it's incredibly dangerous — to the point of being stupid and reckless.

Yes, there are some businesses where it would be very difficult to get any kind of sales at all if they were not online. And there's no real problem with that, because that's no different from a walk-in store having to have buildings to operate from. A good example of this is Mrs. EBG's blog. It would be very difficult to run her little business offline and keep it as simple and profitable. We may experiment with offline advertising at some point, but it would mean going into speciality magazines. This is one reason, of course, we wouldn't focus on this as our main business, even though it has the potential to be much more profitable than it already is. It's too risky and to make the risk acceptable would require more work than we're willing to put in.

But that's really an aside.

My real point is businesses which can get sales and leads from offline sources *should* get sales and leads from offline sources, because not diversifying when you have the opportunity leaves you vulnerable to many things way beyond your control, like power cuts, Internet outages, and even the capriciousness of the owners of the infrastructure we tend to rely on for our online sales: Paypal, Google, and the like. And this is especially true when you have a business in an industry which has hitherto trundled along nicely before the Internet came along (which probably means *most* businesses).

The Medium

So Why the Sudden Downer on the Internet?

Well... I'm actually not on a downer on the Internet at all, as you'll come to see in the following pages. It's more a case I'm on an *upper* on direct mail and offline advertising. And part of *that* is really down to my own hand being forced somewhat by the circumstances in which I find myself.

Fact is, I'm well positioned to be the "go to guy" for small business marketing in Ireland. It would be splendid if I could do this solely by online means in the same way as many friends and clients in my industry have become king of their own hill in other countries. Alas, that's not going to happen, not in my lifetime anyway. Even though there are over 250,000 small businesses in Ireland with 10 or fewer employees (the kind of businesses I'm targeting), there is very little search volume for the relevant keywords. There are businesses out there, and some of them are looking online for the help I can give them, but not enough to make it possible for me to grow my list quickly. There are also niches where there simply isn't *any* online search at all because the problem you're able to solve for people simply isn't top of consciousness for them; or if it is, then the last place they'd look is on this newfangled Internet thing.

A specific example is a highly profitable sub-niche in the Will writing business, for example. It's to do with protecting your Estate from passing to your surviving spouse's *new* spouse on his or her death subsequent to your own, and your children missing out. No one is looking to solve this because they don't know it's possible; worse, even some lawyers don't understand it or know how to prevent it.

On top of all this is the fact not everyone is online.

Even if 75% or 80% or even 90% of people are online and searching for the stuff you sell, the fact remains that leaves

The Medium

25%, 20% or 10% of people who are not.

And when you think in terms of populations of hundreds of thousands and even millions of people, that's an awful lot of business you could be mopping up *as well as* taking advantage of all the cool stuff you can do online.

One Problem with Online Traffic (Especially from PPC and SEO)

This doesn't apply to all businesses but it does apply to a lot. And the thing is, if you're not looking for it, you might miss it. This *could* be something that's damaging your sales and you don't even know it. The people who do notice this are the ones who are religious to the point of obsession about their numbers: they look at this stuff and crunch the numbers to a degree which would drive anyone else insane.

And what they often find is PPC and Search traffic is from people who are just looking for information and, often as a consequence, want to price-shop. Put otherwise, you're advertising in the most crowded place you could possibly find.

The reason you can easily miss this is your conversion rate at the front end to optins can be really high — 20% or more in my experience — but the sales (literally) zero.

A few years ago a client of mine looked into this and found while he was getting 17% optins to his list from Adwords on a high-ticket item, *he made not a single sale.* His results from direct mail, however, were truly spectacular. It *seems* this resistance to online buying is more common in industries where you are dealing with important personal decisions and would traditionally sell in person. These industries seem not to have caught up to the online age, yet (there are some good reasons to retain this old-fashioned approach when you can, too, despite the speed and convenience of automated online

The Medium

systems).

Another good example is the Will writing we just mentioned — most people looking online for Will writing services are not really serious clients because they're looking for a Will as a commodity and so are usually price-buying. We copywriters often have the same problem (which is why we get so many of the "give me your best price because I'm talking to two other copywriters" emails[75]).

It *probably* doesn't apply so much when you're selling off the page, by email, or with online sales letters (although it *may* so it's worth at least entertaining the possibility and checking your numbers).

The wider point here, though, is not only is the *quantity* of online traffic lacking, but the *quality* of it is lacking, too. The corollary to this is *no matter how much money you are making with your online sales, you won't know if you could improve them or add to them or* both *by testing some offline techniques.*

Bottom line: there are some big upsides to offline media, and in particular direct mail.

Direct Mail

Most business owners will swear blind direct mail doesn't work for them. And they are dead right.

The reason they're right and it doesn't work is they do it entirely the wrong way. As a consequence, it's fallen into disfavour in recent times among many business owners because of the Internet. As you are no doubt aware there's a constant search for the next new big thing and right now it's Social Media Marketing. I think one of the reasons Social Media is sticking around so long as there are various different flavours and incarnations of it. Different platforms and so

---

75. And to which the best response is "fuck off".

---

on, and also I think people kind of enjoy it. I'm not going to go into it all again, but just to remind you, it's probably the most ineffective and time consuming way of marketing for most businesses there is and it's amazingly difficult to measure, and that alone means we should be very wary of it. The few people I know who have measured it tell me their results are pretty dire as well. Not to say it can't work so don't just rule out on my say-so and negativity here. Just bear in mind in true 80/20 style there are almost certainly more profitable uses of your time and money.

Five Reasons to LOVE Direct Mail

1. **You have a captive audience.** When someone opens your letter and reads it, or stands there in the hallway reading the postcard they've just picked up off the doormat, you've got their complete and undivided attention.

   That's no guarantee of getting the response you want, but it's a lot better than the short-attention span of someone who's reading your stuff on the Internet — an email comes in, or an Instant Message pings for attention, and you've lost them.

2. **You can target your audience with extreme precision.** Most marketing you do on the Internet is passive. Meaning, you generally wait for someone to stumble across your site and be sufficiently motivated to take action.

   With direct mail, though, it's very easy to acquire lists which are very tightly matched to your specific requirements. I have the set of a publication called *Benn's Media*, and it's packed with endless listings of media publications and outlets on everything from dolls' houses to industrial diamonds.

In other words, it's likely no matter what your niche you can rent a list from a magazine *somewhere* or get yourself a business-boosting mention.

Similarly, there was, once upon a time, a publication called *Lists and Data Sources* (LADS) which is now, sadly, defunct (although I have an old copy). This is just a humongous list of loads of different lists you can rent for direct mail. There are similar publications in the US, and no doubt in other countries, too.

3. **Less competition.** Because all the lemmings are leaping online, there's a good chance your competitors are eschewing offline media and putting all their efforts into online marketing.

    And why not? I mean, it must be the Right Thing to do, because Everyone Is Doing It, and that, by definition makes it Real Smart.

    No.

    Just remember what Earl Nightingale said: *"If you're in a situation and you don't have any clear way forward and want for clear advice, look around and see what everyone else is doing and do the opposite"*.

    If no one in your industry or your competitors in your local area are using direct mail then you are absolutely insane *not* to.

    Even if you balk at sending it as a lead-generation exercise, you should at least be testing it with your existing customers and clients. Not to do so is a dereliction of your duty as the Big Cheese in your business.

4.   **A knock on effect of the last point is what Dan Kennedy calls "anti-search marketing".** What this means is there are people out there who would be interested in buying your products and services if only they knew about them. This means they're not out there actively *looking* for them, so no matter how effective and comprehensive your PPC ad campaigns are, you simply aren't going to get these people as buyers.

The way to find them, then, is by doing the grunt work and using your experience and some logical deduction and guesswork to figure out where you can find them offline and rent the lists to reach them or compile your own; and the way to sell to them is by direct mail, one you have the list.

A good example of this comes from when I started out as a very wet behind the ears copywriter, looking for tech companies to write for. These people weren't *looking* for people like me, so I went to the library, compiled a list of fairly local firms and sent my very first sales letter. One of them landed on the desk of the CEO of one of the firms just as he slammed down the phone on his Project Manager who was lamenting the terrible service being rendered by the incumbent copywriting team. And the rest, as they say, is history.

5.   **It's possible to send more compelling items.** One downside of the Internet is you can send only data. And that's it. That pretty much restricts you to text, images, audio and video.

Sure, they're powerful, but you can also send those by direct mail at low cost, with the added advantage of having their complete attention (ish) if they pop the CD or DVD into the player to listen or watch.

Even if they play them on their computer, they're still less likely to be distracted because it'll be playing in an application as opposed to a browser window which is likely to be just one among many they have open.

But with direct mail, you can send pretty much anything you like with "lumpy mail". In the past I've sent things as diverse as baby carrots and sticks in plastic bags, packets of peanuts, and once I even Fedexed a bowling ball down to Oregon.

Three Tips for Successful Mailings

Of course, making direct mail work for you is predicated on doing it the right way. And therein is the problem: what *is* the right way?

Most business owners have some vague idea of sending "a letter" and somehow magically getting sales from it. Alas, life isn't like that, and if you approach your direct mail in any other way than as a sales process, with all that involves and implies, you're in for a painfully miserable time.

So here are three simple tips to help you create direct mail campaigns that actually work:

1. **Don't let it look like advertising.** Because there's no doubt the buying public is definitely more cynical and resistant to advertising and sales than it once was, and response rates have dropped.

   And if your direct mail looks like an ad or any other marketing piece... then it's going straight in the trash. Moreover, if your direct mail *looks* like direct mail, then everyone from the postie to the ultimate recipient

The Medium

has a good reason for discarding it[76].

See, four things have to happen to make your direct mail successful. It's got to get delivered, opened, read, and acted upon.

So, make your direct mail not only look like something other than advertising, both inside and outside the envelope, but also make it too good to throw away.

Example? Well, maybe use a 'live' stamp and an envelope that doesn't look like it's sent by a business.

You can use handwriting or even labels if you do it right (say, a black or coloured envelope with a label on looks *different*, which is important. Just bear in mind in one test we did, simply using a white envelope instead of a green one with *everything* else being the same, we increased response by 50%).

What we call "teaser copy" on the outside of the package or envelope can help with both delivery and open rates, too. You may have seen this where you get envelopes with things like "Have You Won a Prize?" Printed on the outside; faux stamps like "Private" and "Confidential" serve much the same purpose.

Or you can use 'lumpy' mail putting in objects like pens and keyrings. These not only tend to ensure the envelope is delivered, but that it's *opened*, too.

2. **Be upfront and personal.** Any time you can use someone's name, do so. Our names are important to us and when we see them we pay serious attention to them. One of the most powerful pieces I ever

---

76. In fact, you want to go the other way: *make it too good to throw away*.

The Medium

worked on was a personalised tearsheet[77], where the "article" used the person's name (to the extent they got complaints from recipients, saying "How dare you use my name in the newspaper!?").

Yes, this costs more upfront sometimes, but it's worth it for the long-term ROI (return on investment) of the piece.

3. **Choose your list carefully.** Much as copywriters froth at the mouth when I say this, the most important thing in your mailing is... the list.

   Get your best copywriting team to write the most amazing ad or sales letter they possibly can selling the world's most incredible pork sausage and then send it to a list of vegetarians, and you'll see what I mean.

   The best list you're ever going to get is the list of people who have bought from you before. Don't be an arse and spend your time and money soliciting new business all the time when you could be reaping the harvest you've already sowed.

Conversion Rates and Response Rates

Conversion rates and response rates for direct mail vary wildly depending on the list, the demographic, the offer and, of course the material you send them. I've often seen the figure of 1% bandied about, but I have no idea where that comes from — and frankly it's irrelevant.

Why?

Because... conversion rates for direct mail are deceptive

---

77. A *tearsheet* here is a marketing piece written and printed so it looks like a newspaper or magazine article. They are extremely powerful and typically get three times the response of traditional sales letters.

---

as, indeed, are response rates. The most important measure and the one you really need to be focusing on is your Return on Investment (ROI). And your return on investment is simply the difference between what it cost you to send the mail out and deliver your products and services, and what you brought in from sales (and even this isn't as clear-cut as it seems, as I'll explain in a moment).

So let's look at the two deceptions and why you need to be careful about relying on them and especially careful of marketers and copywriters who like to bandy the numbers about without qualifying them[78].

- **Response rate: is simply the number of people who responded to the ad or direct mail piece.** So if you sent out 1,000 letters and got 20 replies, your response rate is 2%.

- **Conversion rate: is typically the number of people who bought something in response to the ad or direct mail piece.** So if you sent out 1,000 letters and got 20 replies and one sale your response rate is 2% and your conversion rate is 0.1%.

If you're selling "off the page" then your response rate is the same as your conversion rate; if you're doing lead generation (as you really should be in most businesses) then your conversion rate is going to be less than or equal to your response rate.

So, what are considered good response rates and conversion rates? Well, this is the point I'm leading up to: any response or conversion rate that means you have a positive ROI is a good rate. Obvious, yes?

Here are some real-world figures from some of the

---

78. What? Marketers and copywriters lie? Never!

The Medium

campaigns I've done for clients in the past:

- **A 57% response rate and a 46% conversion rate on a £6,000 item.** The ROI was about 36:1 (meaning for every pound my client put in, she got £36 back).

- **A 0.67% conversion rate (we sent them to a web-page where they bought something).** I don't know offhand how many hit the page and *didn't* buy, but that would have been the response rate.

   But this was on a £1,500 purchase and was a 30,000 mailing. So the sales were around £300,000 and the ROI was around 6:1 (it's hard to be exact because I don't have all the figures and there was a complex pricing-model in place).

   Even so, a profit of £250,000 or so for my client... and nice work if you can get it.

So you can see just from these two examples, your ROI is the important thing, not your conversion rate or your response rate. Yes, once you have a winner, you can tweak and test and drive these numbers up, but your ROI is effectively what impacts your bottom line.

A Drop Dead Simple Direct Mail Campaign

Here's a simple direct mail campaign to reactivate existing customers and clients who haven't bought from you for a while. Any business owner can do this:

1. **Send a simple postcard directing readers to a web-page.** On this page you'll have a sales letter making them a special offer of some kind. The offer will have a deadline, or there will be a limited number of widgets available. The postcard itself will be aimed

at the low-hanging fruit, those people who will buy just because you're asking them to at the right time.

2. **About a week later, send a second card.** This may need to be slightly larger and more copy-intensive because you'll be selling yourself to them all over again, just as you did when they first became your customer or client. You'll go through all the reasons they originally chose you above all the others, and reiterate the benefits of doing business with you. You'll also reinforce the limited availability and re-state the offer.

3. **A week after the second card, send a third and final card.** This is your last-ditch attempt and you can afford to be a little edgy with them — because if they don't take action after this, you may as well let them go.

    On this card you'll tell make them the offer once more, push the deadline in their face and tell them if you don't get a response this time, you're going to take them off your list and you'll never make them another offer again. Goes against the grain, I know, but you'll be surprised at how well it works.

    And those who do not respond... let them go.

Print Advertising

Print advertising is a great way to get more business. The problem is most small business owners find it doesn't work for them.

Why?

Well, there are several reasons. First... no one is interested in looking at your pretty ads. Really, they're not. I don't care how gorgeous they are, because there are just three people on the entire planet who care: you, your graphic designer, and your spouse[79].

But readers? Nope.

I hate to be the one to break this to you, but of the endless list of things the readers of the publications your ads are appearing in don't care about, your logo, what you "do", your business, and even you, personally, are probably pretty near the top. Like everyone else on the planet, they are thinking about one person and one person only: themselves.

Anyway, even if they like the pictures and think your ad looks "clever", they can see immediately it's an ad, so they switch off. They ain't interested in buying from you. You've got to do a better job of things than that. But the graphic designers and the creative people in the ad department will be adamant: their ads are "eye catching", make you "stand out" and "get results". But...

- How, exactly, do these people know any of this?
- How do they suppose their ads "get results"?
- How do they measure it all?
- How do they know if anything they do is actually working or not?

The answer is they don't.

Everything they come out with is couched in terms of graphic design best-practice and not marketing best-practice. They may very well be right about everything they say in terms of the design, but what they are dead wrong about is their claims these ads are getting anyone any kind of "results".

---

79. And he or she cares only because it's important you are happy. And if you're not married, then your mother might care, even though she's clueless about what you actually do for a living.

The Medium

This kind of advertising is often called "image advertising", and while it may have a place when you're talking about big firms with multi-billion-dollar established brands like Coca Cola, Virgin, and Reebok, it has absolutely no place in advertising small businesses. They simply can't afford it. Small businesses need to be doing the kind of advertising where the ad hits the paper on the Monday and the very next day money starts dropping into the till. Leave "brand awareness" to the firms with deep pockets and no sense. And stay the hell away from "brand consultants". They're just deep, dark pits waiting for you to throw your money into.

On pages 248 and 249 you'll see two versions of essentially the same ad. It's an ad from one of my Inner Circle Members, Teresa Payne of Parfitt Cresswell Solicitors in the UK. The only real difference between the two is the layout, and the headline. The first one, on the left, is the original, created by a graphic designer. It's aesthetically appealing and is in full colour. The second one is how it looked after I advised her on direct-response best-practice. There's no doubt it's an ugly mofo.

But here's the thing: Teresa ran the ad at the quietest time of year for matrimonial services, most parents staying together until after the kids are back at school. Even so, at the time of writing it's pulled an amazing 2,625% ROI compared to a typical ROI of 500% to 600% with their old-style ads. It would have been interesting to see the results of a true A/B Split, but I really don't think that's necessary.

Alas, this business of ads not working is only part of the problem. Even if we fix that (and if you study Appendix I where we look in detail at copywriting and direct response design, you'll know how easy that is) if we're paying too much to run them, we still won't be making any money.

Most small business owners pump money into an ad in

The Medium

the local press and sit back waiting for the phone to ring and hordes of eager customers to beat an enthusiastic path to their door. After all, the ad rep who called up on the phone said every issue goes to 32,000 local homes and with that kind of readership you can't fail to make a killing, right?

Um… wrong.

There are a number of problems with this idea, and I'll give you the top three now:

1. **Eyeballs are not buyers.** True, most buyers have eyeballs, but they are not one and the same. What you really need to think about is how many of those eyeballs will belong to people who, statistically, are likely to be buyers. For example, if you sell agricultural machinery, there's probably not a lot of point in advertising in a newspaper focusing on Dublin. Similarly, if your business is removing chewing gum from pavements, then I suspect ads in newspapers with a mainly rural readership will vanish without trace or mention.

2. **Most business owners don't know how to write ads.** So they let the advertising department of the publication do it for them. Trouble is, they usually don't know how to write ads, either, so it all becomes a big, embarrassing waste of money.

3. **And in the unlikely event the ad does work, there is usually no way of actually *knowing* how well it's worked.** We'll look at this in a lot more detail in a moment because in some ways it's the most important one of the lot.

I could go on. And on. And on. But by the time I'd reached the end we'd both be old and grey and thoroughly depressed.

So let me boil it down into one, concise statement that'll

The Medium

Why separation and divorce can be a civilised affair

IF you are experiencing the anxiety and loss of a relationship ending and suffering sleepless nights worrying about the future you are not alone.

Almost 50 % of all marriages end in divorce and for many it can be the most traumatic time in their lives. Months and sometimes years are spent deciding whether to separate and then, when the decision has been made, it can take an age to pluck up the courage to take action. Emotions run high and delays are usually down to fear of the unknown and what life will be like after the separation not to mention how you'll cope financially and what you'll tell the kids.

The truth is there is no easy way out. However, the actions you take now and the choices you make will have a big impact on your new life.

Your future is in your hands. You can choose to be reactive to your situation or you can be proactive and take the lead and put a stop to the fighting, anger and hurt.

Divorce and separation is a life changing event and mistakes can be costly both emotionally and financially and you must be prepared to invest to secure your future. To take control you need information and advice from an experienced and trusted advisor which will allow you to make informed decisions about your future.

My dedicated team are hand picked for their experience working with people who are going through a relationship breakdown. They are all members of Resolution which means that they have the legal experience required to give you the best advice and are committed to solving your problem in a conciliatory way if possible - saving you the emotional drain of the legal court battle and the legal fees that go with it. They understand the emotional pressure and stress you are going through and they can help ease the pain and will work with you to achieve the best outcome possible for you to move on with your life.

Our service is confidential, discreet and bespoke to each client and we will never disclose your information to others. Out of hours appointments are available if required.

For a limited period I am offering a selected number of potential clients an opportunity to meet with one of the family solicitors in my team for a free initial consultation to discuss the options available. Due to high demand my team are only able to offer 20 appointments this month and I know that the appointments will book up very quickly.

Choosing the right legal team is key to your emotional and financial future so contact us today to see how we can help you achieve the outcome you want.

The right legal team is key to your emotional and financial future. Family Law Expert Teresa Payne Ref 155301/1

To take control of your future and apply for one of our free consultations just complete this coupon and post it to the address below. Alternatively call or email me today:

Telephone 01753 271 640 or Email family@parfittcresswell.com

Name ....
Addresss ....
....
....
....

Tel. No. ....

Email:...........................

Parfitt Cresswell Solicitors
17/21 Victoria Street
Windsor SL4 1HE
www.parfittcresswell.com

Appointments available in Windsor, Woodley and London

Authorised and Regulated by the Solicitors Regulation Authority No.71480 tell you everything you need to know about print advertising: *it's a big scam filled with dirty little secrets the ad reps really don't want you to know.*

The details differ, but the scam runs pretty much the same way everywhere.

The phone rings or your email inbox makes its funny noise of choice and it's an ad rep from your local rag or some other publication where they run ads. And it just so happens they have a "special promotion" on this week: ads that would normally cost you, say, 300 Groats are only 150 Groats... but it's a time-limited offer, it's Really Popular, and you need to Sign Up Now. Better yet, they tell you, they can let you have seven insertions — meaning they'll run the ad seven times — and knock it down to just 125 Groats per insertion.

What a bargain, eh? A massive 2,100 Groats in advertising for just 875 Groats. You'd be mad to turn them down, wouldn't you?

Actually, you'd be mad to take them up on it but you won't know that unless you've read this book, so you jump at the chance, stump up your 875 Groats (perhaps with additional "creative" costs and maybe an upgrade to full colour) and do the aforementioned sitting back waiting for the phone to ring and hordes of eager customers to beat an enthusiastic path to your door. And when it doesn't work, the ad rep rings again and tells you to be patient... you probably just need to run the ads some more to get more "brand awareness".

Lather, rinse, repeat.

OK, so let's expose the scam once and for all.

Here's what they're really doing: they're selling you space.

A bigger ad costs more money. And a bigger ad using full colour costs even more money. And a bigger ad using full colour run seven times costs heaps of money.

So you can see it's in the ad rep's interests to sell you as

The Medium

many insertions of a big, full-colour ad as he possibly can, especially as often he's paid on commission only.

But by now, since you've been reading this book and paying attention[80], you know what marketing and advertising are really all about: getting a positive ROI and making money for your business. And you've probably also got an inkling big, colourful ads really don't pull as well as smaller black and white ones with an attention-getting headline and lots of compelling copy.

You'll soon realise this means there is a huge conflict of interest in the ad rep's role, a conflict that simply wouldn't be tolerated in any respectable profession (it's about as ethical as politicians approving their own expense accounts).

The Thick Plottens

Something else you'll come up against if you start talking to ad reps is something called the "rate-card". The rate card is basically the price-list for advertising space in magazines and newspapers. Nowadays you can usually download them as a PDF from the publications' websites along with all the technical specifications for ads, how to submit them, and so on.

Great, a price list!

Only... they're a load of old tosh. They are a fiction. They exist only to act as a ridiculously high benchmark against which to compare the "amazing" discounts they offer you on the phone. No one pays rate-card rates except business owners who don't know any better.

How to Get Your Advertising Dirt Cheap

So if advertising is all such a rip off and a scam, why did I

---

80. Haven't you, hmm?

The Medium

say at the beginning of this section advertising is a great way to get more business?

Well, because it is.

Remember, your success in advertising — with all your marketing, really — hinges on it making you more in profits than it costs you in running it.

So, an ad costing you 100,000 Groats to run but leading to 110,000 Groats in sales is cheaper than an ad costing you 100 Groats and leading to only 90 Groats in sales. Ideally you'd want a 100 Groats ad leading to 110,000 Groats in sales, but don't hold your breath.

And there are two ways to increase your ROI and so make your ads pay: increase sales; or decrease costs (and ideally do both at the same time, which is much easier than you think, as you're going to find out).

Here are 7 ways to decrease the cost of your print ads:

1. **Run a smaller ad with fewer (or no) images and lots of copy.** Graphic designers and ad reps tell you to have a big ad with loads of white space and arty-farty images, and they'll use all manner of highbrow language to make the notion sound sophisticated and intelligent. And it's nonsense. White space never sold anything. If it did, then the best performing ad you'd ever get would be just a blank space.

    The fact is the more you tell, the more you sell. Meaning, long copy almost always beats short copy in ads, sales letters, and other marketing pieces.

2. **Don't use colour.** You don't need colour. You may want to experiment with a different colour for the headline, after you have a proven ad that turns a positive ROI, but otherwise start with black and white.

The Medium

If you can't get an ad to be responsive with that, then simply adding colour is not going to have a massive impact. If it does improve things, it will usually be by a small margin only, and you then have to offset that against the extra cost of using colour.

3. **Hammer the reps down on price.** Remember: the rate-card rate is just an in-house placeholder, a hook for the reps to hang their scam on. So don't be shy about snorting down the phone at them and telling them not to be so stupid.

   The first price you hear is, with vanishingly rare exception, not the price you'll end up paying. Simple strategies for doing this range from simply making a stupidly low counter-offer and simply haggling until you meet in the middle; to waiting until (literally) just before the deadline (because any ad space not sold before publication either has to be left blank or filled with content the publication has to find and probably pay for, just as an empty airline seat is worthless once the plane's door has closed. Many reps are remunerated either entirely or partially on commission so ad space going out unfilled can mean a thin month for them). Get this drilled into your noggin: ad reps are not on your side and do not have your best interests at heart. They are sales people and they are selling space. And they want to sell you as much of it as they can at as high a price as they can con you into paying.

4. **Run the ad once only and see how it performs.** Don't buy into the fallacy your ad needs to be "seen" seven times by someone before they'll respond. This fallacy is a conflation of the observation that in general something like 80% of sales are made after 7 or more

contacts between a business and a potential customer or client.

The fact is, if you run your ad once then all other things being equal, the response you get is more or less the response you'll get every time you run it henceforth, with some small variation.

The way the reps have it your response profile would be an upward slope, increasing over time; but this simply is not the way it turns out. If a rep makes this claim to you, just ask them exactly how they know. Your chances of finding one who'll tell you they've tested and measured is about the same as your chances of finding golden coins in goat shit.

5. **Send a cheque "on spec".** What you do is send a cheque for, say, a third of the rate-card price, along with your artwork for the ad you want to run and include a note saying something like, "Here's a cheque for X Groats and the artwork for the ad I want to run. If you agree, cash the cheque and run the ad; otherwise, just tear it up and throw it in the bin". It won't work every time, but every now and then you'll get the cheque cashed and the ad run, especially if you send it close to the booking deadline.

You can even get them to hold the ad "on file" with instructions to run it whenever they get a chance on the condition you won't pay more than, say, 1/3 of rate-card. This is best for tried and tested ads you know get a predictable response but don't get enough to justify running at anything more than the figure you give them and they won't run it that cheaply except under exceptional circumstances.

The Medium

6. **Engage a media buyer.** Media buyers make their living by acting as the middle-man with print publications. And to you, as the advertiser, their services are free — they make their fees from the publications, bizarre as that may seem. The point is a good media buyer will get you space much cheaper than you will get it yourself. Not only do they know the right people to talk to and understand the rules of the game, but they're well-practiced.

A friend of mine negotiates ad space for me and my clients sometimes, and I've known him get an 80% discount in space in a national newspaper before now. His opening gambit when the rep quotes the rate-card back at him is, "What? I think you have the decimal point in the wrong place, mate".

Media buyers will also be able to get you what's called "remnant space" and last-minute placings, which are always cheaper.

7. **Finally... always be prepared to walk away if the price is too high and the rep won't budge on price.** It does happen, occasionally. I know of one media group in England who simply won't negotiate the rate-card at all.

The thing to remember is you must be absolutely ruthless when it comes to making your ads pay their way. No one media publication, or any other single marketing channel or strategy, should have the power to make or break your business.

Don't be sucked in to paying a high price on the promise of "brand awareness". Just bear in mind the next time you go to Dunnes or Tesco they don't take "brand awareness" in exchange for a trolley full of groceries.

They want money. So that's what your ads need to be producing in a measurable and trackable way. And if you can't measure and track the ROI of your ads, you shouldn't be running them. Yes, they might be working... but how can you tell?

At best most ads are glorified business cards; and at worst they are meaningless crap serving only to stroke the already overblown egos of the creative nitwits who design them.

Your typical ad starts with the business's logo and name at the top, maybe has a few words telling anyone who cares how long they've been in business and a list of all the things they "do", and then ends in words to the effect of "and if there's anything you think we might be able to do for you, just pop in and have a wander round".

And all this is usually worked in around some graphic design tomfoolery that's been put together to "get you noticed" and "really get results".

Only... it doesn't.

You know this is true.

Public Relations (PR)

I doubt very much anyone in business does *not* know how publicity in the press and the other media can dramatically boost their business by almost frightening proportions[81]. What you're doing with PR is using the power of existing media networks and channels, like TV, radio and print media to promote your business.

Direct marketing, Adwords, banner advertising, and all the other ways of getting leads and business are fine, but PR

---

81. Frightening because you can find yourself absolutely swamped with work and enquiries and no real clue how you're going to cope with it all.

The Medium

has several advantages business owners often overlook:

1. **It's free.** Or as close to it as you can get. Yes, you have to write the press release and get it to the journalist or producer, but the cost is miniscule compared to the payback if it gets taken up.

2. **It's effective.** One way of looking at PR is it's like one big orgy of testimonials. It's social-proof on steroids. The very fact you're in the media is self-evident proof you're an expert. That's baloney and a complete non-sequitur; but, hey, no one ever lost money by realising the human race is not rational.

3. **It's efficient.** One short and easily written press release can set in motion an avalanche of publicity and media attention worth (literally) millions in terms of advertising. I once got a short mention in an obscure part of the Irish Times and it gave a huge boost to my traffic and my optins; the monthly article I used to write for a local rag was also worth tens of thousands of Euro in business, plus it had the more intangible effect of making me the local marketing expert (and it took me 30 minutes a month to write each one).

4. **It's fast.** Paul Hartunian recounts the story of a press release he sent out once and got a phone call within 13 seconds or something like that. Obviously that's disgustingly fast, but if your press release catches a journalist's eye, then he or she is likely to get back to you immediately, especially if you've put a little scarcity in there (remember, a press release is just a sales pitch for an interview, so you can and should use all the usual marketing stuff in them).

So, we've seen what we want and why we want to do it...

The Medium

but how do we go about it?

How to Become the Media Darling

The first thing to realise is you're already an expert and you don't need any special qualifications to be wheeled out in front of the camera or featured in the newspaper. The fact you know more about your business than the average Joe in the street *makes* you an expert.

The second thing to realise is the media experts you see are no more expert than you are, give or take. The *only* difference between you is they're in the limelight and you aren't. And getting yourself in the limelight is as simple as persuading a journalist or a producer that you have information their audience would find interesting, entertaining and informative. You most commonly do that with a press release.

A press release is simply a short-hand way of telling someone in the media you have a story for them. And this is where most business owners get it horribly wrong. You see, they make the press release all about *them and their business*. But journalists doesn't care about that. All they care about is pleasing the editor and filling the pages with interesting stuff. You aren't even on the radar.

So your press release must be a sales pitch, not for your products and services but for the notion that you have a story the journalist can use to make his or her life easier. We'll look at this in detail in a moment, but the gist of it is your press release should read like any other sales piece, in that it conforms to the AIDA formula[82], has a headline, is benefit-rich and ends up with a call to action (you can even put in scarcity, and it works like a charm).

---

82. Attention, Interest, Desire, and Action. And oldie but a goodie, because it *works*.

The Medium

What the journalist wants is to look good to his or her readers, and if you can make that happen, you've got a friend for life (and this all applies to TV and radio the same as it does to print media).

The Magic of a Press Release

Your press release is really a lead generation device aimed at capturing the interest and response of the media guy with the "back end" product being... *you*. It's important you get this. Because if you think it's about selling your products and services, you're making a big mistake. Journalists and other media professionals will spot that a mile away and treat you like a diseased rat. But you don't have to treat your desire for publicity like the proverbial elephant in the room. Journalists know the score, and they're happy to scratch your back if you'll scratch theirs. What they won't do is give you column-inches just to promote your own agenda without giving the readers something worth reading. They are busy professionals. Treat them with respect and help them do their jobs, and they'll respond in like fashion.

Like any sales piece, your press-release must start with a headline to capture the interest of the media guy and at least get him to read the first line of your release proper.

Why?

Because if he doesn't read the release, you don't get publicity, right?

Right.

So as with all headlines, your release's headline must promise some benefit to the media guy reading on. Remember these people are after material to fill their pages or programmes that's going to interest their audience. If you promise them that, they'll read on all right. And here's the key to all this: the media deal with news. The kind of

The Medium

headline that's going to get you immediate attention is one tying you in to what's already top of the guy's mind.

So, for instance, if you're a tax accountant and the government have revealed yet another raft of tax-rises, a headline like "Outspoken tax accountant discovers 7 unique ways local businesses can legally avoid the latest tax rises", is likely to get someone's attention.

Another useful "trick" is to take a contrarian view to the common wisdom. So if the general feeling is the tax rise is bad for business then a headline with the opposite slant - that it's *good* for business is again likely to get you noticed. Of course, make sure you can back up your statements if you *do* get interviewed (and also be prepared for having a thick skin - if you go against the grain you *will* piss people off and they *will* criticize you, laugh at you, and call you dumb).

Then the body of your release should have three main parts:

An Up-Front Summary.

The reason for putting this in the release is to tell the journalist what your release is all about. Media people are notoriously busy and overworked — that's why they'll *love* you for giving them a well-written press release that hands them a great story on a plate. But it's a two-edged sword. They *won't* take time to wade through a page of impenetrable crap and try to fathom some meaning from it.

A neat shortcut here is to pose it as a problem. For example, if you're selling wooden floors you might (after a suitable headline, which itself, say, ties in with some recent media coverage of how the incidence of allergies is increasing in kids), begin with something like this:

"A new study has shown what practically every

The Medium

parent already knows to be true: allergic reactions in children, some of them life-threatening, are up by 36% from just 30 years ago. Just what has gone wrong with our kids' health? And what can we do to save it?"

Now, I don't know what the exact numbers are, but you see what I'm getting at, right? The whole thing is now presented as a problem... to which you can later (subtly!) offer the solution.

Your Credentials.

This is a brief section where you credentialise yourself and give the media guy a reason to take you seriously. Here's a common misconception: you are not an expert. And it's wrong. You are. You might not be a Nobel Prize winner in whatever it is you're in business doing, but unless you're a complete numpty, you're an expert.

What's more, you don't need permission from anyone to appoint yourself as one (and if you're mad enough to be in a regulated profession where you need some sort of licence from the powers that be to practice, then you can still appear in the media as an expert without treading on anyone's toes or breaking any rules).

The reason for setting yourself up as the expert is to invoke Cialdini's *"Authority Principle"*. One way to give yourself authority status is to be perceived to be an expert.

How do you give yourself expert status in your media guy's eyes? Give him a reason for accepting you as someone in the know by pointing to some relevant achievement. And it doesn't have to be anything spectacular like a bloody Nobel Prize in bricklaying!

The Medium

Examples:

1. **You've written a book.** Easier than it sounds, anyone can (and every business person should) do this. Why? Because it instantly credentialises you as — literally — the guy or gal who "wrote the book" on the subject. There's a reason for that saying, you know — don't trivialise it because it's a trite and hackneyed cliché.

2. **You've written articles on the subject.** Again, easier than it sounds (many free newspapers are crying out for articles as filler). Hell, perhaps not so much now, but certainly in the past and to some degree today, even having a website "dedicated to X" gives a certain amount of kudos. Stupid, yes; but true, nevertheless.

3. **You've written a "free report" on the subject.** Or you're the author of such-and-such a newsletter, dedicated to informing people about your chosen area of business.

Those are just three things, right off the top of my head. The point is you're not credentialising yourself by just being in that business. You need to have something to set you apart from everyone *else* in that business. It doesn't have to be anything spectacular - just something different enough for the media guy to take you seriously.

So, for our second section, we might then say something like this:

> *"But according to Perry Stalsis, author of the 'Living Allergy Free' newsletter, and the owner of the acclaimed 'Living Allergy Free' website, the answer is surprising. Stalsis first stumbled across the secret to living allergy free when his own son, Henry,*

developed a severe reaction to their pet anaconda. Three years later, after extensive research and study, Henry is living allergy free thanks to a simple system anyone can follow"

See, this is just a first pass, but it has all the elements. It credentialises Perry, and gives the whole story a human (and reptilian) interest angle.

You can afford to be a little bit bolder than this. For instance, bullet points often work well (especially "blind" bullets of the "just this one daily exercise can cut down your allergic reactions by 37%" variety).

Call to Action.

As with any sales piece (and never forget your press release is a sales piece, even if it's selling *you* and not your products or services), you want a call to action. In your press release the call to action is for the reporter to call you and request an interview.

It's not hard. Just bear in mind what you're trying to achieve, the benefit to him for letting you achieve it *and* add a bit of scarcity in there, too. Scarcity never hurts.

Remember the old saying, "the one most prepared to walk away from any negotiation holds all the power". So, your call to action might look something like this:

"Perry Stalsis, has helped thousands of kids suffering with allergies break free from their misery and begin to lead happy, comfortable lives once more.

Mr. Stalsis is an outspoken, irreverent and amusing advocate of 'natural' allergy remedies and guarantees an outrageously successful and interesting interview. To arrange an interview call him at XXX-XXX-

> *XXXX as soon as possible. His schedule is always*
> *full and last summer, the height of the allergy season,*
> *he turned away over 130 interview requests."*

As you can see, there's no hype, although there *is* a guarantee and a hint of scarcity.

The benefit to the journalist? Having someone (who's in demand) who also gives an "outrageously successful and interesting interview".

If you make the audience happy, you'll make the journalist happy.

And that, in a nutshell, is it.

As you've seen, it's not terribly different from writing any sales piece — the two main differences are what you're selling and maybe toning down the language somewhat.

Other than that, it's the same as any sales piece (and that's not surprising, because you're just working to get someone to buy into your ideas).

And Then There's Content Writing

Many local publications are crying out for quality content. Remember: every issue they print has to contain enough quality information not only to fill the pages but also to keep the readers, and thus the advertisers, coming back for more in the next issue.

Needless to say, this can be stressful and somewhat trying for the publisher and the journalist.

This is why you'll often find local publications will gladly take your editorial material and print it as a regular column, especially if it's good quality and is useful and informative for the readers. They'll be even happier when they don't have to pay you for it.

I know, I know, every writer out there will hate you for

"writing for free", but screw them, and in any case it's not true. Because you are getting huge exposure, and while you can't have too overt a call to action in your piece, you get instant expert status.

As I mentioned above, I used to write a monthly piece for a local rag. It took me maybe 30 minutes a month, got me essentially a full page of advertising for free, and brought in a €30,000 chunk of work plus some other bits and pieces. And it also gave me content to reuse elsewhere *plus* that coveted expert positioning.

Referrals

Referrals are probably the second-easiest bit of business you'll ever do, coming right on the heels of people you've already done business with.

The problem is that while we love referrals and know how easy they are to sell to, very few of us have a system for asking for them. That's partly because we don't think to ask, and partly because we're a bit embarrassed by it, and we don't like to ask, even if we think to. But it's actually very easy, and, if you do it right, not in the least objectionable, hard-sell or imposing on your customer or client.

What's more you don't necessarily have to offer any kind of reward, other than that of recognition. It's nice if you can offer something, say a fancy meal for two for every 10 people they refer to you, but in some situations you can't do this for legal or ethical reasons. In those cases you'll be surprised at how well people respond to simple "leader boards" and a maybe a special mention in your monthly newsletter.

As for asking for referrals, here's the best way I've found to do it: at the beginning of your relationship, it's perfectly reasonable to say words to the effect of, "I grow my business mostly by referrals from people I've done a great job for. If I do a great job for you, I would hope and expect you will send people to my business so I can give them the same kind of great experience."

Note the important words: "hope and expect".

In other words, set the scene even before you do business.

There's a dentist in Australia called Paddi Lund. You can't just drop in on Paddi. You have to be referred by an existing patient.

And one of the things he does is go through a kind of set interview with you, where he tells you what you can expect from him, and then he tells you what he expects from you. One of those things is he expects you to refer patients. After a short period of time, when you've settled in, done the business and had some results, no matter what you're doing, it's perfectly okay to say, "We said in the beginning you would refer some people to me. Here's a piece of paper. I would like, by the end of next week, the names of five people you know who you don't mind me calling."

You would have this in your "what you can expect from me" bit, and would have words to the effect, "I expect you to give me the names of five people I can contact to do business with."

Let me repeat: there's nothing wrong with saying that.

It's part of your terms of business.

Joint Ventures

Joint Ventures are an excellent way of harnessing the power and potential profits dormant in other businesses' lists. I'm not going to go into the mechanics of how to do all this because it's a fairly advanced topic and for most people it's a good idea to have some solid marketing experience under

The Medium

your belt before you attempt it.

But the principles are simple to understand, and we'll cover them now.

Joint ventures on the internet are very popular and common; in fact I find them so common they've become almost incestuous and often quite nauseating. You know, you get an email from Billy Brylcreem saying, "I just got off the phone with Oily Ollie and I've twisted his arm to give you a great deal on his really hot new product... you need to get in fast because this'll sell out once word gets around. It's a foolproof way to rake in $100, $200, even $1,000 a day on autopilot". The really scary thing is that kind of shit is so easy to write, and there's a certain demographic that just gobbles it up like a pig scoffing truffles.

So, one of the reasons I don't like a lot of JVs you see floating around on the Internet is you've got this small group of "uber-gurus" who are always flogging each other's products, and it all gets a bit incestuous, especially since a lot of it is utter crap. But, there's no doubt they can be profitable and ethical, and this is especially true if you broaden your horizons from the Internet and think about your local area.

In a local area, for instance, businesses are often synergistic. A beautician, hairdresser, suntan place, and even a clothing store — a women's clothing store in particular — are not a million miles apart. Wedding photographers and bridal boutiques are not a million miles apart. Carpet cleaners, decorating places, landscape gardeners and builders are not a million miles apart.

They'd do very well not just to refer business if someone asks, but to have a process in place whereby, for instance, a painter & decorator will write a letter to his customer list promoting someone else's synergistic business. It's as simple as a cover letter, and underneath it is a letter from a furniture

The Medium

maker, carpenter, someone who cleans the windows, or someone who lays carpets.

You could say something like, "Why is your painter & decorator writing to you about a carpet cleaner? Well, if you want your house to look nice and you just had it decorated perhaps your carpet has collected some marks over the years and is not going to show your newly decorated home in its best light now. It would be a shame to spend all that money and not have the last polish, so to speak. And that's why I'm writing to you today — I know Kevin the Cleaner who's the best carpet cleaner in Ireland. I recommend him... and I don't recommend anyone else."

All it takes to do this is a bit of imagination and perseverance. Because a lot of business owners, if you say this to them, will say, in effect, "You're up to something. You're trying to steal my customers. This won't work". That's fine. It's not something they've come across before and they don't have the same view of marketing and business you do. To them it simply sounds too good to be true. So out of every 20 you ask, you might find two who'll take you up in it.

We've already seen how if you have a list of buyers' contact details in your database you have your own personal little goldmine because you can continue to offer them products and services until the cows come home. It's like a licence to print money.

But now think about this: what else might they buy if offered the chance, even though it might be something you don't sell? And then think what stuff of yours might the buyers on other people's lists buy from you?

The Medium

Summary of Chapter 6

1. **There are dozens of ways of getting new business.** You should be testing *all* of them.

2. **If you rely too heavily on any one means of getting new business, you are extremely vulnerable.** I have personally seen businesses vanish without a trace when their one favoured way of getting business was taken away from them.

3. **Every business should be online.** But no business should be solely online.

4. **There's no such thing as free traffic on the Internet.** Paid traffic is far more reliable, controllable, and more highly qualified. If you allow your business exist on the good will of big corporations like Google, then you are a fucking idiot.

5. **Offline marketing, especially direct mail and print advertising are woefully underused by business owners.** With everyone focusing their attention online, they are leaving vast riches for you to pick up offline, no matter what business you're in.

Chapter 7

Getting It All Done

I hope this is going to be the shortest chapter in the book. The first reason is it would be ironic if my suggestions on how to get loads of stuff done in a short time took up a lot of space and required a lot of time to assimilate it.

And the second reason is it's actually all pretty simple.

That said, it's not easy because it's hard work, emotionally uncomfortable, and often counterintuitive. It'll also piss off the very people who are getting in your way right now.

So you wanna know the big secret of how The EBG gets so much stuff done and done so effectively?

Well, it's pretty simple really.

And not a secret at all.

In fact, it breaks down into just a few simple steps anyone can copy (but very few actually will, because it's like, work, you know?).

First, focus on what's important. You probably know this best in its "80/20" incarnation.

Secondly, know where you're going. This does not necessarily mean you have to have some humongous world-changing goal like the shit-eating "gurus" say you have to. I don't, and I do just fine.

Thirdly, have a plan to get there. No plan? Then you might as well not bother, because you're just going to drift around randomly. And on the ocean of life you'll find far more rocky shores than safe-havens.

Fourthly, have a strategy for implementing the plan. I know loads of people with big plans and no idea how to carry it out. Sad. Little wonder everyone laughs at them and calls them rude names.

And fifthly, have the nous, balls, and wherewithal for doing it all (clue: it's not willpower. Because willpower is a poor, misunderstood little thing that just wants to be loved and cuddled).

You Don't Have to Have Big Goals

Earl Nightingale came out with a lot of smart stuff.

And one of the things to make a huge difference in my life and then the lives of others I've passed it on to is the idea not everyone is "goal driven".

That's huge.

Because you know as well as I do the "gurus" have a wankfest over goal-setting and how, usually, it's "got" to be to own a private jet and make shedloads of money because that's how success is measured.

Bullshit.

Don't get me wrong: having money is great. And it's definitely better than having none.

But if you make that your goal just because someone says you should or you think it's what everyone ought to have as a goal, then it's highly likely two things will happen:

1.   You'll most likely fail.

2.   You'll be miserable, regardless of whether you fail or

not.

Moreover — and this is what Mr. N pointed out, much to my Enlightenment — some people simply don't have big humongous life-swallowing goals at all. I'm one of them. There are things I want to do, but there is no One Big Thing consuming my thoughts, dreams and desires.

He called people like me "river people", because we enjoy navigating the river of the topics we find interesting, and while we might have "islands" we want to visit as small and numerous goals, there's no one final destination we hanker for (in fact for reasons I'll explain later if you're lucky, I suspect most people are "river people" and many of the problems we all have is we don't realise it). So here's a bit of homework for you: do whatever it is when you like to think and have a long look at yourself and figure out whether you're really a "river person" or a "goal person".

Are you following wealth, fame, and success measured in someone else's terms because you want to... or because you've been told that's the way it should be? That's the trap I fell into. Well, no: I happily and enthusiastically dived into it headlong, so if you've done it too, then you're in good — or Evil — company. Here's the thing: when I realised I was a "river person" and not a "goal person" and stopped chasing "success" and the money, it meant I got into "flow"... so more success and more money poured in anyway.

Weird, eh?

Alas... being a "river person" doesn't release you from the responsibility of setting goals, unless you want to spend your life randomly bouncing around like a pinball.

It just changes how you go about it.

I found if I set specific and reasonably small goals no more than 12 to 24 months in the future I got the best results. I

Getting It All Done

know from experience any one project I'm engaged in starts to drag after a couple of years, so there is absolutely no point in my setting a big goal that's going to take me 5 years to complete. I'm sure there are people out there who will tell me they can "fix" me with NLP or somesuch voodoo, but I'm really not interested. I like the way I am. If I didn't, I'd change it.

The Big Willpower Myth

Why do I say it's a myth? Well, the myth is anyone can do anything if only they have the willpower to do it.

I think that's all balls. Anyone who's tried to diet hard and been ravenously hungry for days on end will soon tell you how it can grind you down (and this is one reason people fail with crash diets).

See, willpower evolved more for those shit-or-bust moments where you're generally operating at an exponentially higher level of power and effectiveness than you do ordinarily. And very few people can do that indefinitely.

Trouble is, we're often badgered and browbeaten into the mindset that you've not only got to be working hard, but you've got to be grinding it out, too. To be sure, there are times when you have to pull an all-nighter, and that's when willpower comes into its own.

But you're going to get better results long-term by being a little more cerebral about where you apply the effort. Just one more reason for playing the game the 80/20 way: you can get more done with less effort, and leave the constant grind to others. Bruce Lee once said, "I fear not the man who has practiced 10,000 kicks once, but I fear the man who has practiced one kick 10,000 times."

Meaning: get really good at a small number of important

things, and place your focus there.

What's Important? What's Urgent?

As we've already seen most of us are wasting most of our time. We might sit at our desks for eight hours a day and we might be busy all that time... but still at the end of the day we find we've not actually *done* very much. We even say to our colleagues and spouses, "I don't know where the time goes. I've been busy working, but I haven't got anywhere".

Congratulations: you've just discovered for yourself the difference between activity and achievement, something we mentioned earlier. And to look at this in a slightly different way we might say you've been confusing *important* with *urgent*. We often use these two words synonymously, but they have very different meanings.

For example, regardless of what you think about The Revenue, filing your tax returns is *important*. Because if you don't do it, then, ultimately, men with guns will come and drag you off to prison. But if you keep your books neat and tidy and get all your paperwork in well on time, then it's never urgent. Start early and have a schedule for completing everything, and it can be almost painless.

Now imagine you leave it all to the last week, and you've been less than diligent in keeping things shipshape. If you don't file on time you're going to get a fine, and face an audit.

All of a sudden it's become *urgent*.

Of course, although in this case the task is both urgent *and* important, this is just a coincidence. Many things are urgent without being important.

But in the context of our business what *is* important?

Well, that's kind of up to you to decide, because you've got your own ideas, goals, and aspirations, but to me something's important only if:

1. It's taking me closer to one or more of my goals.

2. Taking care of it in good time is going to stop it becoming *urgent* at some point in the future.

Note these two criteria are not mutually exclusive: getting new business might be important because it takes you towards a goal you have, but if you become too lackadaisical about it and you wake up to find you have no customers or clients one day, then it's now urgent.

Below you'll see a simple diagram to help us understand all this. I don't take credit for it, because I've seen it illustrated this way before, but I don't know who did it[83].

---

83. So if you know... by all means tell me and I'll give him or her full credit in the next edition of this book. Mrs. EBG says it's Stephen Covey.

Getting It All Done

As you can see we've got four numbered quadrants and two axes. Here's what they mean in this diagram:

- Q1 — things that are *important* but not *urgent*. An example of this is getting your tax returns filed in good time, as we've already seen.

- Q2 — things that are *important* and *urgent*. Like... leaving your tax returns until the last minute.

- Q3 — things that are *urgent* but not *important*. Although your kids will strongly disagree, the TV going on the blink just before the latest episode of *Stars in Their Eyes* or whatever[84].

- Q4 — things that are neither *urgent* nor *important*. Pretty much anything you ever do on Facebook and Twitter.

Q1: The Sweet Spot

It doesn't take a genius, Evil, Bald, or otherwise to see our most effective use of our time is when we're working in Q1 on *important* but not *urgent* tasks. This is primarily stuff we know is going to move our businesses forwards and make us money. One rule in my own business, for example, is the first couple of hours of every working day I *always* work on my own long-term projects, no matter what other work is waiting. This is all Q1 work and it pays me back enormously.

For the sake of our profits and often our sanity, too, it's vital we avoid urgent tasks whenever we can. If you can prevent something from becoming urgent by tackling it sooner rather than later, then you're an idiot if you don't do it.

So what kinds of things are important and while they might not take our businesses forwards, leaving them to

---

84. I don't have a TV so I'm guessing here.

Getting It All Done

become urgent can cause havoc and cost us a fortune?

Well, one example would be, say, finding my passport and printing off my boarding card for a Ryanair flight. Sounds silly and mundane, but it's got to be done. If I *don't* take care of it in good time and leave it, say, until the night before my flight's due to go, and discover I can't find my passport... then all hell can break loose, because who knows what missing that flight might cost? Sure, I can and do delegate much of this stuff to Mrs. EBG, but the principle is the same: *she* doesn't leave it to the last minute, either, and for the same reasons.

Q2: The Easily Avoidable Quicksand

What I just gave you was actually a classic Q2 scenario: something that's both urgent and important. It's not only got to be done, but it's got to be done *right fucking now!* Any time we spend in Q2 is stressful, usually unproductive, and often costly in terms of time and money. Worst of all, perhaps, with rare exception, any work we do under this kind of stress is hurried and not our best work. If it's client-work, we're not serving them as we should be[85]; if it's our own work, then we're short-changing ourselves. And yet it's almost always avoidable by even a small effort put into planning.

So why, then, do we business owners seem to spend most of our time sinking into the implacable quicksand of Q2? I think there are a number of reasons, but the chief ones are a reluctance to tackle unpleasant or difficult tasks, and the confusion of activity with achievement. These two things together conspire to keep us busy doing nothing while those important tasks we *should* be doing slowly become urgent.

---

85. That said, one of my best ever pieces of work was rattled out in a blind panic when I realised the copy date for the full-page ad I was supposed to be writing was later that day and I'd forgotten all about it. This was more luck than judgement, and I don't recommend it as a strategy to anyone.

Getting It All Done

The easiest way to stay out of the demoralising and enervating mire of Q2 is to focus on Q1.

Q3: The Emotional Train Wreck

If you've ever had the misfortune to watch a soap opera like East Enders or Coronation Street, or you've seen any of those ghastly "reality TV" programmes where you swap wives and shit, then you've seen what Q3 looks like.

Newsflash: there's a good chance you're spending some of your own life in your own soap opera by getting involved in the emotional train wreck of Q3: things that are not important but have a screaming urgency about them you feel impossible to ignore[86].

And you know the most common source of Q3 meltdowns?

Other people's problems — clients', colleagues', friends', and family's.

Here's a typical and example of what can happen if you're not careful from my own business[87]. Towards the end of 2012 I had an email from someone who'd been referred to me, and he was in a blue funk. His business was in dire straits. He'd lost all his Internet traffic and had no other way of driving business. As a consequence his sales were South of the basement, and he thought I was the man to make it all go away for him. And indeed I could have done. Fixing his problems would have meant a lot of work but it was all fairly straightforward. But while it could be done piecemeal, it'd have to have been done *fast*. Hence his panic and urgency.

But the thing is, it wasn't my problem. Without going

---

86. I know people who actually live their entire lives in an existential version of Q3. No kidding. Their lives seem to be an unending sequence of implosions, explosions and utter fuckups. It can be most entertaining at times, especially if you follow the golden rule: Don't Get Involved.

87. And this fellow isn't even a client, and never will be.

Getting It All Done

into details, his business is where it is because of his own misjudgement and lack of foresight and planning. The mistake he's made is one I and others have been warning anyone who will listen about for a long time: don't rely on "free" Google traffic for your business.

Now, for me the answer is simple: desperate as you are, *your* lack of planning and foresight is not *my* emergency[88]. This is a surprisingly difficult attitude to adopt and maintain, because most people have a natural tendency to be sympathetic to and helpful in the plight of others. And I'm only human, after all. But the alternative would be for me to drop everything else I was working on or spend *my time* reorganising and rearranging *my* work and business to accommodate *his* urgent problem[89]. Not only would that wreak havoc in my own business, but it also means I'd be cheating my *current* clients because they would be pushed to the back of the queue by someone else's bad judgement.

You might think this is an extreme example, but it's not. Phone calls, emails, people "dropping by" with a "quick question": they are almost always interruptions from people who want something from you and expect you to drop everything and help them out with *their* problem. And very often these are problems they could and would easily solve themselves if you weren't there to fall back on.

Classic example: someone in the office has a problem with some software and he knows you're pretty sharp with

---

88. Even less politely put as "Sad, but not my problem". I have had several people banging on the door of my business with much the same problem, and they always get the same answer.

89. And I forgot to mention he told me he had no money to pay me at the time, so any remuneration I could expect would depend on his success. Moreover, while this is perhaps cynical of me, I rather suspect *I* wouldn't have been paid until all his other financial problems were solved.

Getting It All Done

it. Before you know it you're sitting at his desk giving an impromptu Microsoft Word training session; or, the phone rings and it's your spouse... the car won't start and she wants you to ring the AA or the garage (and the answer "why can't you do it yourself?" is not conducive to a leg-over at the weekend).

In many ways, I think Q3 activities are even worse than Q4 ones, because at least Q4 activities have the legitimacy of actually having to be done, even if you could almost always have avoided the problem by better planning and structuring of your work.

Every day I guarantee you are being interrupted by other people's problems and emergencies and they are coming to you expecting *you* to take responsibility for *their* emergencies.

And they succeed in doing this *only* because *you* allow it.

Q4: Fatuous Farting About

Let me be as diplomatic and tactful as I can: if you tackle something that's urgent but not important and sacrifice productivity for it, then you're an idiot.

Q4 holds all the pointless, inane, worthless detritus we have floating around in our lives clamouring for attention. In other words, anything in Q4 we should reserve for our leisure time *if* we bother with it at all. We can do it outside of work or in the breaks we take. And with this I'd lump almost all of your Social Media Marketing activity because, you know, most of it simply isn't working (if you could measure it, you'd know this). Liking shit on other people's Facebook pages, posting inane comments about your new hat on your business page, and Tweeting about a great blog post you read (when you should have been fucking *working*) are not *work*. Don't kid yourself they are.

Stuff in Q4 is recreation. Nothing wrong with it, I guess, but there's a time and a place for it, and when you're supposed to be working and focusing on Q1 activities ain't it.

Here's What Works for Me

1. **Find Out where You Are Now (optional).** For the next week I just want you to note down every 30 minutes what you've been doing. Be brutally honest and *non-judgemental*. The point of this is at the end you'll see exactly how bad you are at getting stuff done.

   From this list do your best to label things as we saw in the 4 quadrants e.g. "urgent but not important".

   For the sake of this exercise, *important* means it's an activity that takes your business forwards, and it's *urgent* if it has to be done *now*.

   By the end of it... I sincerely hope it causes you pain.

   Then...

2. **Decide on your 12- to 24-month Goal (you can also do this while you're doing the exercise above).** It doesn't have to be a compelling goal — it can be an island in the river, for example.

   But you do need to have something significant you want to achieve in the next 12 to 24 months in mind. I do recommend an amount of money at least as a starting point because it's something we all understand and tends to enable any other goal you might have.

3. **Then determine what you'd need to get you to that goal.** For example:

   i.   A certain number of clients.

    ii.   A certain number of subscribers on your list.

    iii.   A certain number of website visitors.

    iv.   A certain number of sales.

    v.   etc.

These are the "80/20 tasks" you should be focusing your energy on in the main.

4. **Figure out what you need to do each month to reach that goal over 12 to 24 months.** For example:

    i.   Research 100 keywords and create Adwords ads for them each month.

    ii.   Go to 30 client meetings a month.

    iii.   Make 300 sales a month.

    iv.   Have a list growing by 1,000 subscribers a month.

    v.   Send out one postcard to your list each month.

    vi.   etc.

5. **Now figure out what you need to do to make these things happen every month.** For example:

    i.   Write 30 emails and send them to generate interest.

    ii.   Make 200 telesales calls to people who respond to your emails to get the appointments.

    iii.   Create 4 new products or offers and put them in front of your list.

    iv.   etc.

6. **Break this down into weekly and even daily activities.** In other words continually ask yourself "what do I need to do every day and week so by the

end of the month I've done what I need to do to stay on track?".

While you'll find your own system, I recommend at this early stage you write things down in detail at the level of a month. In other words have your main plan as "what I want to do each month" and then take each day as it comes using the 7-step strategy below.

Ultimately, though, you're going to get to the point where you might know what you're going to be doing (within reason) on any given day several weeks hence.

7. **Now, imagine you were to focus on these activities to the exclusion of all else and ask yourself where your business would be in 12 to 24 months' time.** It's highly unlikely you can do this to the exclusion of all else, but however much time you have to put into your business, you're now going to commit to splitting it 80/20 in favour of the important stuff above and the other, trivial stuff, is going to be done in the 20% of the time.

The more time you can put into this, the more you can achieve. But even if you can put in only 2 or 3 focused hours a day, then I am certain you will achieve *more* in those 2 or 3 hours in terms of taking you towards your goals than you would normally do in a normal 10-hour working day.

I'm afraid this is the bit where there are no shortcuts.

You've simply got to knuckle down to doing the stuff instead of playing on Facebook!

Getting It All Done

A Daily Strategy for Success

Most of us spend 80% of our time doing nothing very much. Instead of that we're going to switch things around: if you have 10 hours available to work every day you're going to take the important things you've identified above and focus on those for eight of those 10 hours. The other two hours you can tackle the unimportant things, like admiring your sister-in-law's new hat on Facebook.

And here's how to prioritise your tasks and structure your day.

1. **Write down the seven most important things you need to do that day.** I tend to do mine the night before because I like to get up in the morning, sit at my desk and get straight into it without having to think too much about what the day's got in store for me. I like to hit the ground running.

   If that works for you do it that way, if it works another way do it another way. I say seven things because most of us can deal with seven (plus or minus two things) in our head — we can grasp that kind of number. If you want to do eleven, do eleven. If you want to do nine, do nine. If you want to do five, do five.

   I don't care, no-one else cares either — it's important that it works for you, and if it doesn't, no-one else cares — find what works for you and use it. And you might have urgent things when you start doing this, but they will shortly become ironed out.

2. **Rank the tasks in the order you need to do them.** The question you need to ask is, "Is this task going to take me towards where I'm going or not?".

And then if you've got, say, seven tasks the next question for each one is, "How far or how quickly is this task going to take me to where I'm going?".

By doing this you're going to rank them in the order of their importance to you in reaching your goals.

3. **When you've got them in the order you want the asks in, pick the one that's going to take you towards your goal faster or more profitably or more effectively...** and start on it.

    And then you stay with it, you keep doing it and you stay with it until you've got as much of it done as you possibly can. You stick with it until it's done or you really genuinely can't get any further.

    And I'm talking about show-stoppers — say you're doing client work and it's a very high value activity. At that moment the most important thing you can do to get you towards your goal is to finish this bit of work for a client, and you get it so far but you have to stop because you need something from him or her (maybe approval, maybe an image, maybe some copy or something like that).

    Well, then you stop and go onto No. 2 in your prioritised list of tasks. But really do put in your best effort to get that one thing done. And if that's the only thing that you get done that day, even if you only get half of it done, that is success because it's a worthy goal and it's progressive realisation of that goal.

Of course, you may not finish all of your daily tasks using this system but if you don't finish them with this one I do find it pretty hard to see how you will finish them with any other.

Getting It All Done

And certainly at least this time you're putting your time and effort on those ultra-high-value tasks that are taking you to where you want to be.

Finally, something else I've found to be invaluable is good health and physical fitness. No, don't worry... I'm not about to go off on some quasi-religious rant about arcane diets and weird exercise routines.

I describe my own regime and how and why I came upon it in more detail in Appendix II, but in short: *everyone* should be pumping iron and eating well[90]. Too much sloth, bad diet, and, especially, alcohol don't make for a particularly healthy body over time, and to get all this stuff done you need to be on good form most of the time.

I've *been* overweight and unfit, and it affects *everything*.

---

90. Women, too. No, you're not going to end up looking like a man, not unless you look like one already or are taking insane amounts of steroids.

Getting It All Done

Summary of Chapter 7

1. **Goal setting is largely BS.** At least in the context of letting others tell you what your goals "ought" to be.

2. **Most of us spend most of our time on important tasks we've allowed to become urgent.** We do this because of poor planning and discipline.

3. **Willpower is a myth.** No one can operate maximal effort all the time. Focusing our time and attention the 80/20 Way makes willpower practically irrelevant.

4. **The best use of your time is on important tasks.** Attend to these in a planned and timely fashion, and they won't become urgent.

5. **You can't do everything at once.** Every day, prioritise your tasks in order of their importance in getting you to the goals you *have* set and tackle them in that order. Stick with them until they're done.

Appendix I

How to Write Ads and Sales Letters that Sell

In this Appendix, we're digging deep into the mysterious and murky world of copywriting... that dark and dangerous power which enables you to mesmerise poor, unsuspecting readers into eating their firstborn and shopping at Wal-Mart in dreadful clothing.

Well, not quite.

But that's the impression most copywriters like to give, *especially* when they're trying to sell you a course or a programme on how you can learn to do it yourself.

I've read dozens of books on copywriting and while some have been excellent, one or two stick in my mind as being dire. One in particular was Joe Vitale's *Hypnotic Copywriting*. Truly a terrible book.

My question to these charlatans is always this: if you can *compel* people to action with your writing, why are you selling $97 ebooks to credulous wannbe copywriters instead of multi-million dollar yachts to Arab Sheiks?

It's a perfectly reasonable question, and one to which I've

never had an answer.

But I digress.

The truth is, copywriting is not the most important thing in any single promotion.

Whenever you send out any kind of marketing piece, from a postcard to a fully-fledged sales letter or even a humble email, the offer, the audience and your relationship with them are all far more important than the words you use. Probably my best-ever sales letter in terms of sales was a 360-something word sales letter for Mrs. EBG, and it converted to sales at over 47%.

Why?

Because of the relationship she had with the list, and the expectation and desire she'd generated for the ebook with her frequent (and purely conversational) emails.

The point I'm making here is although in a moment we're going to dive into the bowels of copywriting and cover structure and content in depth, I don't want you getting all worked up about this and thinking until you're a master of the art, you're not going to get anywhere.

Because nothing could be further from the truth.

There are four stages of learning:

1. **Unconscious incompetence.** You're crap at it but you don't even know you're crap at it.

2. **Conscious incompetence.** You're crap at it and you know you're crap at it.

3. **Conscious competence.** You're good at it, but it's hard work and you have to think about it.

4. **Unconscious Competence.** You're good at it, and you just do it naturally.

One way to get your head around this model is to think

of what it was like learning to drive, going from a kid who has no clue what it's like behind the wheel to a seasoned driver of 30 years who can control the car and follow all the signposts, and traffic signals, and navigate around other traffic while holding a conversation with a passenger — it's all on autopilot.

Now, most business owners are at the stage of unconscious incompetence. Not only are they crap at writing sales letters, but they don't even know it. They assume it's the same as any other "business" letter. But if you look at pro copywriters, including me, we're at the stage of unconscious competence. Meaning, we can do this stuff without even thinking about it. Writing this way is natural to us.

The biggest mistake you're going to make when you start doing this for yourself is to try to measure yourself against people who do this professionally for a living. Do remember we have *years* of experience behind us, plus possibly a certain amount of talent wired into our brains.

So, yes, if you wanted to become a world-class copywriter and work with multi-millionaire entrepreneurs in highly competitive markets where your clients' competitors have hired people just like you, then you do indeed have your work cut out for you. You've a long way to go, most likely.

That's the market I operate in with my big clients and it's a different ball game altogether. But in the vast majority of cases you're dealing with competitors who are so poor at marketing, almost anything you do is going to be better than what they do.

It's like the old story of the two guys hiking in the woods when a bear charges out of the trees. One of the chaps starts to put his running shoes on, and his companion laughs and says, "you won't be able to outrun a bear!". To which the first hiker replies, "I don't have to outrun the bear. I only have to

---

Appendix I — How to Write Ads and Sales Letters that Sell

outrun *you*".

Well, your copywriting, and indeed all your marketing, is like that, really. For the most part, unless you're doing something very new and unique, solving a problem no one knows they have until you tell them, you only have to be better than your competitors... and it ain't that hard.

The most important thing to remember is practice makes perfect. A bit of an old chestnut, and there's no such thing as "perfect copy" but it's true the more you do it, the better you'll get. The classic example is the daily emails almost everyone blanches at when I suggest they write them. And yet every time they actually sit down and do it, they are amazed at how easy it becomes and how quickly it becomes easy.

So please bear all that in mind in what follows.

Because there's a lot of material to get through and you're probably going to feel a bit overwhelmed by it all.

But don't.

Just stick to the rules, and you'll see an immediate bump in your profits and responses.

The EBG's Copywriting Philosophy

Although I'm going to take you through the traditional structure and formulae of how to write sales letters and other pieces, my way of implementing them is very different.

I'll cover this in more detail when I come to the section on Content, but I want you to realise up front my way of doing it is a hell of a lot easier than the other way and is probably more effective for most businesses.

The caveat is... if you're intent on selling "off the page", especially in a competitive market, then you probably DO need all the strategies, tips, tools and techniques so beloved of the "gurus".

You pays your money, you takes your choice.

Personally, I have grown tired of that kind of thing. I can do it, and on occasion I still do. I fairly recently did a 30,000-piece direct mailing of a 22-page sales letter written in the classic way. It took me an age, it was *hard* work and it's not something for the faint-hearted.

I much prefer the softly-softly approach of daily emails and easy sales letters. We'll look at the details of how to do this in a moment.

First, though, let's look at best-practice in design and layout to maximise our responses from any web-page, print-ad, sales-letter, postcard, or other direct response piece.

Design Principles

Graphic designers very quickly come to hate me. That's OK, because very often I'm not too fond of them, either. I don't have anything against their profession, but I get mightily pissed off when some individuals position themselves as marketing professionals when a single glance at their work tells me they're a marketing professional in the same way I'm a giraffe.

The most important thing about designing an ad is not aesthetics. It's *readability*. If your ad doesn't get read, it can't possibly get acted upon, and that means you can't sell anything with it. And in that case pleasing aesthetics are moot.

Unfortunately, aesthetics and readability are very frequently at odds. Graphic designers feel compelled to turn out ads and other materials they describe as "creative", when creativity isn't what we want (in the same way we don't want airline pilots to be "creative" — we want them to follow the rules we *know* tend to work best and to deviate from them only if there's a genuine reason to). Creativity has a place in creating products and services, but it's a positive hazard in advertising and marketing for the most part.

It's easy to see why graphic designers fall into this trap, though, because they quite naturally feel they need to deliver something new, fresh, unique, and exciting to their clients. That I can understand. But this exposes an error in their thinking, because they're focused on delivering a *design* when they should be focused on delivering *results*. And in the case of advertising and other promotional materials that ultimately means delivering *sales*.

So what follows is the result of genuine research and is generally considered to be best-practice for direct-response design for maximum response. This isn't to say other designs and layouts won't do better, but it does say this is the place to *start* because it's the best we've found so far.

Your graphic designer will likely not like or agree with much of this, but that's not something to worry about. These principles are based on *peer reviewed research* published in *Type and Layout* by Colin Wheildon (you can get it on Amazon). So while graphic designers are entitled to their own opinions, they're not entitled to their own facts. If they don't have research of their own — as in objective, repeatable, and independently verifiable evidence to back up their counter-arguments — then you can safely ignore them.

Remember: that which can be *asserted* without evidence can be *dismissed* without evidence.

Layout

The best way to describe this is with an image (see page 270).

The ideal line-length is around 45 to 65 characters, so

---

depending on your font-size, this can mean splitting your page into 2, 3 or even more columns,

Body copy is best fully justified with the first line of each paragraph indented. These are aids to reading because they tell the eye how long the lines are and where paragraphs start and stop. This means your eye very quickly gets into the scanning rhythm and makes reading easier.

Fonts

Use clear, easily read fonts for your medium. If you're online use a sans-serif font like Verdana, Arial, and Helvetica for both body copy and headlines[91]; for printed material always use a serif font such as Times, Corona, and Imprint (which this book is set in). Use a sans-serif or a serif font for headlines.

Set your copy ideally in 11pt font with a 13pt leading, but make allowances for age. If your audience is likely to be over 40 go for a bigger font.

Fonts should be plain black or dark grey and set on a light background: white, light grey, or ivory. Avoid reverse-type except maybe sparingly for headlines, don't have large blocks of all-caps, and never, ever use an image behind the copy.

By all means experiment with different colours for headline-copy, but avoid too much bright red. Red pulls the eye very strongly, and if you have a massive great red headline you can stop people from reading because they feel their eyes continually being pulled towards the red.

---

91. This is much less important now computer screens have much better definition. You can generally get away with a serif-font for online body copy nowadays, so this particular point is perhaps not so important any more.

Appendix I — How to Write Ads and Sales Letters that Sell

Your Headline goes up here

Your optional kicker goes here

Body copy. Fully justified, dark ink on light background. Black on white is fine; black on ivory is perhaps best. We're using a serif font — in this case Adobe Caslon Pro. The main part of the newsletter is in Corona. Font size is 11pt with 13pt leading. If this was going to be for online reading, then the body copy would perhaps be better as a sans-serif font like Arial.

Indented first line of every paragraph, with the exception of the first paragraph under a headline or a body subheading:

A Subheading

The subheading and the main headline are in a sans serif font. In this case it's Helvetica, but Arial is another option. Do not go for fancy, cursive headlines the GD tells you is "eye catching". You don't want people **looking** at it... you want them **reading** it.

The kicker is serif and italics, which is fine, but tests show Helvetica and other sans-serif fonts are OK, too.

The thing to watch with headlines is too many bright colours. There's a balance to be made between eye-catching and comprehension. A bright-red, for instance, can be overwhelming and keep distracting the eye to the point where it becomes impossible for some people to concentrate. Generally I tend to stick to black, Navy blue (hex colour #23238E), or dark red (hex colour #990000). There's also no punctuation at the end of the headline. This is deliberate.

You'll notice we're using three columns. That gives us around 38 characters per column, which is right in the middle of the preferred range (over 20 under 60). The main newsletter has two columns, at about 46 characters per column.

Image

A human face with a caption underneath it is a good place to start.

Image

Something relevant and always with a caption

Terminal Anchor

The place for your CTA or something enticing them on to the next page

Images

Images must always have a caption, since captions get read more often than anything except for the headline. If you don't have captions on your images, you are missing out on the opportunity to put elements of your message in front of your readers with a very high probability of them being read.

Use pictures instead of drawings and if you're selling something with an end-product (say, like a recipe book, DIY tools, and things of that nature) show the end result not the constituent parts; if it's something you *use* then show it in use (like a vacuum cleaner, car, bicycle, etc.).

Images of human faces attract the eye (women's and babies' faces especially attract the eyes of *both* sexes), and if you're using a head-shot have it looking right out of the page at the reader.

If you must have an image at the top of your page, have it full page-width *above* the headline *or* in the top right-hand corner next to the headline.

Another place for images is the bottom left-hand corner. Images pull the eye strongly, but copy in the bottom-left, a "fallow" corner often doesn't get read.

Flow

When a person from a Western culture with left-to-right writing looks at a page, the natural path of the eye is to enter at the top-right corner, flick left, and then scan left-to-right and down, left-to-right and down, continually falling, under what we call *reading gravity*.

And anything you do to make the eye go back *up* again makes reading harder... and that necessarily cuts response.

So ensure your pages have a logical flow, from top to bottom, with your headline at the top (below the image if you have a full-width one, remember), a logical flow of your copy with minimum distractions, and the call to action at the end.

One of the big mistakes I see on sales letters, and web-pages in particular, is a mass of navigation links, sidebars and other distractions pulling the reader away from the course you want them to follow.

So for a starting point, keep your sales-letters and optin pages simple, single-column affairs with a clear top-to-bottom flow.

Copywriting Structure

It comes as a huge surprise to most people to discover the art of selling something has a structure to it.

And copywriting is nothing more or less than selling in print (a "salesman in an envelope", as Dan Kennedy puts it).

Now, there's a common misconception about what it takes to make a good salesman, and that is he has to have the "gift of the gab". He always has something to say, always has a quick answer, and never, ever shuts up. But while this is perhaps a reasonable stereotype of the high-pressure salesman we all know and loathe, it's wholly inaccurate when it comes to describing an effective salesman.

An effective salesman might not work to a script, but he certainly works to a plan. And while the implementation of the plan might mean he has to take some twists and turns, and even backtrack on occasion, he's not just making it up as he goes along. In other words, the "gift of the gab" is irrelevant.

And to the relief of many who want to learn how to write sales copy, it is far more formulaic than you might think, at least in terms of the structure.

Our Old Favourite, the AIDA Formula

Boring and old-fashioned it may be, but it works. And that's why people use it, even the "big name" copywriters.

As you perhaps know already AIDA is an acronym made from the words *Attention, Interest, Desire* and *Action.*

Now, before I get into the nitty gritty of it, I think it's important to understand it's not an arbitrary formula. It actually describes the natural processes going on in mammalian neurology when presented with something new in the environment. We've evolved this way, and for very good reasons.

Picture this: Ug the Caveman is wandering along the forest path and something catches his eye. Back in those days it didn't pay to ignore such things, because you might end up as dinner (the human eye has a wide visual field, but only a narrow focus. When we catch something new in our peripheral vision, our eyes flick to it automatically and outside of conscious control).

So this "thing" now has Ug's attention.

If it then turns out to be something he needs to look at further — say, he needs to determine if it's just a boulder or an animal, and if it's an animal whether it's prey or predator — it gets his interest.

What it turns out to be might then lead to the desire to run away or kill it and eat it... each of which takes action.

It's a logical progression of interaction, in other words.

So it should really not surprise us to find sales messages presented in this form find it easy to engage us, because the path is well-worn.

No magic, no mystery. No special skills required.

So just to sum it up:

- **Attention.** Catching the reader's attention, with the

aim of getting them to read the first line of the body copy. An easy way to do this is to make a big promise about fixing a problem they have, or how they can obtain something they want. In direct response marketing, we typically do this with a headline that clearly encapsulates the problem we're going to solve.

- **Interest.** Giving the reader something backing up the promise you made when you got his attention. For example, you may get their attention with a promise of how you can make them more attractive to the opposite sex, and then get their interest by telling them anyone can do it, and all they need to do is follow a simple seven-step blueprint.

- **Desire.** You've made the promise, you've told them what the solution is and now you tell them you are the "go to" guy or gal for the "how to".

- **Action.** Perhaps the most important of all (because if they don't do this, then everything else has been a waste of time). Quite simply you have to tell them how to get what they now desire.

This, in a nutshell, is it.

A few words of caution: don't assume your pieces have to be split into discrete sections like so much pie.

It can help to do it this way in the beginning, but just remember what I said about unconscious competence: with practice you're going to get so you're writing this way naturally and it'll just "happen" by the time you get to the end of your ad. Remember also we're talking about a fairly abstract process here, one that can be drawn out over several emails and a sales letter. Don't get too hung up on compartmentalisation. Just remember all four *stages* have to be gone through somewhere and somehow.

Let's look at it in a bit more detail and see how the different elements of a sales piece combine to give this structure.

The Twelve Elements in an Ad

Depending on whom you ask, you'll get something like twelve different elements that go together to make an ad, with five of them being essential.

1. A compelling headline (mandatory).
2. A reason for writing or advertising, other than just you wanting more business (mandatory).
3. An offer — the reason to respond (mandatory).
4. A reason to respond NOW (mandatory).
5. A method of responding (mandatory).
6. A compelling first few lines.
7. Compelling body copy.
8. Logically progressive subheadings.
9. One or more pictures, always with a caption!
10. A guarantee (which is sometimes included with the offer).
11. Post-scripts.
12. Testimonials.

Again, be careful of worrying too much about compartmentalisation because simple ads like the one below contain all of the mandatory ones yet are quintessentially minimalist.

You could argue the mandatory "reason to respond *now*" is missing, but then we could also say the urgency is there implicit in the offer:

WARNING!

Broker Makes $731,019.95 a Year Part Time!

FREE Special Report Shows You How:

www.MortgageMarketingGenius.com

This ad ran back in 2007 and was very successful at generating leads from a squeeze page (the site has since changed hands, so what you see there now bears little relation to what was there at the time these ad was running).

So let's look at the 12 essential elements in more detail.

1. The Headline

The very first thing your ad needs is a headline (and by ad, I mean any marketing piece, from a sales letter to an email to a postcard).

The headline is what catches the reader's eye and really determines if he or she is going to read any further. The important point to understand here is this: *the headline is not there to sell your product or service. It's there to sell the idea of reading the first line of the copy.*

If you research headlines, you'll find a bewildering array of rules, templates and strategies for writing them.

But remember what I said before: unless you're going up

---

against stiff competition you don't have to sweat and worry about this overmuch.

Yes, it's important, but when you consider most of your competitors' ads have a headline comprising their logo and business-name, it's not hard to be head and shoulders above them.

That said, it's interesting to note two of the most famous and successful sales letters ever, the Wall Street Journal "two young men" letter, and another, which escapes my memory, didn't have headlines. Just goes to show rules are there to be broken (but break them only when you understand them!).

There's a great list of 100 of the world's greatest headlines put together by Jay Abraham. It used to be available on his site, but I can't find it now. Just Google "jay abraham top 100 headlines" and you'll get loads of copies of the list.

It's the easiest thing in the world to look down this list and choose one that suits your needs, adapting it for your own market.

But perhaps a better way for a small, local business is to think of all the things your market hates about your industry and then promise not to do it.

Don't take offence if your profession is on this list, but here are a few examples, and I'm sure one or two will resonate with you:

- Delivery firms not delivering, or not delivering on time.
- Estate agents who lie, prevaricate and generally muck you around.
- Lawyers who don't call back and charge you for every second they spend thinking about you.
- Marketing consultants and copywriters who promise much but deliver bugger all.

Appendix I — How to Write Ads and Sales Letters that Sell

- Plumbers who do shoddy work, overcharge and then charge you again to come back and fix it (applies to mechanics, builders, electricians and pretty much every other trade out there).
- Restaurants delivering substandard food.
- And so on.

A lawyer, say, who promises your appointment will be free if he doesn't see you within five minutes of the appointed time and promises this in a headline will be so far ahead of the competition they won't know what's hit them.

See, you really don't have to be clever about this.

When I was selling my house in the UK to move to Ireland, I wrote a sales letter to move it quickly, but the headline was simply:

"7 Great Reasons To Live At 19 Dove Gardens"

And then I just gave the seven reasons. It worked, too.

Everyone who viewed the house and had a copy of that letter made an offer on it (my original plan was for the Agent to hand them out to prospective buyers, but he screwed up so I just handed them one when they walked in).

If you're writing articles and Adwords or Bing ads, just bear in mind your headline needs to include your keywords, because not only is that important for "relevance", but it's important for the visitor who's looking for information on specific topics.

Bottom line: writing a decent headline for your business is as simple as making your *big* promise upfront, and it can even be just to promise you won't do the things your competitors do that drive them up the wall.

---

2. The Reason

Obviously you're writing to make sales but if that's *all* you're doing, day after day, then it quickly becomes very tiring.

A good example is the sales letter I get from my bank, as regularly as clockwork.

Not only is it a typically awful letter from a bank, but it's clearly the same thing... Every. Bloody. Time.

Same shiny envelope, same postage frank... and they all go the same way: in the shredder.

They don't even get opened.

Why?

Because I know all they are doing is asking me to buy something I already know I have no interest in having.

It's the same with loads and loads of flyers, inserts and direct mail letters I get every week. They are all trying to sell me stuff, and that's all they ever do. Come online and it's the same old story. You know, Guru Bob and his arsewipe friends all doing a round-robin on the "You've just *got* to get in on this while you still can" emails. It's both amusing and depressing when you're on several of these lists and see the same email come through from a bunch of them.

Now, contrast that with, say, my daily emails. Sure. I'm selling, but I'm also providing tips, interesting comments and observations, and often links to other useful material where I don't benefit directly if you buy it.

I'm skipping ahead somewhat here, but I tell you now, this is a much better way to sell. It's easier, it's cleaner, and my customers and clients like it more. It's the reason my list is so responsive. I don't need any of the slimy tricks and "closes" espoused by the "gurus" and I don't have to hard-sell anyone.

Just something for you to think about.

Appendix I — How to Write Ads and Sales Letters that Sell

The reasons you can give for writing to them with an offer don't have to be educational, though.

For example, you can pick a holiday or an event (birthday, anniversary, etc.).

Or a petshop owner, say, could do something like, "I was walking down the road and I saw a guy struggling to get his dog to walk on a lead; and it came to me... how many people struggle with the same thing when there's an easy solution in the Halti? So I checked through the boxes down in the storeroom... and I was right! I have a box of seven unused Haltis...".

And so on.

See, the emphasis here is on the other person. It's about *you* thinking about *their* problems and offering to help them with it.

3. *The Offer (the reason to respond)*

The offer is the answer to the question "what will the readers get when they respond to this ad?".

In the main it's going to be either something free in return for their contact details, or something they get to buy. But it could be anything, like free coupons, free gifts they have to come to your premises for (the strategy being some of them will buy stuff while they're there), and so on.

But you *must* have an offer... and you *must* have only *one* offer. Robert Collier showed back as long ago as 1937 you can't effectively sell more than one thing off the same ad or sales letter.

Just to be clear about this, if the two products or services are related and have a natural connection or process of ascension, then it's OK; but if they don't, then it's not.

So, for example, standard and deluxe versions of your widgets are fine; but widgets and thingumajigs wouldn't be.

In any case you'll find the more specific your offer is, the better response you're likely to get from more highly qualified people.

In other words if, say, a driving instructor advertises for young men between 20 and 22 who have failed their test once and want a guaranteed pass after a weekend's intensive instruction, anyone replying is pretty much a buyer; but if the ad is for "driving lessons" then you'll get far more tyre kickers (pun intended).

So the rule is, make your offer specific, unambiguous and narrow. It's generally better to send out three narrow and specific offers to three subniches than it is to send one broad offer to your entire list.

4. *Urgency (the reason to respond NOW)*

You need to tell them what they need to do, what'll happen when they do it, what they'll get, when they've got to do it by, and the consequences of *not* doing it or missing the deadline.

And it's the deadline or other constraint on availability that makes the call to action so powerful.

I bet you've seen those coupons — free offers, money off, and all that. They're dated some time 300 years hence. And so you never, ever get round to redeeming them. The same is true, incidentally, of long guarantees. A month's guarantee is a pressing deadline; a year or a lifetime... just fades away. Now, that's perhaps the whole point of giving long guarantees (because they then don't have to keep their promise), but offers with too distant a deadline, or, worse, no deadline at all, rarely do as well as those where the deadline or other scarcity strategy is tight.

I love scarcity.

In my experience it's perhaps *the* most powerful "kick up the butt" call to action strategy there is.

Appendix I — How to Write Ads and Sales Letters that Sell

Another one of the many quirks of human nature is, by and large, we'll fight harder to keep something we have than we will to attain something we don't have. And scarcity is a way of using this to our own advantage, because once people see they might lose the opportunity to have something... they want it. They often are so discomfited by the thought of losing that chance, they'll buy things and rationalise to themselves they have it "just in case". I've even done *that* myself.

How do you use scarcity?

Simple: either set a deadline (preferably tight, usually within a week to ten days) or do it numerically by restricting the number of widgets available.

So if scarcity is so powerful, why do so few business owners use it?

Because they're scared to.

They think by telling people they might miss out on offers, they, themselves might miss out on sales.

And, yes, you can shoot yourself in the foot slightly by setting the limits too small (which is one reason I prefer to use a deadline rather than numbers; but sometimes I'll use both, as you'll see).

Gauging the right time and numbers is really a matter of experience. Testing, in other words. Just be aware you'll almost always get a better response than you thought you would.

Two big no-no's of scarcity: first, to break your promise (read: lie about it); secondly, making up some bullshit excuse why you have it in the first place. The first makes you look repugnant and the second makes you look stupid.

To me, there are few things more aggravating than to see Guru Bob and his pals suddenly announce "we managed to open up a few more spots" or "some of the credit cards were declined so there are some free spots" or "our web-guy managed to tweak the servers so we can accept 7 more people". It's so fucking annoying... because they're treating you like an idiot. If you have eleven places, then keep your word and offer no more. Learn the lesson that next time you need to offer more of them!

And bullshit reasons for scarcity? It's saying you have limited amounts of things which are quite clearly to all intents and purposes unlimited (like downloads). It's not hard to think of genuine reasons for having scarcity on most things, though, even downloadable ones. For example, if you tweak the offer so you include some kind of personal support, then it's reasonable to want to limit sales (it also adds enormously to the value of the offer, meaning you can charge a higher price — yay!).

This is exactly what I did with *Online Sales Supremacy*, a series of teleclasses I ran several years ago, and it sold out quickly. I *should* have offered more than the 10 places I did, but a promise is a promise.

How effective is scarcity?

Enormously.

I haven't done any numerical analysis of it, but I can tell you from observation you get around 80% of your sales in the last 20% of the time before the deadline. It's so predictable but none the less scary for that, because you often spend the first few days watching the responses just trickle in and begin to worry it's going to flop.

5.   *The Method of Responding*

A few years ago Dan Kennedy included a scan of a postcard in one of his newsletters. The card was well presented and had a truly great offer: free overnight delivery anywhere in the continental USA of printed materials.

Brilliant.

The only trouble was... no way to respond. Worse: no contact details at all. Worst of all: no company name or anything you could use to find them on the Internet or anywhere else.

In other words, it was absolutely, utterly and 100% anonymous. A guaranteed 0% response rate to that one.

You can laugh (and perhaps we should), but the response mechanism is absolutely vital — and it's vital to get it right.

There are dozens of different ways to ask for response but what we've seen, at least in the business-education niche, is an overwhelming move towards wanting to be sent to a website. Responses dwarf all other methods.

But beware: don't take that as being true for your market. For example, in my work with the Wills, we found older people wanted to get on the phone and actually talk to a human being (best responses were when the phone was answered by a young woman with a local accent).

So test different ways of getting them to respond and bear in mind the general rule that the more ways you give them to respond, the more responses you'll get (and don't forget you must *track* response!).

6.   *A Compelling First Few Lines*

Joe Sugarman put it this way: the headline exists to get your reader to read the first line of the copy; the first line exists to get them to read the second line; the second line, the third, and so on, until they're on the slippery slide to the sale.

I'm paraphrasing, but that's the gist of it.

So your first line of copy has to give an immediate payoff in terms of rewarding them for reading on past the headline.

In other words, the headline makes a big promise of a benefit to them if they read further; and the first line of the copy begins to deliver on that promise in a big way.

You'll find copywriters tend to have their own favourite techniques, and I am no exception.

What I've found works very well, especially with my Premier Positioning and style of selling is to say something like this:

> Dear Friend,
>
> If you're struggling to get traffic to your website and frustrated at the amount of sales you're making — and the number you know you're missing out on and just don't yet know how to attract — and you know one small but important step in the right direction is going to be enough to make it all start happening for you… then your day is about to get a lot better.
>
> Because… regardless of the "competition", "recession", or the economy, the truth is your website can be your own personal "gold mine", whether you're an online— or offline-business…
>
> … BUT… if and only if you master a surprisingly small number of simple skills and put some very easily copied strategies to work for you in your business.
>
> And in a moment, I'm going to share with you exactly how you can make this happen… but first… I want to put you off if I possibly can.
>
> See, this message is NOT for everyone.
>
> Why?
>
> Because at the end of it I'm going to ask you to make a substantial investment in the future success and even survival of your business.
>
> And if you're not the kind of person willing to invest in your business… then what follows isn't for you and reading it will just be a waste of your time.
>
> What's more, this message is definitely NOT for you if [...]

Appendix I — How to Write Ads and Sales Letters that Sell

And then I'll give three criteria that might disqualify them. I've used this formula several times with excellent results, most recently on the sales copy I wrote for Mrs. EBG's Inner Circle.

7. *Compelling Body Copy*

If the first few lines are to get you onto the slippery slide to the sale, then the body copy is the slide itself. And there's no magic or mystery in it, either.

Alas, there's not a lot I can usefully say about it in terms of *structure*, other than to say begin with saying the thing can be done (interest), segue into saying you're the one who can do it for them (desire), and end with a call to action.

But what I am going to do is share something with you I call my "million pound email". The history of this is interesting. He was referred to me by an existing client, another high-flyer, so from that perspective he was already predisposed to working with me (the guy who referred him was one of Dan Kennedy's Platinum members).

So I spoke to him on the phone after looking at his existing copy. This guy is very much a "thing" person — he referred to his potential clients as "buying units". His sales letter was very much "thing" orientated, too. The only *person* he spoke about was... himself.

After I spoke to him I wrote this email, all based on what he'd told me, and using much of his own language back at him. I was literally "speaking his language".

Here it is:

```
Hi XXX,

Here's my Action Plan.

I've been over everything with a fine tooth-
comb and looked into a lot of the detail and
now I can see various specific things I can do
```

to eliminate your problem.

There's lots of choice and I think we can solve the biggest difficulties fairly easily. It's a LOT of work, but I don't think it's a tough "sell", if you see what I mean. You're in a strong position from what you said. I think we just need to talk to your prospects the right way, don't you?

So, as well as fixing the copy, which I think we know needs to be done, you might want to consider beefing up the entire marketing process: ads, squeeze page, autoresponder sequence, sales letter, and even the application form.

As I mentioned on the phone, time is very very short and to get done what needs to be done, it necessarily means I'll have to drop a lot of stuff I'm doing to give you maximum attention to get this problem licked.

This month - and into March - I had intended to use my recuperation from foot surgery to best advantage and had scheduled 50/50 with client work and my own projects. I'm presenting at Infusion's Momentum 2007 Event in May and I have a product to create for that, plus I have my own mentoring/coaching group to launch. I also have some regular commitments to clients, but I can work around those. So I'm kinda pressed for time on all fronts.

However, because you've been referred to me by X and Y and because I can see you need to get this fixed now and are stuck in a hole, I'll drop my own stuff until I've got yours done and rearrange some of my clients' work, effectively meaning I can give you 80%+ of my time over the next few weeks - until your Discovery Day - to get this fixed.

As I say, ordinarily I'd not be able to do this but as a favour to X and Y, and indeed YOU, and because I've kept Feb/March relatively free of clients' work (until now!) it IS possible with a bit of pushing and squeezing.

Appendix I — How to Write Ads and Sales Letters that Sell

But, XXX, I'll be upfront with you and tell you I AM charging you a premium on my normal fee simply because of the time constraints and knock on effects at my end.

We need to jump into this right away and I can see some very long days and late nights in the next few weeks, and the knock on effect is going to be a big hit on my time even AFTER this is done and I've got your problems fixed.

That's OK. Sleep is for wimps, and I love coffee... but it's really going to make for a much busier three months than I'd anticipated. But, hey, I won't become the world's most famous copywriter by not grasping a few nettles, will I?

So ordinarily I'd not sting you quite this much - as you'll find out as we work together in the future. I think it's a reasonable fee, and still probably less than you'd have to pay for one of the "bigger named" but no more-talented copywriters out there, although only you can decide it's fair from your own perspective. And no-one is going to give you more commitment and better service, that I promise.

If you've any doubts, you might want to consider checking out my testimonials and even asking XXXXX or XXXXX XXXXXXXXX of XXXXXXXX if you want to prove to yourself the kind of ROI and level of service I've been giving them.

Basically my aim is to get all this done FOR you leaving you free to concentrate on the task of solving the other pressing problems of hosting your Discovery Day. XXXXXX even has me dealing direct with some of his vendors (like advertising reps and the like) from time to time - it's all part of the "done for you" service.

This late in the day it's really a case of just jumping in and getting it all done. What do you think? I know what needs to be done and while of course only you can decide on the final copy, experience shows it's best if we just get on and do it.

So, here are the details of what I propose to do to your marketing process to get as many people along for the Discovery Day as humanly possible:

1. Change the squeeze page to increase signups. I can see several ways of doing this.

2. Rewrite sales letter to increase conversions. This is a big job, XXX. I'll go into the detail if you like, although you might like to consider doing that once I have the draft. Right now, I think we just need to get it done.

Some of the subtle language I use will mean I'll need to talk to you for maybe a half-hour and ask you some questions. Some might seem odd, but that's normal ;-). The thing to remember here is linguistic wizardry is my forte.

I'll also adapt this so you can send it out as a sales letter/info package. See point 7, below.

I'll format the sales letter in the draft although it's best if you get your web-guy to HTMLise it on the actual site. I CAN do it but it's a longer and slower process for me. I can liaise direct with the web guy if you want me to.

3. Completely rewrite the email autoresponder sequence. I currently have a client who's emailing his list of 12,000 TWICE A DAY and making regular sales. I think we need to be hitting YOUR signups at least once a day until the day before your Discovery Day starts. We don't want to be shy about this. What do you say?

We actually want dual-streams: people who've not given us their postal details we'll want to keep hitting until they DO as well as promoting

---

Appendix I — How to Write Ads and Sales Letters that Sell

them to sign up. These folks will get TWO emails a day. One to get them to sign up, one to get them to give you their postal details.

4. Rewrite your full-page ad for the March magazine. If you want me to I'll liaise direct with the ad departments. All you'll have to do is approve the copy.

5. Write a minimum of 6 postcards and 6 faxes for you to blast out (you're using Infusion, aren't you?). Scripts for voice blasts? No problem.

6. Work with you on sundry bits and pieces that occur to us as we go on. Stuff is bound to come up. I'm a can-do guy and solve your problems.

7. Only you can decide, XXX, but I STRONGLY recommend you might like to consider multivariate testing to quickly optimize your conversions. This is going to allow us to tweak your copy (headlines etc.) in record time. It lets us get optimised results by testing many possibilities easily and quickly.

I do this using software that works seamlessly with your HTML pages to "serve up" different versions of the copy to different users.

Unless you're using something really exotic and bizarre on your web site, this software will plug right in - it's php based and installation is easy. Once it's up the site visitor never knows it's even there, and even your web guy won't need to touch it - I'll handle all the "snippets" that get tested for you. I see from looking at how your web page is put together that you're using a CSS style sheet - and that makes it even easier.

Any given visitor will always see the same copy; different visitors will (with a non-zero probability) see different copy. So it's like a traditional split-test on steroids. You have loads of options and gives you practically unlimited possibilities in the testing.

Appendix I — How to Write Ads and Sales Letters that Sell

The advantage of doing this is twofold: first your web site quickly converges on the maximum conversion rate; one of my clients improved her overall results by 1108%.

Secondly, once we've run one big test (probably the NEXT ad that runs plus the next 20,000 email blast), we'll have optimised copy we can use... for a direct mail piece (your information package).

It means you completely avoid the problem of sending out an untested sales letter. That's HUGE and saves you a fortune.

Most people don't "get" this point. I sense you will. One client pays me almost $7,000 every month to write simple daily emails but won't spend $200 to install even the basic version of this software to test the conversion of the sales page my emails prompt his readers to click through to.

Again, you won't have to do anything except perhaps review the stats with me - you don't even HAVE to do that because the testing process means you automatically get the optimum copy. I'll run all this from my end, do it for you.

One thing you might not know about me is I'm an ex-computer programmer and come from a scientific and mathematical background. The upshot of this is I understand the testing process and the technology so I don't get stopped by technical issues. If I can't fix them myself, I know how to find and talk to the guys who CAN.

OK, so that's it in a rather large and detailed nutshell. My guarantee is ALWAYS if the first piece doesn't pull, I'll rewrite it for free; and then if THAT doesn't pull, I'll rewrite it again.

This is less relevant in some ways for the multi-variate tested sales letter because that gets tested continuously so in a sense I'm constantly "rewriting" but if it needed a complete rewrite, that's what it'd get, no worries.

As I say, my main concern is your success – and candidly, given we're both in Gold Peak Performers and we're both visible to "big players" (hey, you ARE one!), including Dan himself, my whole reputation is riding on this, so I'm not taking any of it lightly or taking advantage.

So, for all this (and more, because I'm 100% committed to making a big success of this for you), my fee, including the "drop everything and give up sleep for a month" premium is just $34,997.

Usually I take a 30% deposit before starting work.

However, because it's urgent if you think it's reasonable now and accept this Action Plan I'll start work IMMEDIATELY and trust you to wire the deposit over in the next few days.

Anyway, that's it. Let me know what you want to do – the sooner I know, the sooner I can get started. If there's anything you want to ask me about it, call me on 011 44 1449 XXXXX and I'll pick up. Right now it's Sunday night, but call anyway if you want – I know how important and urgent it is, so what the heck.

His response to this was an immediate, "I love everything you say. Go ahead".

Since then I've modified this and used it over and over again. It's been worth hundreds of thousands of pounds to me, and it could be worth the same to you, too.

8. *Logically Progressive Subheadings*

Huge chunks of unbroken text can be intimidating.

What's more, some people scan the copy and pick up the "story" from the subheadings. Others, like me, just read the whole thing, even if we jump around from section to section.

The trick to subheadings is to have them tell your story, standalone. In other words, if you removed all the copy, the bare bones of the "story" would be there in the subheadings.

It's no more complex than that.

9.   *One or More Pictures (always with a caption)*

Pictures can be a great addition to sales copy, but with some caveats.

The first caveat is they have to support the sales message. It's true pictures of sexy women pull the eyes of male and female readers alike, and that is necessarily going to increase readership. What we don't know and does seem quite unlikely is that they actually increase sales.

A second caveat is your pictures really need to be photographs rather than illustrations, and they must have a caption. The reason for this is photographs draw the eyes, especially if they're of human faces or eyes. And any captions under them get very high readership.

An excellent strategy, then, is to put a human face (say, your own) in the top right hand corner of the page with a caption in the form of a quote, where the quote is, say, you repeating the promise in your headline or stating your guarantee.

In this instance there's a very high probability your caption is going to get read immediately after the headline, if not actually before it. If you're going to include a big image, say one occupying the whole width of the page, then have it right at the top. If you don't then the eyes get drawn to it and then they move down.

So if you have a headline or copy above the picture, then the chances are it won't get read because the eyes have to fight the natural "reading gravity" (which for English is left-to-right and down).

Finally, before-and-after shots work well for many niches, like weight loss and other "health and beauty" niches; and if you're selling tools and equipment, show them in use rather than just standing there looking pretty (by the same token, show cars being driven, food prepared rather than as ingredients, and so on).

10.   A Guarantee (sometimes included with the offer)

Guarantees are one of the most underused and fear-provoking sales strategies out there. As an example of how safe they can be, Mrs. EBG gives a lifetime money-back guarantee on all her products, and has a refund rate over 24 months of under 2%.

In general the longer and more comprehensive your guarantee, the more persuasive it is for sales *and* the less likely you are to get called on it.

The reason guarantees are so rarely used is business owners are afraid they're going to get ripped off. But this almost never happens, because the kind of person who'd rip you off will do it anyway, guarantee or no. In any case, so what if they do? Imagine you get ripped off three times for every hundred sales you make, and it costs you 3,000 Groats... but your sales have doubled because of your guarantee and for every 3,000 Groats you "lose" you're actually making 50,000 Groats in increased revenue.

So the obvious question, then, is why don't I offer a guarantee all the time? If you're familiar with my work already, you might have spotted this and wondered why I'm not always following my own advice.

Well, it's a positioning thing. If I don't offer a guarantee, I don't just quietly forget about it: I make it plain there is *no* safety net. What this means is I get a better class of buyer. They're more committed and they work harder. The upshot of this is they get better results... which means they're more likely to buy from me again.

I am not as daft as you look.

11.   Post-Scripts

Ah, the famous P.S.

Research shows P.S.s get very high readership, second only to headlines and captions.

Why?

Because a typical reading pattern for a letter is to look at the front, check out the headline and the picture with its captions, then turn to the back and see who it's from before deciding whether to read it or not. And it's at this point, right when they're looking at whom it's from they see the P.S.s... and read them.

So your P.S. Should not typically be an afterthought or an add-on. For a long-copy sales letter it should summarise your entire sales message and offer.

One of my recent strategies has been to use the bullet points from the body of my sales letter as being the meat of the P.S.s. It works very well (although I haven't split tested this, so I have no idea if the P.S.s in this form make any difference at all. All I do know is the sales letters I've done recently, with the P.S.s done this way have done very well indeed).

12.   Testimonials

I get lazy with these myself, and I also know in the US it's getting harder and harder to use them. But they're still useful and powerful and I encourage you to test them.

In my experience testimonials work best when your relationship with your reader isn't quite so strong.

Why?

Because it's about trust. People do business with you when they like and trust you, and a big part of testimonials is the warm and fuzzy feeling people get when they hear others saying nice things about you.

What's more, what other people say about you is far more believable than what you might say about yourself.

On the other hand, when *you* are looking to buy... don't trust testimonials. It's not because the givers are lying. Rather it's because of something called "self justification". Someone who's spent a lot of money on something is more likely to sing its praises than someone who hasn't — not because it's necessarily good, but because they'd look pretty damned silly saying, "no, it was rubbish. I was hoodwinked".

I recommend the excellent book, *Mistakes Were Made but Not by Me*, by Carol Tavris and Elliot Aronson.

Copywriting Content

I just want to make something very clear before we start, though: these are just ideas and guidelines. They are not laws or rules to be followed slavishly. That said it *is* important to understand them and to have mastered them before you start breaking them.

Something else I want to make clear is what I'm about to share with you is very different from the style of copywriting you've perhaps aspired to in the past, especially if you're in or seeking to enter the profession yourself.

I think one of the problems is people read a sales letter for a copywriting course and assume they have to be writing in the same style, even if they're selling hearing aids or whatever.

To repeat what I said before, in case you missed it: if you're intent on selling "off the page", especially in a competitive market, then you probably *do* need all the strategies, tips, tools and techniques so beloved of the "gurus".

The Four Essential Emotional Hooks

If you thought the AIDA Formula and the essential elements we've already seen was all you needed to know... then I have some bad news for you.

Because if you cast your mind back to a previous chapter you'll remember we saw how people buy only for one reason: to solve a problem. And when someone has a problem we have to get them caught up on four emotional hooks: the Pain, The Commitment, the Cure, and the Reason to Believe.

Unlike the AIDA Formula, these don't have to come in any particular order, but they must all be present if you want to maximise your chances of making the sale.

The Pain

The Pain is simply the effect of the problem your reader's facing. The fact it might not strike a chord with you is irrelevant. I know there are people out there who spend a *lot* of money chasing cures for baldness because their loss of hair is, to them, emotionally traumatic. Some people claim it's even ruined their lives; me, I find it all rather mystifying.

I mean... you're bald.

So what?

I guess if you're a woman and you lose your hair it's rather different; but, then I'm not a woman and I know from long experience men and women are not even remotely alike, and I don't pretend to understand the fairer sex for a moment.

So a guy getting genuinely upset about going bald?

Nope. I just don't get it.

That's not to invalidate the feelings of someone who is upset by it, though. The point is... I don't feel or share his pain.

Appendix I — How to Write Ads and Sales Letters that Sell

But that wouldn't stop me being able to *use* it in a sales letter.

So, every time you write any kind of sales piece, from the lowliest email to the most labour-intensive and complex multi-page sales letter, you must be clearly addressing the pain ownership or use of your product or service is going to ease. There's no point sending anything where the problem you're ultimately going to solve for the reader isn't clear.

I'll often talk about copy having no "focus", especially on websites, and when you do nine times out of ten it's because there's no obvious *point* to the page, no obvious problem it's promising to solve.

The Commitment

The Commitment is the promise you make to solve the problem or ease the pain. If we use the previous example again, if the problem is baldness and the pain is the emotional trauma, then the commitment is *what* you're going to do to fix it for them, and, sometimes, even *how* you're proposing to do it.

I've heard of all sorts of cures for baldness, from rubbing with some very strange concoctions, to transplants, to Lord knows what. In each case these are the hooks you'd use, the commitment to easing their pain. In effect you're saying, "If you're sick of being bald, then this is my promise to fix it for you".

The Cure

The Cure is simply what they get when they take action to get you to meet your commitment. It's the *quid pro quo*: "if you want me to cure your baldness, then you need to phone this number and ask for your free report, *Three Steps*

---

to the Hairiest Head Ever"[92]. In that instance, the "cure" is the free report, and the problem would have been a lack of information of how to get a hairy head.

A sales piece without a call to action asking them to accept the offer *is not a sales piece*. This is probably the second most common mistake business owners make, usually because they're squeamish when it comes to sales and asking people to buy.

Remember: people buy when they want to buy and not when you want to sell, so you need to jockey them along sometimes to make their "want" bubble up to the surface (this is why we use *scarcity* in the form of deadlines and limited availability).

Your offer must be clear and unambiguous: you need to tell them what to do, why they need to do it (and do it right *now*), what'll happen after they've done it, and what the consequences are of *not* doing it.

The Reason to Believe

The Reason to Believe gets you over the subtle but very important hurdle of *mistrust*. Liking and trust are two of the most important elements in any sale. Even if a prospective customer or client loves the look of your products and services, if he or she doesn't like *you*, then you can kiss the sale goodbye.

It doesn't make much logical sense, but, then, who said we humans were logical and sensible?

That's the bad news.

The good news is people *want* to believe. All they need is the reason or the excuse to trust you to solve their problems.

---

92. And, yes, this is *quid pro quo* because their contact details are valuable to you.

Appendix I — How to Write Ads and Sales Letters that Sell

How do we provide this reason?

The two main ways are with testimonials and guarantees.

Testimonials give them the reason to believe because what someone else says about you is far more believable than what you say about yourself; and guarantees act as *risk reversal*, as we've seen, putting the risk of things going wrong back onto the seller[93].

A third way of giving them a reason to believe is with objective third-party recommendations, studies, qualifications, and certificates. I did some work many years ago with an engineering firm whose products had been the subject of testing at some university or other, and one of the things I had my client do was get permission to use the results from the study in his marketing to give his prospects a reason to believe his products were up to the job.

A Very Few Additional Words About Structure

Everything I'm going to share with you now you should consider in the light of what we went over in the last section: the AIDA Formula and the 12 elements of a sales letter (five of which are mandatory, as we saw), and the four Emotional Hooks you have to get in there.

But while it might be useful to think in terms of compartmentalisation in the beginning, don't let yourself get bogged down in it.

So long as the elements are there, you don't have to be able to draw boxes around things and say, *"there, that's where I get their interest!"*. With practice this will all come naturally. Interestingly, just recently I had to write a load of copy for a client, which was *deliberately* features-orientated and not

---

93. Of course, they have to believe you're going to honour your guarantee, but that's another story.

---

benefits-orientated.

Ordinary copy, in other words.

You know what?

I found it harder than writing sales copy. And I hated every minute of it.

This is a good thing in my business (and probably in any business) and comes only with practice, practice, practice.

The Most Important Lesson You'll Ever Learn about Writing Sales Copy

Is... write like you speak.

Yes, it really is that simple.

We all leave school able to write. More or less.

Even though I am aware there are truly illiterate people out there, I have yet to meet any adult who literally cannot read and write.

But there is a big difference in being able to read and write to the minimum standard and being able to communicate effectively.

I've mentioned this before, but the stats are scary enough for me to mention them again: in the US and the UK the average reading age for adults is... 10½. I find that truly frightening.

But, I think there's actually a second problem over and above the problems with literacy — and in some ways it kind of goes the other way. I'm talking about educated, intelligent and (supposedly) literate people who write like pompous asses! Speak to them in real conversation and they talk like normal human beings.

But put them in front of a keyboard, typewriter or sheet of paper with a pen in hand... and they almost start "writing in tongues". They churn out rubbish which is English in as much as it contains English words, but other than that it's gobbledegook.

Why is this?

I think there are 3 main reasons.

First, schools and teachers don't have a clue about writing. I really don't know where to start with this — there is so much screwed up about the whole endeavour.

Not only are teachers not terribly bright in my experience (one at my daughter's old school didn't realise to write a sign saying *"there is headlice in the early years unit"* is not the best advertisement for her literacy skills, and another could see nothing wrong with her sign saying *"knive's, spoon's, and fork's"*), but the way they teach us to write up reports in the sciences and humanities is a crime against good taste. We're taught to write formally in the third-person passive.

But no one actually *speaks* like that!

Science pretty much proves our intelligence stems from when symbolic language first appeared. We've been communicating using spoken language for a very long time, certainly many tens of thousands of years longer than we've been writing.

It's clear if we're to communicate in writing most effectively, it behooves us to look at the way we speak.

Secondly, evolution has made us a gregarious and tribal species (which is why global catastrophe actually touches us very little when we don't know the people involved — it seems we can "care for" and live in groups of about 150 people before we start wanting to fight them[94]).

Anyway, when we "belong" to a modern "tribe" — say, lawyers — we tend to slip into the lingo of that tribe. It's OK writing legalese to another lawyer perhaps, but writing it to

---

94. Or, in the case of Haggis, my Jack Russell, that's just 3 people.

Appendix I — How to Write Ads and Sales Letters that Sell

your client makes you about as popular as haemorrhoids.

Thirdly, there is the myth of "professionalism". Many years ago, only the learned could read and write. It was a sign of an almost aristocratic status.

This hangover has... hung over. To be "professional" is to be "learned", and to sound learned, you have to write like a pompous ass. But it's B.S.

Richard Feynman, for example, was an Nobel Prize winner and one of the most learned men on the planet.. But he wrote like a real live human being; so does Richard Dawkins, Dan Kennedy, Nido Qubein, and a gazillion other great communicators.

Being "professional" is about serving your clients' needs to the best of your ability. That means communicating with them clearly, honestly, and openly. You can NOT do that while you're writing with euphemisms and hiding behind obscurantist phrases. This means using contractions and apostrophes, slang appropriate to your audience and as simple a vocabulary as you can get away with (the reason being the people who understand the big words also understand the small ones, but the reverse is not always the case).

So regardless of what the teachers told you, your colleagues tell you and what all the "professionals" out there say, write like you speak, like you're having a conversation with a friend or a favourite Aunt and you'll find your words having a much greater effect than you ever dreamed possible.

So: write fast, and don't edit until the end.

Here's a great exercise to do (and please do it. I even got Nido Qubein, the President of High-Point University and the Great Harvest Bread Company doing this and he was blown away). You can do it on paper or use a word processor.

1.   Get a kitchen timer. Set it for 5 minutes.

Appendix I — How to Write Ads and Sales Letters that Sell

2. Get a piece of paper and a pen. Then write down these three words: *bicycle, fire, sandwich*.

3. Start your timer and begin writing. Write as fast as you can and do not stop to edit. Write anything that comes into your head. The only rules are:

    i.   Pick one of the three words above as the *first* word you write. This *must* be the first word of the first sentence you write.

    ii. The other two words must appear at least *once* in the *first* paragraph.

    iii. There is no third rule.

4. Write for the whole 5 minutes. Do not stop to think. Do not stop to edit. Do not stop, full stop!

When the timer has stopped, take a look at what you've written. I think you'll be very pleasantly surprised at the quality.

Some of my very best work has been done at breakneck speed and under tight deadlines.

Don't Make It Seem Like Work

People don't want to work.

They want their problems solved *for* them by the latest gizmo, widget or doodad.

A great example of this is in the weight-loss industry. To lose a pound of fat means burning 3,500 calories from your body's stores.

And no matter which way you look at it, it's not easy — even if you do no exercise, you've got to go hungry while the fat comes off. And even though they know it's true, they don't *want* to believe it, and they'll flit from product to product and diet to diet hoping to get it all done for them.

So when writing sales copy place the emphasis on the product (which also includes *you* if you're in a service industry).

For example, compare the two following sentences:

> *Using tearsheets you can get up to a 300% better response than you get when you send ordinary direct mail*

And,

> *Tearsheets typically give you a 300% better response than ordinary direct mail*

The meaning is pretty much the same, but the way we present it is very different.

Similarly, compare two calls to action:

> *Write your details on the form below, put it in the envelope and send it to us and we'll send you a free widget*

And,

> *Just pencil your details on the priority reservation, slip it into the post-paid envelope and drop it in the mail... and it'll bring your free widget right to your door by return*

Again we're describing the same thing, but in a much gentler and easier way.

Don't lie, though. By all means warn them it *is* work if it is. Tell them upfront as I do. Just make it *sound* like it's not.

Appendix I — How to Write Ads and Sales Letters that Sell

Sell to the Problem

In almost all cases people will be coming to you to solve a problem — and that means they're in "away from" mode.

When someone comes to you in your capacity as consultant or purveyor of problem solving products and services they are *usually* moving away from pain — this is why the *problem, agitate, solve* formula for sales letters is so powerful.

That's it, plain and simple.

And, depending on your product, the pain they have to feel to spur them to action can be immense.

For example, in the finance industry the pain of debt almost has to be at the point of bankruptcy before some people will act.

Let's face it, no one actively *wants* a mortgage, or dental work, or insurance, or new tyres for their car... they're making these *grudge purchases* because they have to.

Occasionally you *will* get people who are seeking you out because they are goal orientated and you'll usually know this from the way you've positioned yourself.

So, given your prospects are almost always going to be moving *away from* I suggest you use words like *solve, fix, avoid, leave behind, drop, stop, get away from* and other similar words.

Incidentally, research has shown us people will tend to work harder to keep something than they will to attain it (which is one reason scarcity works so well).

But in headlines, in all the testing I've done, it's better to couch the headline in terms of achievement rather than avoidance.

Why?

I have no idea. But that's how it pans out with me and my business.

Appendix I — How to Write Ads and Sales Letters that Sell

Use Lists and Bullet Points

Lists and bullet points are very effective in getting a lot of information packed into a very small space.

But don't make the rookie-copywriter's mistake of having just a long list of features. Play around with them — bullet points of features with the attendant benefits; bullets where you black out or omit important words (e.g. "Page 9: Just _____ the _____ and get an instant £9,000 a month CASH boost to your bottom line". These drive people nuts); and occasional bullets where you give away a real meaty secret (e.g. "Discover how to get maximum 'oomph' from your website images (tip — always use a caption reinforcing some benefit of what you're selling)".

If you want to see a "bullet point master", check out Ben Settle's work. His bullets turn me green with envy. No kidding[95].

Use "I" Rather Than "Us" and "We", and Use "You" in Preference to Any of Them

Even if you're part of a company, write the letter from an individual, and write it *to* an individual. As I've said elsewhere over and over again, you need to be cultivating a relationship — and you can't have a relationship with an anonymous group of people (unless you go to certain parties I've heard about).

However, do use the word "I" sparingly. It's a temptation to write about ourselves, our products and services and what we want, but no one but us gives a stuff. You know the kind of thing I mean — success "gurus" who write things like "My mission in life is to...". No one cares. All they care about is themselves. So instead of "I" and "me", then, think about

95. Learn more about Ben at www.bensettle.com

writing "you". Step into the other person's shoes and write about his problems, fears, pains, and struggles.

Here's an exercise for you... and it's much harder than it seems. Write an email or other short sales piece without using the words "I", "me", "my" etc. at all. You're highly unlikely to create something immediately usable from this exercise, but you'll be close, and I think you'll be amazed at the power of what you do write.

Avoid Using Words that Obviously Mean They're Spending Money

I see this so often: *order now, buy now, sign up now...* it's a mistake.

When people are using a credit card it's not real money, is it? So you'll do better by not reminding them it really *is* money.

Consider instead using words like *invest, apply, join me,* etc. Similarly, instead of *cost* or *price* say *amount* or *fee*.

And calling it a "small" amount is often effective, too. I find it useful to put the price in smaller font than the rest of the copy, and any savings in a larger font.

Keep Humour Out of It

Your "amusing" little jokes and comments aren't.

Spending money is serious business so treat it that way.

The exception to this is when it's part of your persona *and* you have a relationship with the person you're writing to.

If you look at my work carefully you'll notice a few things about my use of humour.

First, is it's irreverent and almost unbridled.

Secondly, I never use it in a sales letter, no matter whom I'm sending it to. Yes, it's on my blog, on a couple of my optin pages, and in my articles. It's also in the *Business Supremacy* monthly newsletter, this book, and in my daily emails.

But it's *not* in my sales letters.

A really talented young copywriter I know and mentor used to have the habit of injecting silly jokes into his sales letters right in the middle of the call to action. Not only did it irritate the hell out of the reader, but they indicated he was perhaps not completely happy with the product.

Don't Talk Down to or Insult Your Audience

The instant you talk down to them and make out you're better than they are, you've immediately got their backs up — especially if you're writing to and for men.

Far better to take the attitude, "I'm cool and you're cool, now let's see how we can make you even cooler".

Voice their Objections and Overcome Them by Using Events They're Familiar With

No one is going to believe you just because you tell them you're honest.

When you're trying to get them to part with money, they are going to be sceptical. In other words, they're often not bothering to listen to you, even: they're too busy thinking of reasons you're wrong.

So, if you're hoping to persuade them to give a different form of marketing a go because the "usual" kind doesn't work, perhaps suggest they look at the Yellow Pages and observe how all adverts in their niche (including their own) are pretty much the same.

Let them see it for themselves.

If it's a price objection, then perhaps use the analogy of how servicing a car "costs" but is cheaper than repairs (most people probably know this from bitter experience).

One of the things I frequently do, if you recall, is I make the point I do the right thing not *only* because it *is* the right thing, but because it's in my own rational self interest to do so.

Honesty pays.

Isn't that a bit more believable than telling you to trust me because I'm a Really Nice Guy and I'm bursting with Universal Love and Light?

Exactly.

It's the truth, the whole truth and nothing but the truth, and everyone can relate to it.

Appendix II

In Fitness and in Wealth

This is perhaps where we get a bit odd. Or so it might seem at first. But bear with me, if you will.

See, I'd finished this book, or at least the preview, and sent it to a few people I trusted for review. The book you now have in your hands is the final, slightly more polished result. Most of the comments I got back were about marketing and a few things I'd either not covered in enough detail or had missed completely.

But one reviewer, my friend, lawyer, and Inner Circle Member, Flor McCarthy said this:

> *Hi,*
>
> *I know this is a little out of left field and too late, but the one thing that struck me as missing reading the book was any fitness element.*
>
> *I say this because your cycling was a huge influence on me at the start and still is. Taking responsibility for and action over the things we can control seems to me to be the key to all of this and taking control of yourself has for me been a vital first step.*

Perhaps it's not right for this book, but it is for me an essential part of the EBG whole. I thought you could just add a section to Getting It All Done and add in something like that gut buster download thing you have as an appendix. It may be getting carried away but it's just a thought.

All the best,

Flor

And he was dead right.

See, for me, things really started to take off in my business when I started getting *serious* about my fitness. I don't know why it had that effect, but it did. And it's not just me, either: this is something I bring up fairly often with my Members, and the ones who also begin to take it seriously report the same thing: it makes a *huge* difference to everything.

So I'll keep it as brief as I can and simply offer it to you as an idea you might want to think about.

You Don't Need a 300 Page Diet Book or a Complicated Workout Schedule to Get Excellent Results.

It's the 80/20 rule, as always — you'll get 80% of the results you want by putting in just 20% of the effort you'd need to put in if you were a fitness model or pro-bodybuilder.

In other words, if you're just an average Joe or Josephine and you want to look and feel better than you've ever looked and felt before, and better than probably 99% of the people you'll see walking by you down the street, then you don't have to enrol in some bizarre fitness religion or spend your days eating rabbit food.

Proof?

At the time of writing this I'm 48, 5'5" tall and have average genetics[96]. I like my wine (perhaps a little too much) and like almost every other middle-aged man or woman out there, I tend to thicken around the middle more easily than I ever have before.

Gone are the days when I could shovel anything into my face in any quantity and still look like Adonis.

So, there came a point where I was 12½ stone (which is 175lb) with a 39½ inch waist and I felt — and *looked* like shit. My business was doing OK, but progress was glacially slow. No energy, no enthusiasm, happy just to keep turning the handle.

I'd become fat and lazy.

Now, there's a strange thing about us humans: we don't tend to change anything until the pain of staying as we are is worse than any possible pain of change. You see this with relationships and employment, too: people stay in horrible situations they know they ought to get out of, but the pain of change is too much... *until* something happens to make the pain of inaction suddenly worse. For me the tipping point was reading an article on the BBC website about a bloke who was both older and far fatter than I was who had done Amazing Things after buying a bike[97]. So that's when I set about taking control of my weight. That very day I got my old bike out and took it for a spin. I didn't get more than a mile or so up an embarrassingly gentle hill before I had to stop, get off, and prepare myself for imminent death. I felt awful. But I persevered and the next time I went out, a few days later to let the saddle-sores go down, I managed a bit

---

96. I'll probably stay 5'5" and my genetics are fixed, but I sincerely hope to add substantially to my age.

97. The article is here www.jonmcculloch.com/gybf/fat-bloke-article

---

Appendix II — In Fitness and in Wealth

further. And then a bit further still. Within a few weeks I was happily doing a dozen miles a day, and we have some pretty serious hills around here.

Fast forward a few months and I was down to about 10½ stone (147lb) with a 31 inch waist. And the weight-loss was net — I'd put on a lot of muscle so my *fat loss* was a lot higher.

Fast forward even further, and I have a six-pack, something I've not had for over 20 years, and I can squat, ass-to-grass, well over twice my bodyweight. As you may already know I also continued with the cycling, between 12 and 25 miles a day. Where we live, in County Cork, it's nearly all hills. Now you don't have to do this, of course. As long as you stick to the simple rule of eating fewer calories than you expend, you will lose weight. You must. The Laws of Physics say so, and they don't lie. I cycle because I like to be physically fit, I find the time out on the bike mentally therapeutic, and I wanted to lose the flab as quickly as possible! But the point is, if you don't cycle or do something else to increase the calorie deficit, then it'll just take longer. That's all.

On top of the cycling I still hit the iron three times a week, although at 48 I'm now thinking that might be too much for recovery. No matter — twice, three times, makes no huge difference. It's all really very simple.

First...

Measure Everything

So head on over to www.fitday.com and get yourself a free account. It's worth tracking *everything* you eat and do. Anything measured improves (I got Mrs. EBG, doing this against massive resistance and female hissy-fits and emotional tears, and now she steals my whey powder and is in the garage with the weights as often as I am).

Then, you need to figure out your diet and exercise regime.

I got all the stuff below from a really good friend of mine, a British amateur bodybuilding champ I've known for the last 15 years or so. He's a PhD at Cambridge in the UK and one of the smartest people I know.

No, I'm not going to give you his name here, but if you're burningly sceptical and think I'm making this up, you can email me and I'll maybe tell you.

The Specifics of Your Diet

High protein… every day.

Protein not only builds new muscle, but it also helps stop you losing the muscle you have when you're dieting. Using the schedule and diet below, I've lost fat and gained muscle at the same time. That's more common in rank beginners, but I did have a long layoff.

Nevertheless, the calorie-cycling means everyone but the leanest and most highly-trained individuals will manage to put on muscle and lose fat at the same time, at least for long enough to improve your shape dramatically.

So… high protein… for me that's 200g, about 1.5g protein for every lb of bodyweight. Mrs. EBG is taking a little less, because she's lighter.

Contrary to popular myth a high-protein diet is *not* bad for your kidneys *unless* you already have an underlying problem. At least, that's what the current research suggests.

Other than that, she works out and eats the same as I do (only lighter — and she can't do chins or dips, so does rows and press-ups instead. And she does deadlifts instead of squats. The point is she trains heavy with real weights, no pink-vinyl girly-nonsense. There's no truth to the myth women should train differently from men).

Appendix II — In Fitness and in Wealth

On workout days it's high-carb, low fat.

The high-carb/low-fat is important around your workout because you want insulin high to drive protein into the just-worked muscles and fat low so it doesn't get stored as body fat[98]. My total calories on a workout day are about 2000.

On non-workout days it's low-carb and tends to be higher fat. Calories are about 1600.

The way to do it is fix your protein, fix your carbs (for me, 250g on a workout day, about 75 on a non-workout day), and then the rest is fat. It's easy. Ignore the rubbish you hear about "fat-burning foods" and all that.

Good sources of protein are whey protein (you can get 10kg for about £80 from www.bulkpowders.co.uk), red-meat (probably not on workout days unless you go extra-lean), chicken, turkey, eggs, and fish.

Good sources of carbs are starchy vegetables like peas, sweet-corn and potatoes; bread; pasta, rice... all that good stuff. You don't want too much in the way of high-GI carbs except around your workouts (see below).

Your daily calorie deficit can be anything that works — meaning if you're still losing weight or you're changing shape, then it's working.

I find I can get up to 1500 calories a day deficit with cycling, but if I keep it up for too many days weight-loss stops and I feel like crap (lethargy, etc).

Then I'll eat more or exercise less (I prefer to eat more and then exercise more rather than feel hungry, but that's just me — you can do it either way).

Once a week we'll have a "free meal".

So, on a Saturday we'll perhaps have lasagne and chips

---

98.   It's more complex than that, but that's close enough.

Appendix II — In Fitness and in Wealth

(fries, to my American friends), red wine, and then ice-cream while we watch a video.

Or maybe we'll nip to the local chip-shop and really live it up with some deep-fried death-fodder.

A Typical Day's Food

It varies from day to day, depending on whether or not I'm working out.

On a Workout Day

Breakfast (about 90 minutes before I work out)

All told this wants to be something that gives you about 60g protein with 30 to 40g carbs, most of them complex, but with a little fructose, too.

So...

Porridge with fat-free milk, banana, and a touch of honey. Then 75g of 80%-protein whey.

Post-Workout

Then 25g of 80%-protein whey with 10g glucose

Wait about 20 minutes and then snack periodically on ham, pitta bread and a fat-free relish.

Dinner

Typically chicken curry with basmati rice, or pasta with chicken.

On a Non Workout Day

Breakfast

Yoghurt, raspberries, with 3 scoops of 80%-protein whey.

Lunch

Pitta bread, ham, cheese, and mayonnaise. Occasionally avocado.

Snack

Piece of chicken with avocado, tomatoes and some mayonnaise.

Dinner

Chicken in mushroom sauce (with mushrooms and onions), green beans, pureed cauliflower with butter; or perhaps steak with mushrooms, onions and tomatoes with pureed cauliflower.

My Workouts

There's nothing magical about these exercises.

They're chosen specifically because they all, with the exception of the biceps curls, involve many muscle groups (they're often called "compound exercises").

The only other thing of note about them is you'll see they alternate in terms of being push-pull. The reason for this is simply practical: the pushing muscles get a rest while you're doing the pulling exercises, and vice versa.

In the Workouts below you'll see two numbers, separated by an 'x', say 3 x 5. What this means is simply "three sets of five repetitions each".

Workout A

Weighted Dips   3 x 5[99]
Bent-Over Rows 3 x 5

---

99. Press-ups if you can't do dips yet

Shoulder Press	3 x 3
Squats (heavy)	4 x 4
Biceps Curl	2 x 12
Bench Press	3 x 5

Workout B

Squats (heavy)	3 x 5
Squats (light)	2 x 12[100]
Weighted Chins	4 x 4[101]
Shoulder Press	4 x 3
Biceps Curl	2 x 12
Bench Press	4 x 5

Workout schedule

Mon A
Wed B
Fri A
Mon B
Wed A
Fri B

And so on.

As you'll see, you're working out three times a week on alternate days, except for the weekends when you get a couple of days off.

Correct form in all these exercises is essential for both safety and maximum results. There are loads of online resources (just search YouTube), but I strongly recommend the book *Becoming a Supple Leopard* by Kelly Starrett and

---

100. Should be front-squats or split-squats, but I can't do these owing to a missing toe-joint — surgically removed.
101. Rows if you can't do these.

Glen Cordoza. A very odd title, to be sure, but an excellent guide to form and function of exercises (and it contains a lot of vital information on mobility, too). It's not cheap, but you won't regret it since it's an awesome investment in your own fitness and health.

Further Resources

Now, I realise what I've written above seems too good to be true — it's too brief. Nothing that simple can be that effective, correct?

Well, no.

It works — and by following what I've outlined, you're going to get 80% of the results you want. Yes, you might find you have to dicker with a few things here and there, but this is substantially it.

But some readers, I know, are going to want more.

If you're feeling the need for something more cerebral where you have to do a bit of thinking for yourself, I recommend anything and everything by a fellow by name of Lyle McDonald because he probably knows more than anyone else on the planet about fat loss and muscle gain — www.bodyrecomposition.com.

This is real science, not faddy popular nonsense for middle-aged women riddled with angst. It's easy to read and not hard to understand, but it's not about making you feel good — it's about educating you.

Get them all if you're feeling flush, or if not leave out *Applied Nutrition for Sports* and *The Protein Book*. All the rest will be useful if you're just an amateur like me.

I warn you, though: this is not Mr. Comfy or Dr. Phil like platitudes which tell you how you can lose weight with no effort. Like my approach to marketing and business, it's gritty, stark and brooks no bullshit.

I have all his books save *The Protein Book*, and I think I'm correct in saying Lyle's work is the foundation to my bodybuilding chum's own work.

In terms of the iron-pumping, more recently I've been following the StrongLifts 5x5 programme — www.stronglifts. com. The reason for this is I've reached a point where progress is otherwise slow, so I need a proper structured approach to continual strength increases. You can use my original workouts or start with the StrongLifts ones — the most important thing is you *do something*.

Disclaimer

I shouldn't have to put this here, not in a sane world, anyway. But the world isn't sane and there's always some fucking idiot who feels the need to blame others when things go wrong.

So... following these guidelines has worked well for me and has worked for Mrs. EBG. They've also worked well for other people I've shared them with... which is why I'm sharing them with you now. To the best of my knowledge they're correct and will do you no harm. But I am not a doctor or a sports professional so please view this entire Appendix as "entertainment" and not "information" or "advice". You're a grown up and make your own choices. And by choosing to follow any of the health and fitness ideas in this Appendix, you accept full responsibility for your actions and any consequences arising from them.

If you're in any doubt, consult a professional, pay him or her well, and follow the advice you're given.

Afterword

Thank you for investing in *Grow Your Business <u>FAST</u>* and taking the time and trouble to share this journey with me. I realise it's been something of a roller-coaster ride and you've likely had many of your preconceptions, beliefs, and assumptions challenged and, ultimately, changed for the better.

But the journey isn't over yet.

And it never will be.

Because there's always something more to learn, always another mystery to solve. That's why it's always going to pay you to be the eternal student, and that's no bad thing.

Most business owners who read this book won't take even the simplest action on the tactics and strategies they learn, and will continue to struggle unnecessarily. That's frustrating for me, personally, of course; but by far the bigger frustration is that which they will experience themselves in their businesses as they continue to grind away at the same old ineffective marketing strategies and methods and continue to get the same inconsequential rewards and suffer the same avoidable failures.

But I hope *you* are one of the few who *will* take action. In fact, I hope this is the start of a very long and mutually profitable relationship between us (and that's why the information I've included in these pages is worth thousands of times the price of the book — I *always* over deliver).

So if you've enjoyed *Grow Your Business FAST* and are keen to get started, I have a very special gift for you at the end of the book, right after the index.

It really is free and there's no catch or strings attached. I sincerely hope you'll accept it.

Jon McCulloch,
Co. Cork, 2013.

P.S. If you've enjoyed *Grow Your Business FAST* to the extent you want to obtain copies in bulk at a substantial discount to give as gifts to your own clients, then email me here: gybf@jonmcculloch.com.

More About The EBG and His Work

I am not generally available to work on new clients' projects. Any projects I *do* work on are subject to a minimum project fee and always begin with a full day of consulting either in my office or in yours.

If you wish to enquire about my availability to work on your projects, please use one of the methods over the page and clearly state your name and contact details (fax or email only), and give an outline of your business, as well as a brief paragraph saying how you think I can help you. Please don't embarrass yourself and annoy me by offering an "equity stake" or a "share of future profits" in return for my help and advice on your "guaranteed winner".

It might come as a surprise for you to learn this is not a new idea, and it's about as appealing to me as a cup of cold dog vomit. If you don't have the cash to pay my fees *plus* an ongoing royalty on the materials I create for you, then you don't qualify to work with me. *No exceptions.*

If your needs are less onerous you may qualify for a one-hour telephone consulting session. I also have a very limited number of one-off consulting days available, and

I am available for appropriate speaking engagements and interviews. Please contact me for availability.

Finally, if you have a question about the Business Supremacy Inner Circle, you can get more information here:

www.jonmcculloch.com/inner-circle

All other services are described along with fees, availability, and qualifying criteria on my website, here:

www.jonmcculloch.com/service

How to Get in Touch With Me

You can get in touch with me by any one of these methods:

Email: contact@jonmcculloch.com
Web: www.jonmcculloch.com/contact
Fax: +353 (0) 21 238 0554

Please note: I do *not* accept incoming telephone calls without appointment.

Index

Domino's Pizza, 89
Explicit, 89
Remington Razor, 89

V
Vitale, Joe, 291

W
Website
  Traffic, sources of, 159
  Two things it needs to do, 158
Willpower
  Myth of, 274
Words of Warning, 19
Workouts, 348
Workout schedule, 349
Writing Sales Copy
  Most important lesson of, 329

A Special Free Gift from the EBG
Help Yourself to an Amazing €291 Profit-Boosting Information Package

*G*row *Your Business **FAST*** contains everything you need to increase your profits and business success starting right now.

But it's also true many of the strategies require a more detailed knowledge than I've been able to provide you with here if you want to get the maximum results possible from them. So that's why I'm giving you these remarkable *free* resources — my gift to you for having the grit and determination to change your business once and for all.

1. **Pay Per Click Supremacy.** If you're looking for more business but you're struggling to make Google Adwords and Bing Advertising pay, then this is the Guide you've been looking for — *Pay Per Click Supremacy* is your short-cut through the confusing, bewildering, and often frustrating maze of PPC advertising on the two biggest and most popular platforms.  Normally €97, this Guide is yours, FREE from the *GYBF Owners' Inner Circle.*

2. **Remarketing Supremacy.** If you are not harnessing the power of Remarketing in your business, then you're losing out on a *lot* of sales you'd otherwise be making. In short, Remarketing allows you to place banner ads on prestigious and high-traffic sites all over the Internet and have them shown *only* to people who have already visited your site. Best of all, the flexible display rules mean you can hone and fine-tune your Remarketing ads for extreme accuracy and precision. *Remarketing Supremacy* is yours FREE from the *GYBF Owners' Inner Circle*, saving you €97.

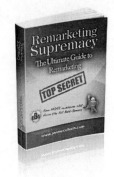

3. **Direct Mail Magic.** Struggling to make your Direct Mail pay? Then *Direct Mail Magic* has the answer with its detailed Blueprint on how to create direct mail campaigns giving you an easy 300% on response. You can claim your own copy of *Direct Mail Magic* for free from the *GYBF Owners' Inner Circle* — another €97 saving.

To claim your free gifts and your complementary Membership of the *GYBF Owners' Inner Circle*, visit this web page:

www.jonmcculloch.com/gybf

And follow the simple on-screen instructions.

A Special Free Gift from the EBG